The Power of the Plan

The Power of the Plan

BUILDING A UNIVERSITY IN HISTORIC COLUMBIA, SOUTH CAROLINA

RICHARD F. GALEHOUSE

Foreword by Patrick L. Phillips

THE UNIVERSITY OF SOUTH CAROLINA PRESS

Published by the University of South Carolina Press in cooperation with the University of South Carolina Bicentennial Commission

Published by the University of South Carolina Press
Columbia, South Carolina 29208

www.sc.edu/uscpress

Manufactured in Korea

28 27 26 25 24 23 22 21 20 19
10 9 8 7 6 5 4 3 2 1

Library of Congress Cataloging-in-Publication Data
can be found at http://catalog.loc.gov/.

ISBN 978-1-61117-970-5 (cloth)
ISBN 978-1-61117-971-2 (ebook)

THIS BOOK IS DEDICATED TO THE BUILDERS

The university trustees, the presidents and senior administrators, faculty, alumni, philanthropists and friends who have brought their love and talents to building a great public university for South Carolina.

CONTENTS

FOREWORD

The contemporary American university is many things: a center of traditional undergraduate learning, a focus for scholarship and research, a source of state and local pride and prestige (often due to success on the athletic fields), and an important engine of economic development. The physical place where this all occurs, the campus, conjures familiar images of quadrangles, dorms, lecture halls and libraries, and yes, ivy-covered walls. The best campuses foster a strong sense of place, often through memorable public spaces and a few iconic buildings, and a cohesive and contextually sensitive use of materials.

Yet today's campuses are increasingly complicated and intertwined with their surrounding communities, both physically and economically. The modern research university, particularly in its state-flagship form, is a small city in itself, one that must fit within a complementary, but distinct, social and economic milieu. From an urban-planning standpoint, this is a mighty challenge. Addressing the programmatic requirements of the institution itself is hard. Doing so in a way that not only mitigates the impact on the surrounding community, but advances opportunity and quality of life in the metropolitan area is sufficiently complex to have emerged as a distinctive specialty within the urban-planning field.

This challenge has also expanded the role of university officials, who must not only raise the resources to help their institution adapt and change but must also develop new leadership skills and organizational capacities in real estate investment and development, planning and urban design, the management and programming of public spaces, and community relations.

The rewards are clear for those universities and cities that successfully tap this symbiotic relationship. In today's knowledge-driven economy, the outsized success of places like Silicon Valley, the Research Triangle, and Greater Boston make the linkage obvious. But civic and university leaders know there is no formula, no recipe for this kind of success. Building a mutually supportive relationship between town and gown takes time, leadership, money, and—perhaps most importantly—a clear vision and plan. Or, rather, it requires a series of plans that build on a consistent set of principles, but allow for adaptation and change.

This book tells the story of such a process. Over 20 years or so, the City of Columbia and the University of South Carolina have worked to fulfill an ambitious agenda for growth and development, improve the quality of the physical environment, and boost the stature and competitiveness of both city and school. Like the process of urban development itself, the story is not finished—there will be many more chapters—but as Columbia works to establish a more productive relationship with its university this helps us understand the challenges and opportunities ahead for other institutions.

Patrick L. Phillips,
GLOBAL CHIEF EXECUTIVE OFFICER 2009–2018
THE URBAN LAND INSTITUTE

Patrick L. Phillips served as Global Chief Executive Officer of the Urban Land Institute and president of the ULI Foundation from 2009 to 2018. Phillips has a career in the economic analysis of real estate and land use that spans more than 20 years. Prior to his service at ULI, he was president and chief executive officer of ERA AECOM (formerly Economics Research Associates). In that role, he coordinated all aspects of ERA's organization, strategy, business development, and service delivery. His own consulting practice focused specifically on the intersection of private investment and public policy. Phillips is a frequent speaker on urban development issues and is the author or coauthor of eight books and numerous articles.

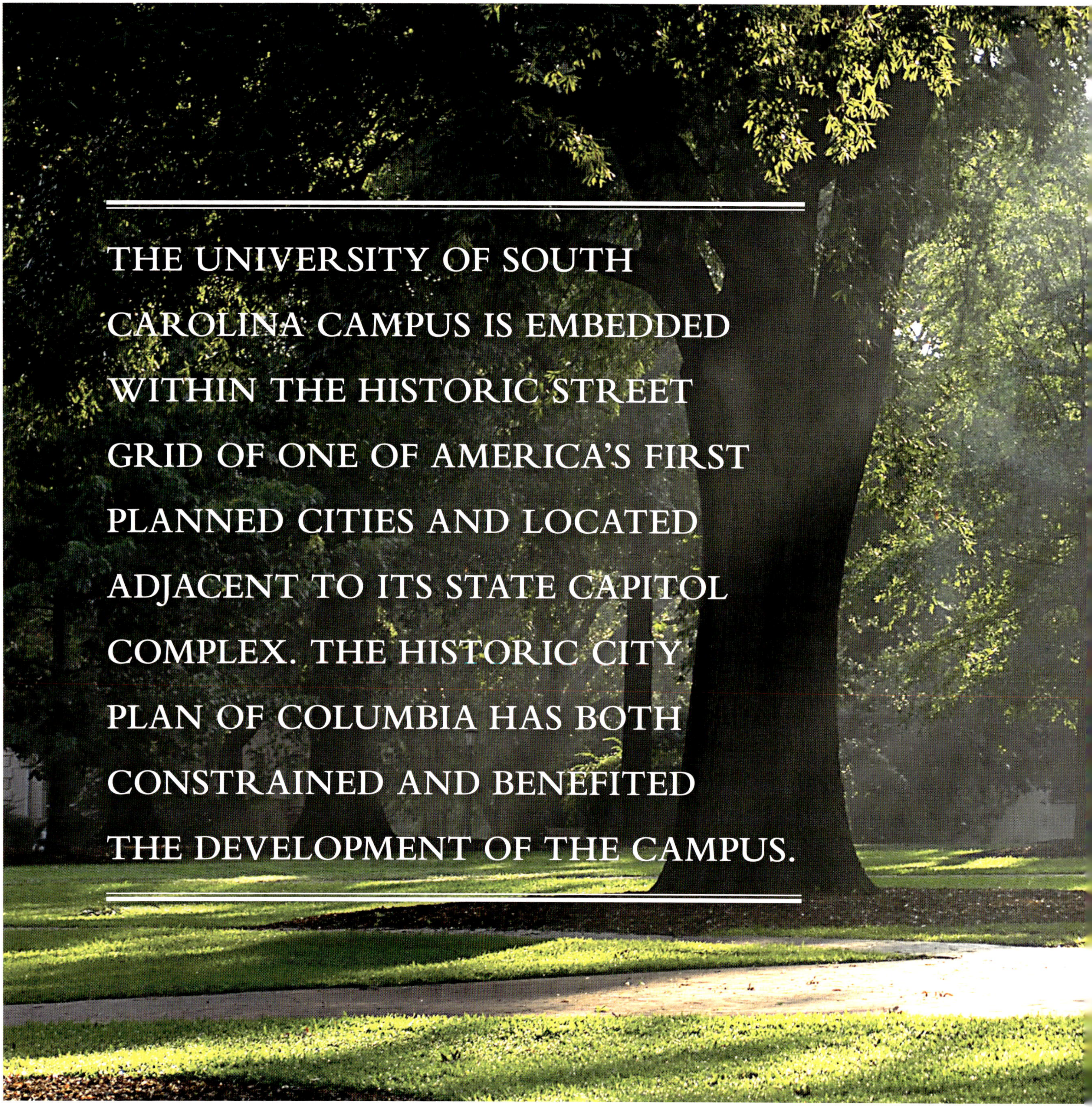

THE UNIVERSITY OF SOUTH CAROLINA CAMPUS IS EMBEDDED WITHIN THE HISTORIC STREET GRID OF ONE OF AMERICA'S FIRST PLANNED CITIES AND LOCATED ADJACENT TO ITS STATE CAPITOL COMPLEX. THE HISTORIC CITY PLAN OF COLUMBIA HAS BOTH CONSTRAINED AND BENEFITED THE DEVELOPMENT OF THE CAMPUS.

PHOTO COURTESY OF CREATIVE SERVICES

View of McCutchen House
IMAGE COURTESY OF KEITH MCGRAW

Introduction

Each university campus has a distinct personality that is rooted in its history, campus traditions, the quality of its physical environment, the emphasis of its academic programs, and the historic context and culture of its host community. The physical configuration of a university campus directly impacts its operational efficiency and the programs that can be offered. The environmental design quality of the campus, its architecture and landscape, plays an important role in educating students, supporting recruitment, and retaining the loyalty of its alumni.

Urban public universities have faced powerful forces shaping the physical configuration and environmental quality of their campuses: the explosive growth in student enrollment in the post–World War II period that led to neighborhood conflicts, "suburbanization" in the age of the automobile, management of the process of facility programming and design, the impact of their "builders" (the dedicated men and women who strive to bring their universities to greatness), and the evolving face of university community outreach in their host cities.

In the second half of the twentieth century, the University of South Carolina, founded in 1801, has faced similar forces, as well as forces distinct to its history, culture, and physical context. The university's explosive growth from its pre-war student enrollment of 2,200 to 22,700 students by 1974 was particularly challenging. Landlocked in the heart of the city of Columbia, the university thrust outward from its historic campus into adjoining residential neighborhoods, displacing African-American neighborhoods to its south and west under the umbrella of the City of Columbia's urban renewal program. While this neighborhood conflict was similar to that experienced by other urban universities, the conflict was greatly amplified in South Carolina by the civil rights movement that prevailed at the time.

The University of South Carolina campus is embedded within the historic street grid of one of America's first planned cities and located adjacent to its State Capitol complex. The historic city plan of Columbia has both constrained and benefited the development of the campus. In 2006 the family heirs of John Gabriel Guignard, who planned the City of Columbia in 1786, entered into a partnership with the university to plan a research park as part of a new urban neighborhood adjacent to the campus containing a mix of university and private development.

This is the story of how a maturing public urban university, the University of South Carolina, addressed the challenges of growth and development within the city of Columbia, SC, in the latter half of the twentieth century.

Civic Outreach. The relationship of the University of South Carolina to its host city of Columbia and the state of South Carolina has evolved over the last quarter century from an institution inwardly focused on its academic mission to one with a growing awareness of its larger responsibility to the state of South Carolina for economic development. In 2006 a unique partnership between the university, the state, the city, the Guignard family, and other private property owners initiated the planning for a new urban neighborhood, Innovista, adjacent to the campus to be used as a center for research, innovation, and contemporary urban living, a challenging task that has met with mixed success to date.

Architectural Design. The programming and design of new campus facilities is one of the most challenging management tasks facing university administrations. Historically the development of architectural "styles" has been a direct response to the culture of the area, the building materials that were available, and the building technologies of the times. Today, with the advent of computer-aided design tools and an unlimited palette of building materials, architects have nearly infinite license to experiment with new architectural forms. The University of South Carolina possesses a family of beautiful historic antebellum buildings framing its historic Horseshoe. In the Post World War II period, the university, as did many other universities, teamed nationally prominent architects with local professionals to design "modern" buildings for its campus. Disenchantment with that approach has led the university to participate in an ongoing discussion on the merits of mandating an historic architectural vernacular, an unresolved issue prevailing on campuses throughout the United States.

Vision. Traditional campus master planning, which brings an analytical grounding and physical order to a campus, typically has a ten-year time horizon. The long life of institutions makes the need for long range vision imperative. In the words of Daniel Burnham in his "Plan of Chicago," "Make no little plans for they have no magic in them to stir men's hearts ." No better example of a sustaining long range vision exists than the university of South Carolina's historic campus "The Horseshoe." The Bicentennial Master Plan published in 1994, which was the University's first contemporary comprehensive master plan, drew from the qualities of the historic Horseshoe in articulating a series of sustaining planning/design principles to govern the long range development of the university's campus.

Quality of Place. The quality of the neighborhoods framing the University of South Carolina campus, and urban campuses throughout the country, has been a source of concern, indeed conflict, since the end of World War II. The relationship of urban universities to their host communities has slowly evolved into a mutual understanding that "quality of place" impacts both the university and the community: the institution's ability to attract and retain faculty, staff, and students and the community's desirability as a place to live in attracting and retaining talented men and women for today's knowledge economy. Richard Florida makes the case for "quality of place" in his book *Cities and the Creative Class,* "Today, it is the ability to attract human capital or talent that creates regional advantage: those that have the talent win, those that do not lose. In this regard, the quality of place, a city or region, has replaced access as the pivot point of competitive advantage." [1]

The Builders. Master plans are primarily two dimensional instruments designed to bring order to the process of developing campuses. The campus's "builders" bring the third dimension: its buildings and landscape. From the time of its founding, a distinctive characteristic of the University of South Carolina has been the "personal interest and affection"

The Historic "Horseshoe" at the university serves as an outdoor classroom. PHOTO COURTESY OF USC CREATIVE SERVICES

that the state, civic leaders, and community-minded citizens have taken in the development of the university campus. State leaders in particular took a "personal interest" in the founding of the university. "In antebellum decades they looked upon South Carolina College as a department of state government, lavished money upon it and often attended academic functions."[2] This interest and dedication persists to the present time. William Hubbard, a long-serving Trustee of the University of South Carolina, exemplifies the dedication, indeed passion, of trustees for their university. When asked as to what motivated his more-than-twenty years of service as a trustee of the university, he replied, "You can't have a great state without a great University."[3]

The "Power of the Plan" lies in its ability to gather the work of the "builders" into a coherent whole within the framework of the campus master plan.

In 1992, Sasaki Associates, an interdisciplinary professional planning and design firm from Boston, Massachusetts, was selected by the University to prepare the Bicentennial Master Plan (published in 1994) in partnership with local Columbia South Carolina professionals. Since that time the university has carried out an intensive planning program, including the development of an urban neighborhood plan, Innovista, in 2006 and an update of its comprehensive master plan in 2010.

This story focuses on the last twenty-five years of campus development at the University of South Carolina. The prior history of campus development at the university has been well documented by others. Sections I and II provide a brief history to bring the story up to the early 1990s, when the trustees and the university's new president launched a long range strategic planning process for the campus that embraced both academic and physical planning dimensions. Section III describes the university's strategic master plan, the Bicentennial Master Plan, and highlights the leadership responsible for its development. Section IV describes the university's intensive planning efforts in the last quarter century and identifies the key leadership responsible for each period of planning and development. Section V promotes the idea of "the city" as the twenty-first-century campus of the university.

Section I

A NEW CAPITAL CITY FOR SOUTH CAROLINA

Bird's-Eye View of the city of Columbia 1872

GRAPHICS WITH PERMISSION OF THE SOUTH CAROLINIANA LIBRARY, UNIVERSITY OF SOUTH CAROLINA

Chapter 1

The Planned City of Columbia 1786

The Guignard Family. French Huguenots, Gabriel Guignard and his family immigrated to Charleston, SC, in 1737 to escape religious persecution in France. His son John Gabriel Guignard became Surveyor General of the state of South Carolina. When the State General Assembly in 1786 made the decision to move the state's capital from coastal Charleston, SC, to a more central location within the state, John Gabriel Guignard was charged with finding a site and preparing a plan for a new capital city.

Since that time the fate of the Guignard family has been intertwined with the city of Columbia and the University of South Carolina.

John Gabriel found the location of the present city of Columbia on the Congaree River in the central part of the state. "John Gabriel hung around and acquired land."[(1)] Other family members also settled in the Columbia region, acquiring hundreds of acres of land in and around Columbia. James Sanders Guignard, son of John Gabriel Guignard, accumulated over 10,000 acres of land in the counties of Orangeburg, Barnwell, Lexington, Edgefield, and Richland for his plantations. James founded the family brickworks in 1803 on the west bank of the Congaree River.[(2)] Though the family sold the brick-making business in 1974, some of the historic "beehive" brick kilns have been preserved and can be seen today on the west side of the river in the city of Cayce, SC.

Historic "beehive" brick kilns of the Guignard family in Cayce, SC

PHOTO ©JEFF AMBERG

Over the centuries the Guignard family has been an important contributor to the development of the Columbia community. Their contributions include helping to found and build the Trinity Episcopal Cathedral, the donation of land and a mansion for the Still Hopes Episcopal Retirement Community, donation of land for parks, and donation of land on the west side of the Congaree River to the state for the construction of the Blossom Street Bridge. Many historic buildings in Columbia are said to be constructed of Guignard brick, including the buildings of the University's historic Horseshoe built after 1850, the State House, and the historic cotton mills along the Congaree River. The University of South Carolina owns the second-oldest house in Columbia, the Horry-Guignard House, built in 1813 and located on the site of the university's new law school. The 1957 book *Planters and Business Men: The Guignard Family of South Carolina, 1795–1930* provides an intimate portrait of the Guignard family. The book tells the saga of an emigrant family who upon escaping religious persecution in Europe thrived in their adopted homeland of South Carolina.

Guignard heir Charles Thompson, manager of Guignard Associates (the limited liability company [LLC] that holds land on the east bank of the river, adjacent to the university campus), made land available to the university for its new baseball park in 2005, and in 2006 entered into a partnership with the university for the planning of a new urban mixed-use research district, Innovista, adjacent to the campus. While the Guignard family necessarily looks out for its own financial interests in this regard, there has been more than a touch of noblesse oblige in their commitment to partner with the university and city in realizing the ambitious plan for Innovista.

Location of the New City of Columbia. In 1786 South Carolina followed the lead of the other thirteen colonies in moving its state capital to a more accessible central location within the state. John Gabriel Guignard selected a site on the Congaree River at the fall line between the Piedmont plateau and the coastal plain of South Carolina. The site for the new city was near Friday's Ferry, below the confluence of the Broad and Saluda Rivers. In this location the Congaree River provided navigable waters from Charleston on the Atlantic

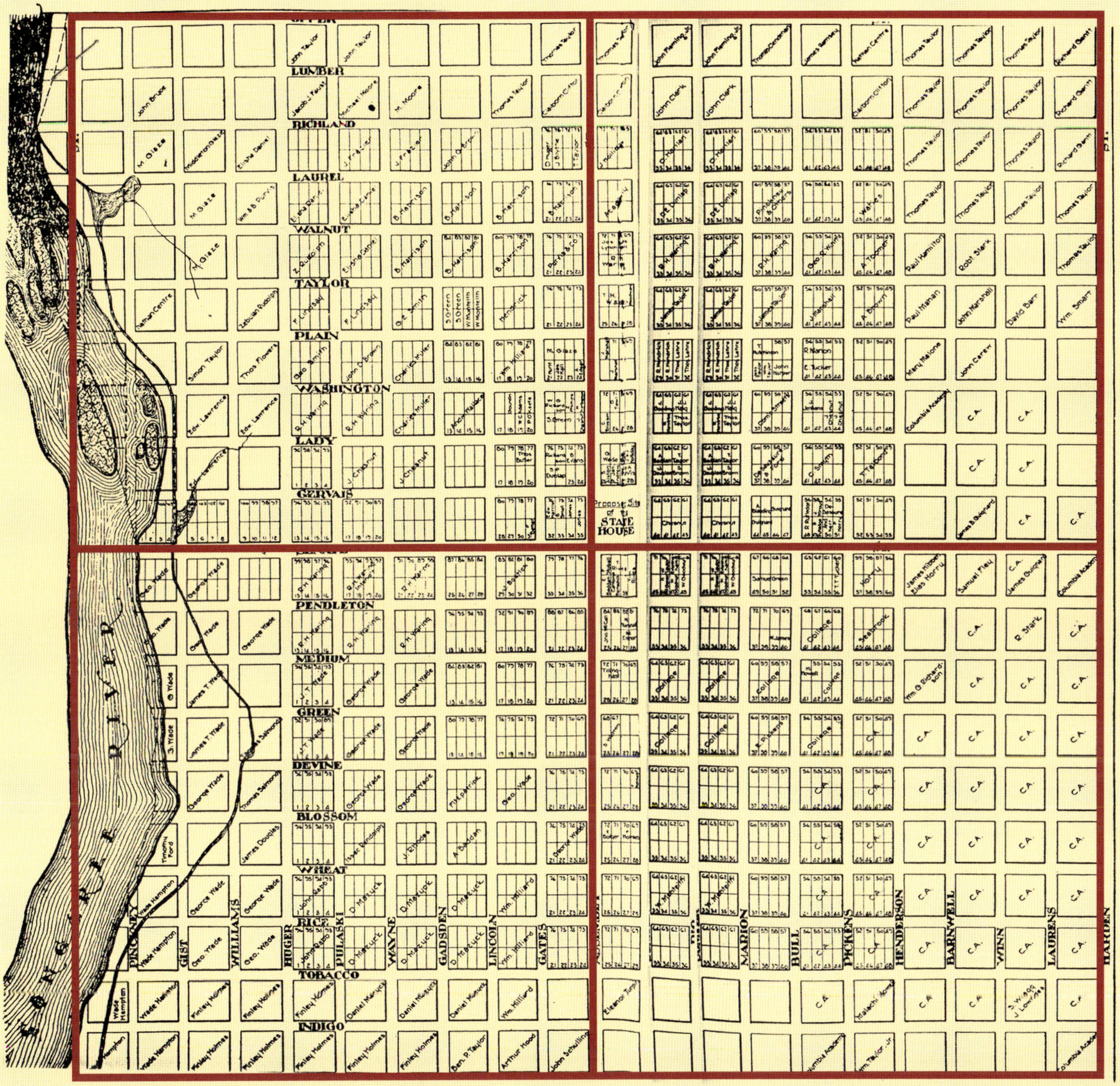

1786 Foundation Plan for the city of Columbia, as laid out by James Gabriel Guignard GRAPHIC COURTESY OF SASAKI ASSOCIATES, INC.

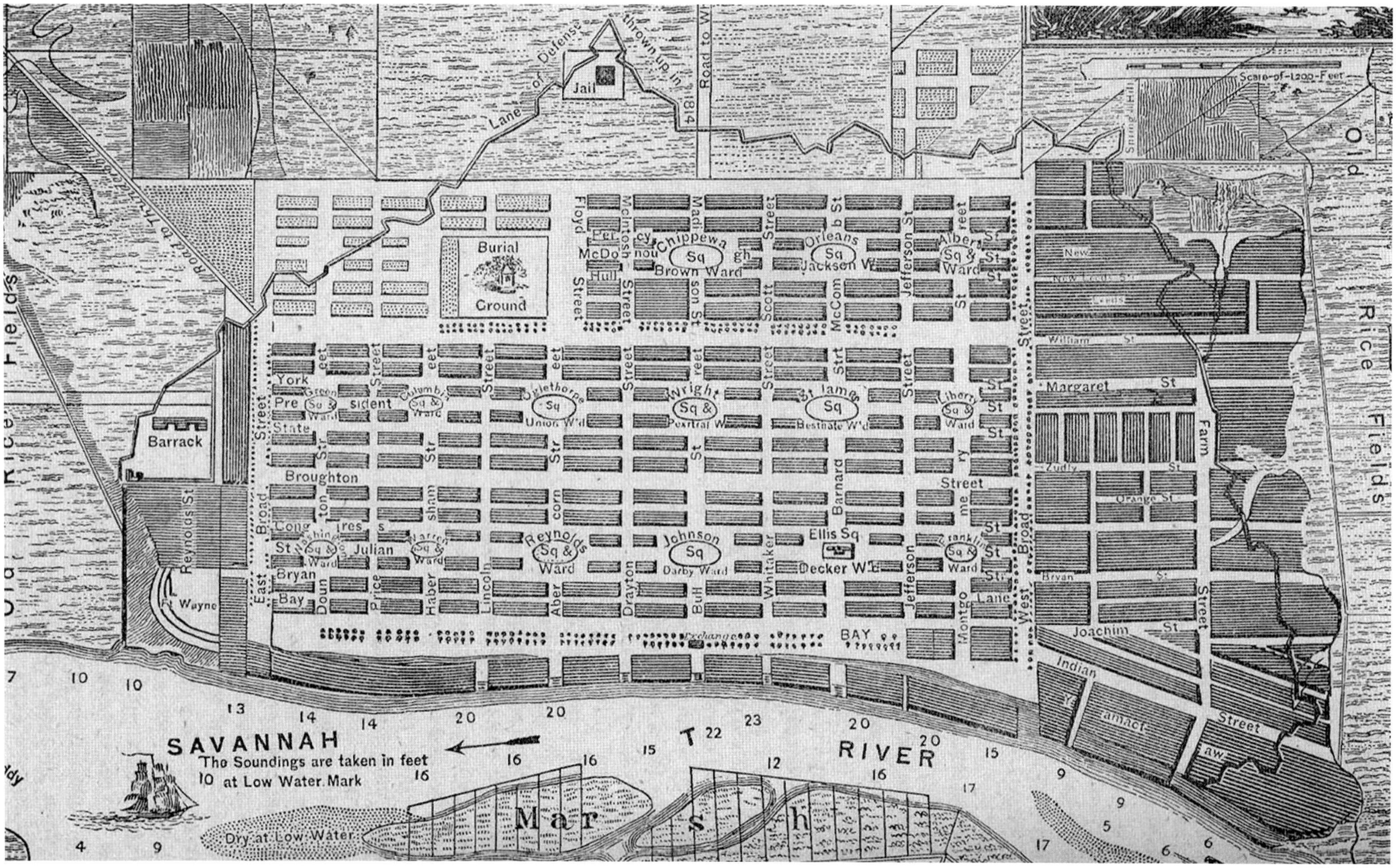

"Grid" plan of Historic Savannah, Georgia

IMAGE COURTESY OF WIKIPEDIA

coast to Columbia, while the Broad and Saluda Rivers to the west provided navigable waters to Columbia for the farmers in the Piedmont region.

The central location of Columbia and the fact that it is the location of the university afford it a special status in a state with deep diversity of economies and social character. Historically it has mediated between the aristocratic coastal low country around Charleston and the economically booming upcountry around Greenville and Spartanburg. The University of South Carolina was deliberately placed in the new city as a way to bring citizens from the coastal plain together with citizens from the Piedmont area. The Innovista endeavor illustrates a university shedding its inward focus and acknowledging its role in helping to make Columbia the "hub" of a vibrant economy in a state that is rich both in history and entrepreneurship.

The Plan of the City of Columbia. The master plan for Columbia by John Gabriel Guignard reflects his profession as a surveyor—a classic orthogonal grid of streets in a two-mile-square frame laid without regard to the rolling topography and a bend in the Congaree River. The master plan's street grid of ten streets to the mile created a pattern of 400 equally sized blocks. Street rights-of-way were 100 feet wide, with the exception of 150 foot rights-of-way for Senate Street and Assembly Street, which divided the city into four equal quadrants. The commission appointed by the South Carolina Assembly to acquire the land for the new city subdivided the property and sold half-acre lots to pay for the purchase of the land.

Charles Thompson believes that John Gabriel's plan for Columbia, which was drawn before the age of the automobile, was based on the conception of a "garden city" with its wide rights-of-way allowing for shade and prevailing breezes.[3] This original intent can be seen in the adjoining residential neighborhood east of the university where streets are characterized by narrow pavement, broad street lawns, and a canopy of shade trees.

Origin of the "Grid." The design plan of the "grid" for Columbia had its origin in ancient Greece. The Greeks attributed a philosophical value of equality to the grid, utilizing the grid plan to secure and organize property rights outside of established urban settlements. It was later adopted by the Romans for their military encampments. The plan of the earliest Spanish settlements in the United States (in St. Augustine, Florida) was governed by "The Law of the Indies," a detailed prescription by the Spanish crown for the design of cities in the new world using a modified grid plan focused on a town square.

Town planning in America has had a long history of embracing social experiments and experiments in design form. James Oglethorpe, for example, utilized a basic grid in his plan for Savannah, Georgia, in 1733, overlain with a sophisticated political construct of wards and focused upon landscaped squares. The wards provided lots on the north and south sides of the squares for the colonists' private homes, and lots on the east and west sides for public buildings and churches. The beautiful urban landscaped squares framed by historic homes and public buildings that remain today are Savannah's enduring legacy.

Benjamin Franklin saw "democracy" in the use of the grid for his plan of Philadelphia. In 1791 Pierre Charles L'Enfant imparted an extraordinary civic scale to his grid plan for Washington, DC, by overlaying a series of diagonal avenues and landscape squares, and adding the great Mall oriented to the Potomac River.

The state of Florida has been the source of continuing experimentation in town planning since the 1930s. The grid

Pictured Left
The Capitol of South Carolina

Pictured Below
The plan of Columbia was concieved as a "garden city" with its wide street rights of way allowing for shade and prevailing breezes

IMAGES ©JEFF AMBERG

plan for George Edgar Merrick's Coral Gables incorporated a series of existing natural features and a location for a university within its plan. Planner John Nolan, a Harvard educated landscape architect, prepared town plans for more than six Florida cities in the mid-1930s, including the present-day cities of Sarasota, St. Petersburg, and Venice. All featured variations of a grid plan overlain with diagonal avenues and civic open spaces. In the present era the New Urbanist movement has embraced the grid with a religious fervor.

The sustaining vitality and maturing beauty of these planned cities over the decades is a testament to the power of their town plans, which projected both a vision and a strong physical framework.

Pictured Right
Suggested system of inner and outer parks for the Township of Columbia

Facing Page
Showing the capital buildings, the use of South Main Street for "future" civic buildings and the extension of the Horseshoe to Assembly Street.

HISTORIC PLANS COURTESY OF CHARLES THOMPSON

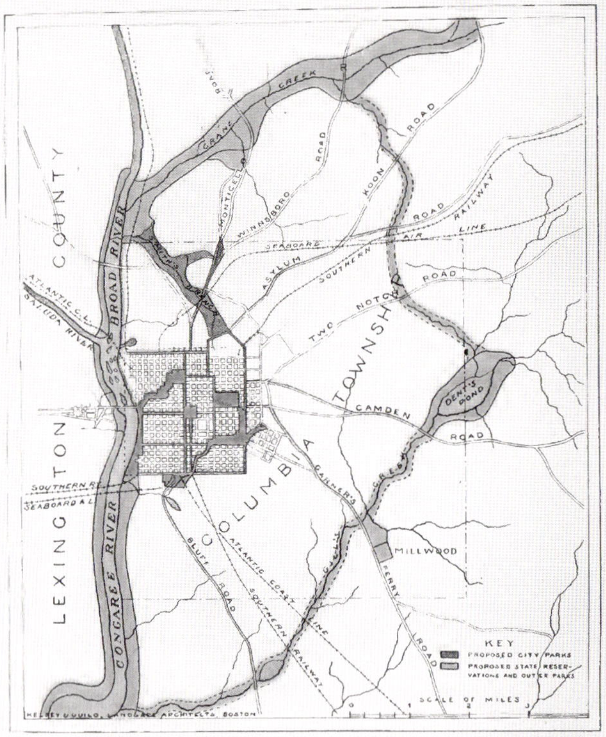

Plan Showing a Suggested System of Inner and Outer Parks and Reservations, and Connecting Roads and Driveways

The grid plan for the city of Columbia was an expedient and proven real estate formula designed to address the financing of the new city through the sale of lots. John Gabriel Guignad's plan was unadorned by civic gestures. The exception was the configuration of Senate Street and Assembly Street, which were designed as boulevards. The presence of the Congaree River and the rolling topography of the area did not influence the design of the plan for Columbia as, for example, the Potomac River did to L' Enfant's plan for Washington, DC. Public gathering spaces, town squares, or parks, were also absent in John Gabriel's plan.

Development of the City of Columbia. The new capital city developed slowly despite the economic stimulus of the state government and the presence of "South Carolina College." By 1830 the town of Columbia had 3,310 residents and its host county of Richland claimed 14,772 residents.[4] In the following decades, the capitol complex and "South Carolina College" spurred the growth of distinctive residential neighborhoods, such as University Hill and Wheeler Hill, adjacent to the State House and the college campus. In support of the burgeoning industry developing along the banks of the Congaree, mill village neighborhoods developed around the mills to the south of the college and west of Assembly Street. On the west bank of the river the Guignards established the region's brickworks. John Hammond Moore in his book *Columbia and Richland County: A South Carolina Community, 1740–1990* chronicles the growth and development of Columbia from its founding through the Civil War period, and its growth and development in the twentieth century up to 1990. By the year 2010 the Columbia Metropolitan area had grown to 750,000 residents.

The Kelsey and Guild Plan. In 1919 a second comprehensive planning effort for the city of Columbia was undertaken by the Boston, MA, firm of Kelsey and Guild, landscape architects. In a report to the "Civic League of Columbia" the Kelsey and Guild firm recommended a comprehensive plan of improvements for the city. The focus of the plan was a comprehensive "Inner and Outer Parks and Reservations" plan, including recommendations for street landscape improvements and a plan for a civic center, "Capital Park and Mall," for the State Capitol complex. The concept for the "Capital Park and Mall" featured a dramatic extension of the university's Horseshoe—to the proposed Mall and across Main Street to Assembly Street.

The Kelsey and Guild firm saw urban design opportunities in the hilly topography and natural drainage patterns in Columbia. Their report lamented the lack of attention to the topography and other natural features of the region in John Gabriel's master plan. "It is extremely unfortunate, however, that the plan was arbitrary, with apparently little, if any, consideration given to the topography of the land."[5] Also, in support of the proposed plan of parks and reservations, the report decried the loss of Sidney Park, which at the time had been given over to the railroads. "Sidney Park has disappeared, and a scarred, sunburned hole, of doubtful use as a railroad dump, coal chute, and ice factory shows the sad results of indifference and lack of foresight now bitterly resented by Columbia's citizens."[6] Sidney Park, today known as Findlay Park, stands beautifully restored.

The Post-World War II Period. The Post–World War II period saw Columbia lose large parts of its historic fabric downtown. Suburbanization and white flight brought the abandonment of in-town neighborhoods in favor of the suburbs. Hulking freestanding parking structures servicing new and existing office buildings provided in-town parking places for the suburbanites. The abandonment of the mills and consolidation of the railroads left blocks of vacant and underutilized land to the west of the capitol and the university in the Vista area. Columbia's "City Beautiful" movement after the war was launched after a flurry of planning activity, including a comprehensive planning concept by the internationally known planner Constantinos Doxiadis. It led to the development of the "Congaree Vista" plan for the area between Columbia's traditional Main Street and the Capitol complex with its view west to the Congaree River. The redevelopment of Arsenal Hill near the Governor's Mansion and the Columbia Housing Authority's redevelopment of Wheeler Hill and Ward One adjacent to the university coincided with the consolidation of multiple rail lines that traced a path through the Congaree Vista, the area now branded as Innovista. The 1970s led to the highly successful redevelopment of the city's historic mercantile buildings along the Gervais Street corridor as Columbia's restaurant/entertainment district.

Columbia has continued to make progress in its efforts to achieve a contemporary urban quality for its center city. However, Columbia was a frontier town at the time of its founding and remnants of those characteristics persist today. Its wide arterial streets, vacant undeveloped blocks, surface parking lots downtown adjacent to the state capitol, and stand-alone office buildings tied with bridges like umbilical cords to their parking garages are reminiscent of the auto-centric character of America's western frontier cities. Despite its role as the state capital and the presence of the state's flagship university, Columbia does not yet possess the beauty and urbane qualities of Charleston, SC, or the urban liveliness that redevelopment has brought to downtown Greenville, SC. ■

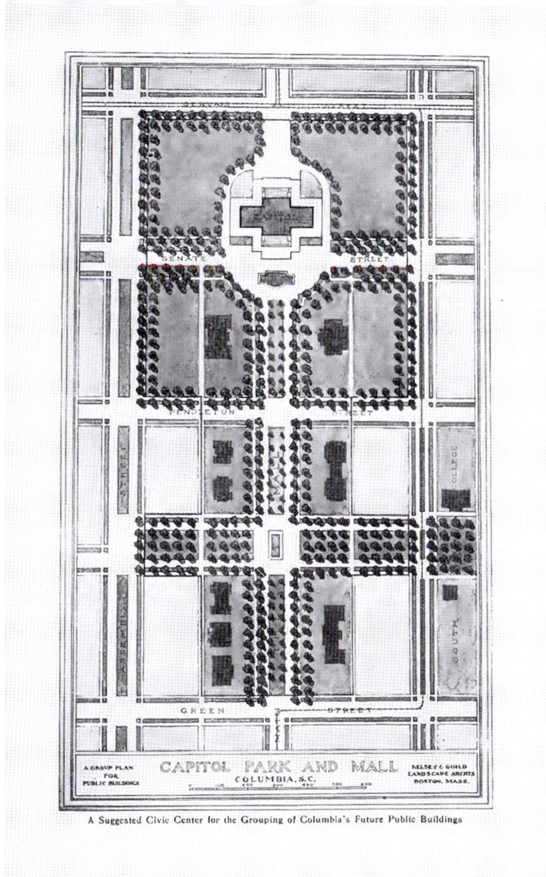

Pictured Below
View of the South Carolina State Capitol on South Main Street in 2015

PHOTO ©JEFF AMBERG

View of the historic hydroelectric power plant which powered the nation's first electric cotton mills

PHOTO PROVIDED BY THE AUTHOR

Chapter 2

The Legacy of the Congaree River

The River. The Congaree River, which gave birth to the city of Columbia, is located four blocks west of the university's campus. The river is considered Columbia's and the university campus's greatest untapped physical asset. The Kelsey and Guild report of 1919 noted, "The Congaree River is undoubtedly the most notable landscape feature of Columbia and should receive first consideration in any general plan adapted." (1)

The river and its falls, tamed by the Columbia Canal, provided the transport and power for the development of a robust mill industry of cotton, textiles, and flour in the middle of the nineteenth century. Today the riverbank, its floodplain, the remnants of the Columbia Canal, and the uplands on the east bank of the river between Gervais and Blossom Streets lie fallow and undeveloped. This area of the riverfront, which is controlled by the Guignard family, is the missing link in the region's existing 12-mile-long Three Rivers Greenway. Charles Thompson has incorporated the greenway into his concept plan for the property controlled by the family as part of the Innovista Master Plan.

Clockwise from Left
The "Columbia Canal"

The "Duck Mill," the world's first electric powered cotton mill which has been adaptively reused as the South Carolina State Museum

They hydroelectric plant at the head of the Columbia Canal

The historic "Palmetto Compress" cotton warehouse being adaptively reused for student residences

Dam & power station at the head of the Columbia Canal

CENTER IMAGES ©JEFF AMBERG
OTHER IMAGES PROVIDED BY THE AUTHOR

The Mills. The completion of the Columbia Canal in 1824 provided the means for farmers in the western part of the state to bypass the rapids on the fall line at Columbia. Sixty-six thousand bales of cotton were reported to have been transported to the coast through Columbia via the canal in 1833.[2] The canal also became the source of power for the mills developing along the east bank of the Congaree from Gervais Street south to Whaley Street. That area is now being planned as "Innovista," the urban mixed-use research and development district that is a principal subject of this book.

By 1910 Columbia was the home to seven mills employing 3,600 people.[3] The remnants of the mill district can be seen today in the Columbia Mill (which has been adaptively reused for the State Museum), the Adluh flour mill, and the Palmetto Compress Building which has been adaptively reused for residential apartments. Employees originally walked to work from the villages that developed around the mills. Today, the ability to walk to work is a goal of contemporary urban planning.

With the Columbia Canal also serving as a source of hydroelectric power, Columbia achieved international prominence in the nineteenth century with a series of distinctive technological innovations in its mills. The Columbia Mill, for example, became the first electric-powered mill in the world.[4]

The Innovista Master Plan seeks to build on this historic legacy and reinvigorate the mill district as a mixed-use live/work research district with contemporary technological innovations drawn from the university's research capabilities.

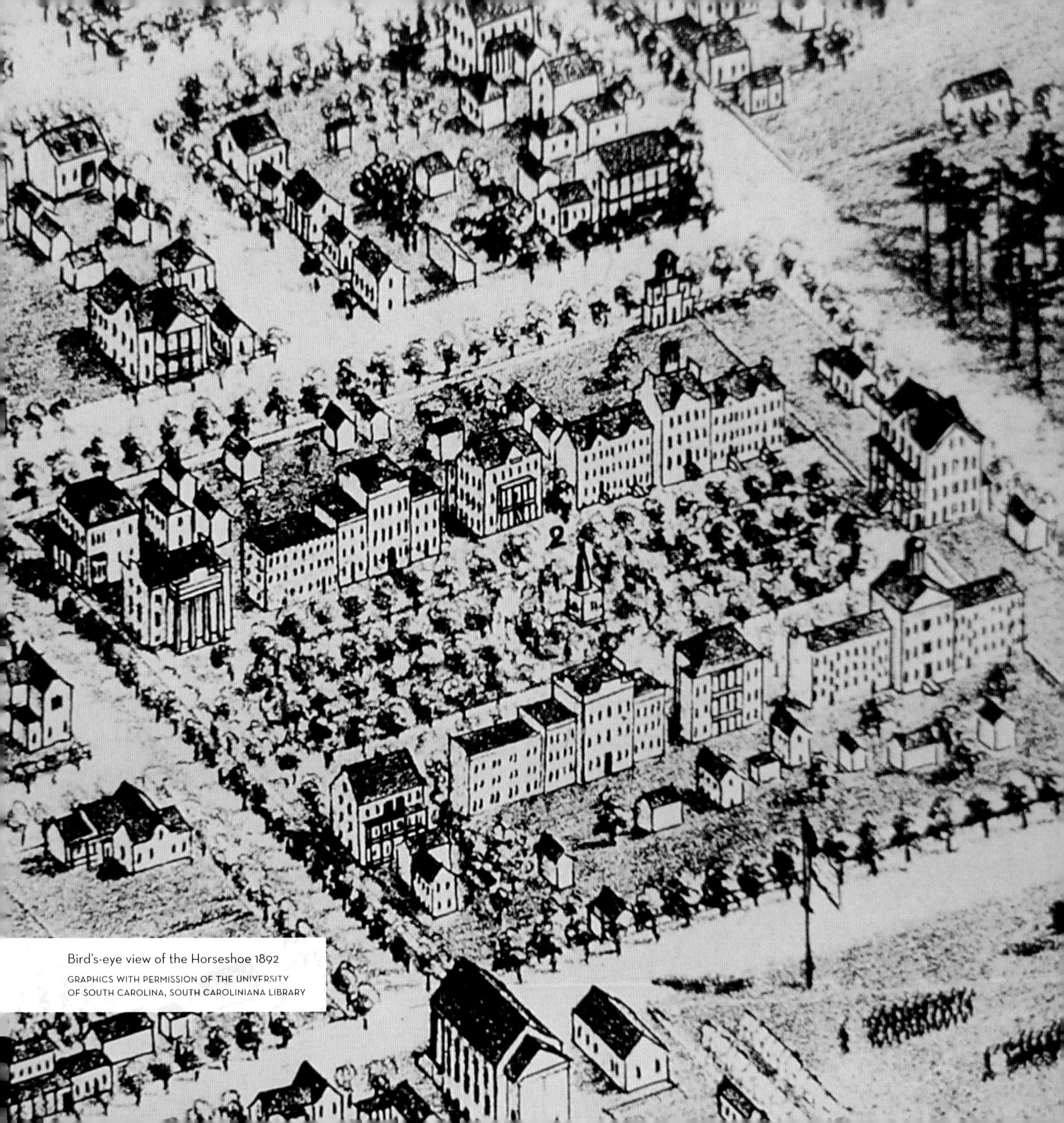

Bird's-eye view of the Horseshoe 1892

GRAPHICS WITH PERMISSION OF THE UNIVERSITY OF SOUTH CAROLINA, SOUTH CAROLINIANA LIBRARY

Chapter 3

A New Public University—South Carolina College

A College in the City. Under the encouragement of then President Thomas Jefferson, South Carolina followed North Carolina and Georgia in founding a public college. The South Carolina Assembly authorized the college to acquire undeveloped lots within the new city of Columbia. The university founded as South Carolina College in 1801 was placed on a 26-acre site two blocks southeast of the state's new capitol building. Like Thomas Jefferson's University of Virginia, founded several decades later in 1819, South Carolina College was centrally located in the state and carefully designed to espouse democratic ideals and a sense of destiny for the still-young United States of America.

The first colleges in America, primarily founded in New England, were privately sponsored religious colleges and were typically located in small villages or on the frontier, deliberately shunning the cities. "Cities were regarded as centers of irreligion and discord."[1] The General Court of the Massachusetts Bay Colony that authorized the new nation's first college, Harvard, in 1636, selected a site in Newtowne (later renamed Cambridge), a small village four miles from Boston.[2] Dartmouth was placed in a wilderness setting. William and Mary (1693) was located located in the small village of Williamsburg, which, at the time, was the state capital of Virginia. Yale (1701) was founded in the small town of New Haven.

Two early exceptions to the rule of private colleges in small communities were Kings College (1754), now Columbia University, in New York City and the College of Philadelphia (1755), now the University of Pennsylvania, in Philadelphia, PA.

The two public state colleges that preceded South Carolina College, the University of Georgia (founded in 1785) and the University of North Carolina (founded in 1789), were placed in rural settings. State leaders in North Carolina specifically stipulated that "…the University of North Carolina be located five miles from any seat of government."[3] The founding fathers of South Carolina College located Carolina College within the city of Columbia as part of a deliberate strategy to address the social and economic divide between urbane Charleston and the farming communities of the Piedmont. "The choice of Columbia was no accident; for a prime goal of the patricians who guided the bill of incorporation of the College through the general Assembly in less than a month was to unite up country and low country."[4] The coastal plain of South Carolina had been settled by the English with Charleston as its center of activity. Farmers of German descent had settled in the midlands and the Scotch Irish in the Piedmont. "It was almost inevitable that friction would develop between two societies so different in outlook. The German Lutherans and Scotch Irish Presbyterians resented paying taxes to the established Anglican Church. The refusal of the low country authorities to respond to demands for representation in the General Assembly, additional courts and law enforcement agencies, fairer tax laws, and location of a new capital aroused great resentment."[5]

The Master Plan for South Carolina College. In order to develop a plan for the new "South Carolina College," the trustees advertised a design competition in the ***Washington Federalist*** on the 27th of March, 1802, to wit: "In pursuance of a resolution of the board of trustees of the South Carolina College, Notice is hereby given that a premium of three hundred dollars is offered for the best original plan of a College, which shall be transmitted under seal to the president of the board, on or before the 4th Monday in May next, and which on examination may be approved of and accepted by the Board. In projecting the said plan, due attention must be paid to the expense of erecting the same in stone or brick, at Columbia, in this state which must not exceed fifty thousand dollars; and the building must be so calculated as to be capable of accommodating the greatest possible number of students, besides having rooms adapted to the studies and exercises of the institution, and for the accommodation of the Professors. The Premium will be paid to the author of the best original plan, which on being received is approved by the Board as meeting the purposes hereby required."[6]

The notice elicited at least ten building proposals, which were reviewed by a select committee appointed by the board of trustees. Proposals included that of Robert Mills, a young architect, who worked from time to time with Thomas Jefferson on his plans for Monticello. A native of South Carolina and the first federal architect, he later served as the designer of several of the earliest buildings on the Carolina campus, including Rutledge and the South Caroliniana Library, the nation's first free-standing college library. All of the proposals envisioned the campus as a single large building. However, "[t]he select committee did not recommend the adoption of any of the proposals submitted. Instead, they drafted their own plan which was both presented and endorsed by the Speaker of the South Carolina House of Representatives at the meeting of 26 May 1802.'"[7] "Instead of the Building of one continued Front reported by the Committee there shall be two Buildings fronting each other at such a Distance apart, as will be suitable to the Land to be procured not exceeding three hundred feet."[8]

The Horseshoe. The master plan of South Carolina College had as its focus a landscaped quadrangle named the "Horseshoe." One of the great campus quadrangles in America, it is so named because of the rectangular shape of its plan, featuring an interior greensward framed by buildings on both sides. The president's house stood at its head and the quadrangle was open to the community at its foot. Ranges for gardening stretched from the rear of the buildings to Pendleton and Greene Streets, which surround the Horseshoe.

John Morrill Bryan reports in his book *An Architectural History of the South Carolina College* that a diary entry by Edward Hooker from November 6, 1805, contains the first known graphic reference and description of the intent of the trustees to have buildings fronting each other across a landscaped green 160 feet apart, with the president's house at the head of the green and with additional buildings to be added in line as necessary—hence its "horseshoe" shape. Paul

View of South Carolina College 1850 GRAPHIC COURTESY OF THE UNIVERSITY OF SOUTH CAROLINA, SOUTH CAROLINIANA LIBRARY

Venable Turner in his book *Campus, an American Planning Tradition* reports that Jefferson was aware of his protégé Robert Mills's submittal for South Carolina College and was in all likelihood strongly influenced by the Horseshoe in his brilliant design of the lawn framed by the "academical village" at the University of Virginia.

Development of the Horseshoe began in 1805 with Rutledge and DeSaussure Colleges facing each other across the lawn at Bull Street. It was completed with the construction of Lieber and the South Caroliniana Library in 1836 and 1840, respectively, at Sumter Street. As the campus continued to grow new buildings were placed within the ranges behind the buildings fronting the Horseshoe.

The composition of the space, architecture, and landscape of the Horseshoe is a classic illustration of "place." The simple but beautifully proportioned historic buildings framing the Horseshoe act as a stage backdrop to the greensward they embrace. A canopy of monumental oak trees provides a roof and cooling shade. What distinguishes the Horseshoe from the Lawn at the University of Virginia is the broader canopy of trees, which filter the sun, creating an extraordinary quality of light. The space and the light has a deeply personal effect on those who enter the space.

Justin Fay, Sasaki's project planner for the university's 2010 Master Plan, offered a fresh observation of the Horseshoe on his first trip to the University of South Carolina in 2009. "The trees are extraordinary and while there is no one element that is remarkable, its beauty lies in the composition of the whole ensemble. Also the oasis like quality of the Horseshoe in contrast to the wide streets and vacant lots of the surrounding City of Columbia sets it apart."[9]

A monograph, *Buildings of the Columbia Campus,* authored by Derek Gruner, university architect, eloquently defined "campus": "By contemporary inference, 'campus' more naturally connotes the symbiotic presence of buildings and their surrounding grounds. It is the campus that circumscribes the scholastic experience, creates a 'spirit of place' and ultimately gives form to our memories. The importance of thoughtfully conceived and interconnecting open spaces cannot be overstated. It is these voids between buildings that establish rhythm analogous to moments of repose between chords in a musical composition. The nature of these spaces

The canopy of the monumental oak trees on the Horseshoe creates an extraordinary quality of light

IMAGE COURTESY OF USC CREATIVE SERVICES

It [the Horseshoe] is a brilliant plan which in its embrace of the city reflected the goals of its founders to "unite up country and low country." The mall form that was created not only influenced Jefferson in his design of the Academical Village at the University of Virginia but remains as one of the most widely used urban design forms in the hands of architects and campus planners.

continually bestows opportunities for beauty and character. Textured and narrow spaces allow passage; articulated facades define intimate spaces which can be celebrated as gardens and courtyards while the largest green spaces, such as our iconic Horseshoe, timelessly inspire awe as the heart of our institution. It is the omnipresent green spaces, courtyards and stately buildings which both give form to our spirit, weaving a sublime campus fabric that memorializes the University." Gruner describes the experience of the Horseshoe as "absolutely spiritual, as though one is moving within the serene landscape of a painting."(10)

Campus Precedents. The urban design principles displayed in the Horseshoe—mixed-use academic and residential buildings framing a beautiful pedestrian landscaped open space, complemented by a beautiful historic architectural vernacular—are as relevant today as they were in 1801.

The word "campus," the Latin word for field, branded the unique design form of the American colleges: separate buildings around a greensward. The American system of higher education derived from the English medieval system, in which teachers and students lived together in a "boarding school" environment. The English system in turn had been derived from the monastic tradition characterized by linked inward-looking buildings creating a cloistered environment. "Harvard's founders followed by Yale and Princeton also implanted a preference for residential education that seeks to shape the whole person."(11) In the development of the Harvard campus, the founders, though graduates of the English collegiate system, "believed in the Puritan ideal of community and felt that the college should be part of the town that surrounded it."(12) Harvard Yard, with its separate buildings fronting a greensward, thus became the prototypical planning model for the American campus.

South Carolina College in Columbia followed in the "boarding school" tradition with its early buildings serving as multi-purpose residential and teaching facilities. The design form of the early Carolina campus, the Horseshoe, however, was unique: a two-block-long landscaped "mall" framed by buildings facing each other across a landscaped green with the president's house at its head and open to the Columbia community at its terminus on Sumter Street. It is a brilliant plan that in its embrace of the city reflected the goals of its

The President's House, one of the beautiful classical buildings framing the Horseshoe

IMAGE COURTESY OF KEITH MCGRAW

founders to "unite up country and low country." The mall form that was created not only influenced Jefferson in his design of the Academical Village at the University of Virginia but remains today as one of the most widely used urban design forms in the hands of architects and campus planners. The Horseshoe's ensemble of buildings and green space was placed on the National Register of Historic Places in 1970.

"Had we built a barn for a college and log huts for accommodation should we ever had the assurance to propose to a European professor to come to it? To stop where we are is to abandon our high hopes and become suitors to Yale and Harvard for their secondary character."[(13)] Thus wrote Thomas Jefferson in response to critics questioning the cost of his Academical Village at the University of Virginia, highlighting the importance of great architecture and landscape in the design of American campuses.

For architects and urban designers, the sustaining attributes of the plan of the Horseshoe include four features: first, the mall form of the open space, which allowed for incremental growth of university facilities for well over a century in which each phase of development was complete in itself and ultimately led to a completed ensemble that was both functional and beautiful. Second, the physically compact pedestrian form, which allows for quick and safe pedestrian movement among the academic facilities. Third, the aesthetic quality of its buildings and landscape plays a subliminal teaching role in the education of young students and plays a direct role in their recruitment and retention. Fourth, the concept of mixed-use buildings where academic, residential, dining, and recreational spaces are co-located in compact pedestrian environments promoting communal opportunities, which are essential to today's contemporary teaching and community-building environments. ■

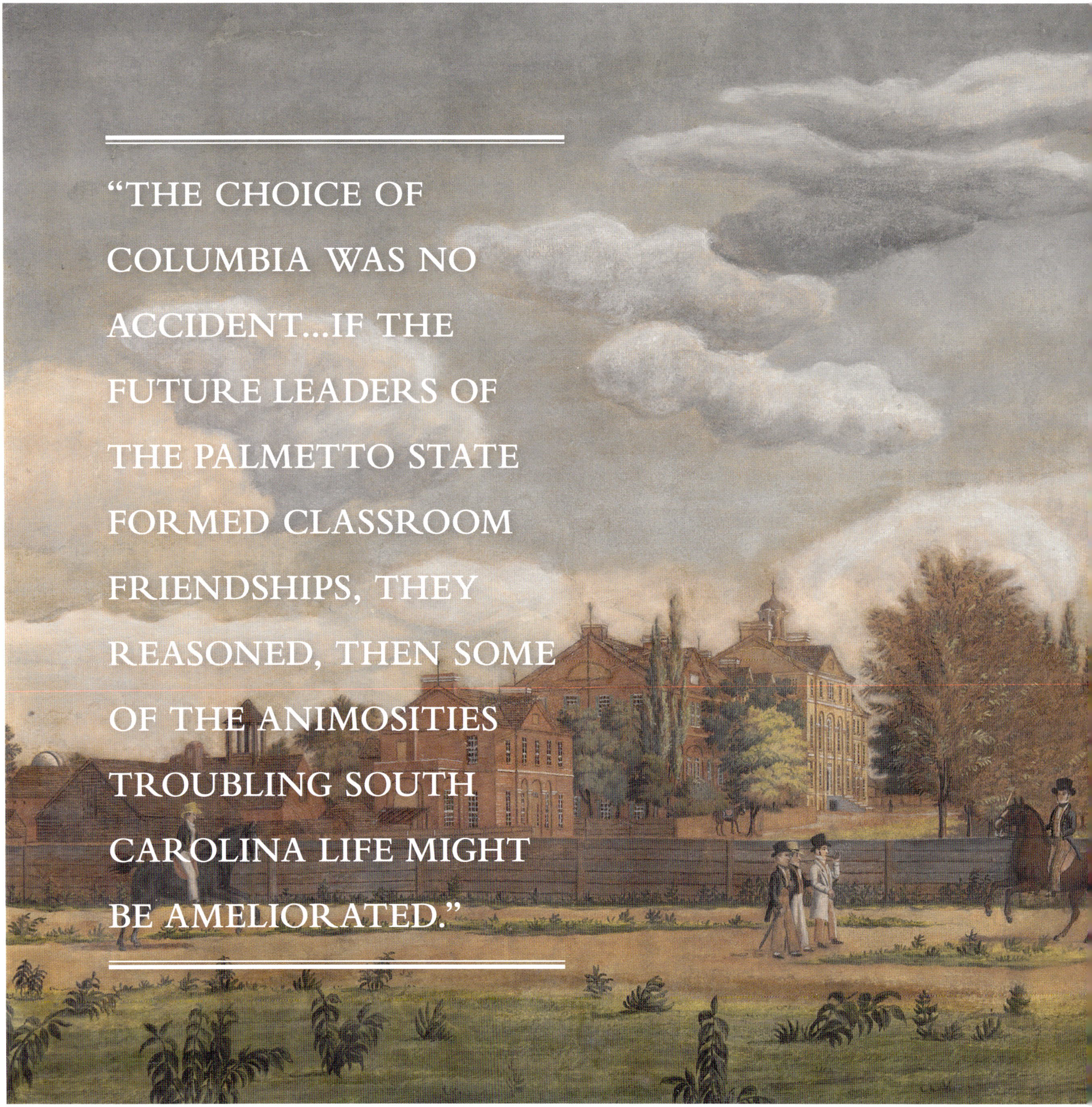

"THE CHOICE OF COLUMBIA WAS NO ACCIDENT...IF THE FUTURE LEADERS OF THE PALMETTO STATE FORMED CLASSROOM FRIENDSHIPS, THEY REASONED, THEN SOME OF THE ANIMOSITIES TROUBLING SOUTH CAROLINA LIFE MIGHT BE AMELIORATED."

View of South Carolina College 1820
GRAPHIC COURTESY OF THE UNIVERSITY OF SOUTH CAROLINA, SOUTH CAROLINIANA LIBRARY

Section II

BEST LAID PLANS

“Shotgun” houses on the 900 block of Assembly Street in 1957

PHOTO COURTESY OF UNIVERSITY OF SOUTH CAROLINA, SOUTH CAROLINIANA LIBRARY, JOSEPH WINTERS COLLECTION

Chapter 4

The University of South Carolina in the Twentieth Century

The Crisis Era. South Carolina College flourished in the antebellum period, becoming one of the South's most important educational institutions. The campus had grown to encompass twelve buildings around the Horseshoe prior to the Civil War. Columbia, the capital of South Carolina, and the adjoining college were also the intellectual center of the secessionist movement in the southern states. Maxey Gregg, a prominent local citizen, helped draft the resolution in favor of secession on December 17th, 1860. The Civil War and the Reconstruction Era that followed effectively destroyed the pre–Civil War institution. Carolina College was closed for the school years of 1863, 1864, and 1865. The use of campus buildings on the Horseshoe as a hospital is credited with saving the college in the burning of Columbia in February of 1865 during General Sherman's "March to the Sea." Despite its reopening after the war, the college suffered in the Reconstruction Era and the decades that followed, experiencing both closures and reorganization with a significant decline in enrollment. At the turn of the twentieth century, with enrollment once again growing, the state re-chartered the college as a university in 1906.[1]

With enrollment growing and the campus lacking additional building sites in the area of the

Pictured Above
Aerial view of the University of South Carolina campus in 1940

PHOTO COURTESY OF THE UNIVERSITY OF SOUTH CAROLINA, SOUTH CAROLINIANA LIBRARY

Pictured Right
Dessauseur, one of the historic buildings "saved" on the Horseshoe

PHOTO PROVIDED BY THE AUTHOR

Horseshoe, the University moved outside of its original grant of 26 acres in 1909 and created a new campus quadrangle, Gibbes Green, with the construction of Davis College and LeConte College east of Bull Street. The constraints of the city's "grid" of streets was addressed by closing the intervening street, Bull Street, between Pendleton and Greene Street. The new quadrangle created a rectilinear green space three-quarters the length of the Horseshoe, placed at right angles to the Horseshoe. In contrast to the Horseshoe, Gibbes Green was designed as a garden with a canopy of trees, curvilinear paths, and flowering plants. Gibbes Green also represents the last true campus quadrangle developed on the South Carolina campus. While some of the later campus building programs created courtyards and smaller green spaces, they tended to be "stand alone" schemes unrelated to a larger vision.

In anticipation of university growth as World War II neared its end, and in response to the constraints of the university's urban location and the small size of the campus, the House Speaker of the South Carolina legislature, Solomon Blatt, proposed selling the existing campus and moving the university to a 1,200 acre suburban location. At their December trustee meeting in 1944, ". . . the board of trustees immediately approved Blatt's sweeping new and greater university proposal with only two dissenting votes."[2] However, "... alumni reacted with horror to the idea of destroying the traditions of the antebellum campus whose buildings dated to 1805, by selling it off and moving"[3] and the proposal ultimately failed.

While the university administrators faced with operating and maintaining old buildings understandably respond positively to the prospect of new "modern" buildings, the timeless character of historic buildings on university campuses cannot easily be duplicated today and the traditions and lore associated with the buildings are irreplaceable.

The nature of the university crisis at the beginning of the century took a dramatic turn in mid-century with the need to accommodate the tidal wave of returning veterans on the GI Bill.

Rapid Growth of the University. The post–WWII period beginning in 1945 with the enactment of the GI Bill saw a rapid growth of enrollment; it reached 7,300 students in the fall of 1962 and 22,700 only 12 years later in the fall of 1974. In 1965, in order to accommodate these dramatic increases, the university, under the direction of dean of administration Harold Brunton, developed a long-range campus development plan, illustrating blocks of land to the east, south, and west that the university proposed to acquire. In order to acquire the needed property, a private corporation, the Carolina Research and Development Foundation (CRDF), was chartered to buy property for the University's expansion. Each of the areas designated for acquisition were long-established residential communities of single family neighborhoods.

Saving the Horseshoe. The condition of the historic buildings framing the Horseshoe had reached crisis proportions by the 1960s, having "settled into a seedy, dilapidated state of benign neglect with paint peeling off the exterior walls and stucco surfaces with great blotches of heavy mildew."[4] Consideration was given by the administration to tearing down and replacing the buildings on the Horseshoe with modern buildings.

Better heads prevailed. In what might be considered the University of South Carolina's most significant campus planning decision since "An Act to Establish a College at Columbia" in 1801, the decision was made to restore the historic buildings of the Horseshoe, one of the greatest campus ensembles of space and buildings in the United States.

In an emotional and sentimental appeal to a meeting of the senate finance committee at the State House in the spring of 1972, Harold Brunton, the university vice president of administration, single handedly secured funds to start the restoration of the Horseshoe. He was asked at the hearing, "How much money would it take to do what you are talking about?"[5] Harold Brunton later said, "I didn't have the slightest idea of what needed to be done, never mind how much it would cost. Speaking completely off the top of my head, I said, 'Two point eight million dollars.'"[6] A few weeks later the senate finance committee authorized "Two point eight million dollars for the renovation of the Horseshoe dormitories."[7] Hal Brunton, chronicles the restoration of the Horseshoe in his book *Renovation and Restoration of the USC Horseshoe: A Memoir.* It is a remarkable personal account of this defining effort.

The value of the Horseshoe to the university cannot be overstated in retaining the loyalty of its alumni, aiding in recruitment, and serving as a subliminal teaching model for young students. Thomas Stepp, longtime secretary of the university and its board of trustees, echoed Thomas Jefferson's admonition of his critics at the University of Virginia when he said, "The Horseshoe and the quality of the Carolina campus dramatically impacts the university's academic mission and the view that parents and prospective students have of the University."[7] ■

View of Capstone from the adjoining University Hills neighborhood

IMAGE ©JEFF AMBERG

Chapter 5

Conflict

Neighborhood Conflict. "This is what we have decided and are going to do."[1] This was the opening statement of the University of South Carolina Development Foundation in its first meeting with the University Hills Neighborhood Association in describing their proposal for a new inn in the historic University Hills neighborhood adjoining the university. The proposed university inn on Pendleton Street required demolishing a historic home and the historic Kirkland apartments, to be replaced, in the words of John Stucker, president of the association, "with a proposal for an Inn that looked like a CVS pharmacy on steroids."[2]

This meeting in 2002, forty-five years after the University of South Carolina's initial disruptive incursion into the University Hills, Wheeler Hills, and Ward 2 neighborhoods, characterized the relationship of many urban universities with their host communities after World War II. The central lesson of "Town/Gown" relationships in the post–World War II period is the need for dialogue and for forging new partnerships. The experience of the University of Chicago in Chicago, IL, the University of Pennsylvania in Philadelphia, PA, and the University of Notre Dame in South Bend, IN, all of whom partnered with their communities to address conflicts, resulted in a wide range of successful strategies to effect needed change.

The University of Chicago campus in the Hyde Park and Kenwood neighborhoods of Chicago, Illinois, and the Midway Plaisance

PHOTO: NATIONAL AGRICULTURE IMAGERY PROGRAM (NAIP)

University of Chicago. The University of Chicago in Chicago, Illinois, was among the first to realize the seriousness of its neighborhood problems after WWII. In his "State of the University" address to the University of Chicago in 1945, Chancellor Hutchins said, "For the past eleven years the University's neighborhood has steadily deteriorated until today I am ashamed to say the University has the unfortunate distinction of having the worst housed faculty in the United States."[3] The University of Chicago feared that its deteriorating Hyde Park and Kenwood neighborhoods were becoming a ghetto. Their deterioration was accompanied by a "sharp decline in undergraduate enrollment and loss of prominent faculty."[4]

The University of Chicago, founded at the end of the nineteenth century and endowed by John D. Rockefeller and leading Chicago merchants and industrialists, was located on the south side of downtown, the "Loop," several blocks from Lake Michigan. Its Hyde Park, Kenwood, and Woodlawn neighborhoods, which had grown around the university, were characterized by owner-occupied single family homes and apartments, as well as university-supported commercial development. Most of the faculty and students, and many of the staff, lived in the adjoining neighborhoods.

A distinguishing feature was an Olmstead-designed plaisance, the Midway Plaisance, a mile-long one-block-wide linear park that bisected the campus, connecting it to Chicago's great waterfront park on Lake Michigan.

World War II brought a flood of new residents, primarily African Americans from the southern states, to defense jobs in Chicago, bringing about a dramatic racial change to Chicago's historic eastern European immigrant culture. "From 1940 to 1960 the African American population in Chicago jumped from 278,000 to 813,000 persons."[5] Hyde Park, Kenwood, and Woodlawn were popular destinations for the newly arriving workers, many of whom came from poor rural environments.

In response to deteriorating physical, social, and civic conditions in the neighborhoods, the university established the South East Chicago Commission (SECC) and launched a program with the City of Chicago to improve street lighting and security and support the conservation and rehabilitation of strategic neighborhood blocks. This program was followed by redevelopment when the commission's first director secured the power of eminent domain for the university. "In 1958 the City of Chicago approved the commission's proposed urban renewal plan which encompassed nearly 900 acres and

The University of Pennsylvania across the Skulkill River from Centre City, Philadelphia, Pennsylvania

PHOTO: NATIONAL AGRICULTURE IMAGERY PROGRAM (NAIP)

anticipated clearance of 100 acres with the displacement of 2500 families and local businesses."[6] While the university achieved its goal of securing land for expansion and stabilizing the neighborhood, "the displacement of many African Americans from the neighborhood and the perception that the University was acting dramatically only in its own interest led to deep tension between the University and the African American communities of Chicago that has persisted for decades."[7]

While the University of Chicago's community outreach over the last five decades has been successful the university has once more stirred its communities' concern with the request to utilize city park land for the Barack Obama Presidential Library—a request that was approved by the City of Chicago.

On the east coast, not even the storied Ivy League was free of post–World War II conflict.

University of Pennsylvania. The experience of the University of Pennsylvania, located in West Philadelphia across the Schuylkill River from Center City Philadelphia, was similar to that of the University of Chicago. When the university found its surrounding neighborhoods in serious decline from the mid-1950s onward, its first response, like other urban universities, was to participate in the then-popular federal urban renewal program. Under urban renewal it first cleared twenty blocks for university expansion in an adjacent African American neighborhood. Recognizing the conflict that it was generating, the university and other institutions in West Philadelphia in 1959 reached out to its neighbors and formed the West Philadelphia Corporation to create a "University City" and a redevelopment program that emphasized revitalization rather than clearance of the neighborhoods.

Despite the work of the previous decades, when Judith Rodin assumed the presidency in 1994 she found that "University City" had been in a state of serious decline since the 1950s. "From the mid to late 1980s the area had become increasingly blighted and unsafe. One in five residents had income below the poverty line. Shops and businesses were closing, pedestrian traffic was vanishing, middle-class families were leaving and more houses were falling prey to abandonment and decay. The streets were littered with trash, and abandoned homes and buildings became canvases for graffiti artists and business addresses for drug dealers."[9] The social infrastructure of the neighborhood was in disarray, with poor public schools, insufficient street lighting, poorly maintained public open spaces, inadequate city services such as street cleaning, and public safety a major concern.

With renewed incentive the University of Pennsylvania, along with the city and public and private stakeholders, began what is perhaps the most comprehensive program of neighborhood revitalization ever undertaken by a university: the West Philadelphia Initiative.

The West Philadelphia Initiative articulated five challenging goals: "First, to improve neighborhood safety, services, and capacity; second, to provide high-quality diverse housing choices; third, to revive commercial activity; fourth, accelerate economic development and five, enhance public school options."[9] It was an extraordinary initiative in which the university agreed to take the lead. "It boiled down to this: if Penn did not take the lead to revitalize the neighborhood no one else would."[10] The plans for extensive neighborhood re-investment "required capital, supportive services, and committed management over a long period of years."[11] Rodin said, "I was asking the faculty to trust me in the early days, to believe that a vastly improved neighborhood would benefit Penn academically, facilitate reinvestment, and energize the campus."[12]

In addition to traditional methods of improving public safety with increased policing, the University in partnership with the city and utility companies launched an extensive street lighting program and searched for ways to make the streets more attractive and inviting. Penn took the lead in creating a special services district, the University City District (UCD), incorporated as a not-for-profit and designed to become the management entity for a 2.2 square-mile special district. Unlike the prototypical special district it was not supported by an additional tax, but by volunteer contributions from all the institutions in the district.

The university updated its 30-year-old mortgage guarantee program for faculty and staff and, in partnership with the city and community groups, acquired, improved, and placed back on the real estate market nearly 400 renovated homes. In 1999 the university created both a "Neighborhood Housing and Development Fund" to acquire and renovate rental housing units and a professionally staffed Office of Community Housing, offering outreach and supportive services to the community. The university balanced its neighborhood initiatives with an increase in undergraduate and graduate housing on campus to relieve pressure for student rentals in the neighborhood. The results were significant with "[t]he average home sales price in University City increasing from $78,500 in 1995 to $175,000 in 2003."[13]

In order to revitalize retail, the University retained a professional team and employed its own capital in developing a mixed-use retail, office, housing, and hotel project—Sansom Common. The university added some 25 new stores and 150,000 square feet of complementary retail space between 1999 and 2003.

In what President Rodin characterized as its greatest gamble, the University intervened directly to develop a K-8 public school. Penn leased a five-acre site to the school district for $1, and over the course of ten years provided $700,000 in annual operating support, as well as academic support through the university's Graduate School of Education.

Echoing the University of South Carolina's Bicentennial Master Plan, which redirected the growth of the University of South Carolina to the Congaree River, the University of Pennsylvania redirected its growth eastward to the banks of the Schuylkill River. In 2006 the University of Pennsylvania retained Sasaki Associates to build a master plan for about 14 acres of industrial land that it had purchased on the Schuylkill Riverfront across from Center City in Philadelphia. The master plan, "Penn Connects," introduced the "Bridges of Connectivity," which links the campus to the riverfront, downtown, and the city's regional trail system.

Pictured Left
Aerial viewing the University of Notre Dame campus showing Phase 1 development of the Eddy Street Commons at the bottom of the photograph

PHOTO: USGS HIGH RESOLUTION IMAGERY

Pictured Below
Eddy Street Commons and the south edge of the Notre Dame campus

PHOTO COURTESY OF GREGORY HAKANEN

The University of Pennsylvania's extraordinary neighborhood revitalization program has been characterized by university initiative and leadership, a willingness to commit university capital and seed money to initiate the revitalization programs, a remarkably sophisticated understanding of contemporary urban planning, and an understanding of the needs of its diverse community, how to incentivize the real estate forces at play, and the need for transparency and inclusiveness. The university clearly recognizes that "quality of place" of its framing neighborhoods is essential to achieving its academic mission.

University of Notre Dame. At the onset of his presidency the Reverend Edward A. Malloy (1987–2005) of the University of Notre Dame established a priority of improving the university's relationship with the city of South Bend, Indiana.

In the post–World War II period, South Bend saw a continuous erosion of its manufacturing base. The city never fully recovered from the demise of its automobile industry, the Studebaker Corporation, in the 1960s or, later, the 1990s recession. A homelessness problem in the central business district, typical of many cities, combined with the flight of traditional downtown retail to suburban malls, had a depressing effect upon the entire community. The Northeast

Neighborhood, located immediately south of campus at the university's "front door," deteriorated badly.

Unlike the University of Chicago, the University of Pennsylvania, and the University of South Carolina, the University of Notre Dame did not require additional land for expansion. Driven by both self-preservation and moral considerations, the university's first initiative in 1988 addressed the homeless issue by providing financial support, administrative talent, and—over time—hundreds of student volunteers annually to the South Bend Center for the Homeless, located in the southern portion of the downtown district. The Center for the Homeless has since become a nationally recognized model. In 2001, the University developed the Robinson Community Learning Center in the Northeast Neighborhood, a 7,500 square-foot facility that provides educational programs, training, and a place for neighborhood residents to gather.

To combat the physical deterioration of the Northeast Neighborhood, the university partnered with the City of South Bend, three local medical institutions, and neighborhood residents to create the Northeast Neighborhood Revitalization Organization (NNRO), a 501(c)(3) non-profit organization. The governing board of 14 members includes seven representatives from the founding/funding institutions and an equal number of neighborhood residents. The NNRO sponsors redevelopment programs in the neighborhood by acquiring vacant or depressed properties, clearing dilapidated homes, and developing new homes for sale under affordable housing programs. The NNRO also sponsored The Triangle, the mass redevelopment of a blighted neighborhood near campus, when complete, will result in 52 new homes, 30% under affordable housing programs and 70% at market rates. In all, the NNRO has sponsored construction of approximately 75 new homes.[14]

Independently, Notre Dame sponsors the Notre Dame Avenue Housing Program (NDAHP) in which the university acquires blighted properties, recycles or demolishes deteriorated homes, and sells buildable lots to full-time faculty and staff who build new homes according to established guidelines. In order to catalyze the program, the university initially offered lots at low prices and provided buy-back guarantees, but these incentives were not required after the first four homes. The NDAHP has contributed another 50 new homes to the neighborhood.

At the intersection of campus and the Northeast Neighborhood, Notre Dame engaged an Indianapolis real estate developer to develop a mixed-use, new-urbanist district called Eddy Street Commons. Eddy Street Commons offers 82,000 square feet of office space, 88,000 square feet of retail/restaurant space, 266 high-end apartment units, 200 for-sale townhouse and condominium units, and a 120-room limited-service hotel, with a second 165-room full-service hotel scheduled to be built. Eddy Street Commons provides a secure shopping, dining, and entertainment destination for students, faculty/staff, and neighborhood residents in a convenient location close to campus, downtown, and within walking distance of student residence halls.

President Malloy's program of reaching outside Notre Dame's campus boundaries to partner with its host city, its institutional neighbors, its neighborhood residents, and private developers to address social infrastructure as well as physical planning issues was distinctive. Social infrastructure is more typically an area of avoidance for colleges and universities.

University of South Carolina. Like the other schools mentioned, the University found itself facing a similar crisis in its need to expand the campus. The question was where to expand. The small campus imbedded within the street grid of the planned city was framed on three sides by established residential neighborhoods. A decision was made to move outward from its traditional campus boundary in three quadrants. The State Capitol complex effectively blocked movement to the north. President Russell in 1953 appointed a "committee of local citizens including Susan Guignard to help negotiate the purchase of adjacent property."[15] The first land acquisitions in the early 1950s were carried out by the university through negotiated purchases of individual homes and properties.

In 1959 the Columbia Housing Authority, working under the federal urban renewal program, began acquiring property by eminent domain to the south in the Wheeler Hill neighborhood and to the west of the campus in Ward One, a predominantly African American community. The acquired property was made available to the university. According to Dr. Bobby Donaldson, university professor of history, some residents were given but one month's notice to vacate their properties. Additionally, property owners felt they were not

Pictured Left
"Shotgun" houses on Wheeler Hill 2015

PHOTOS ©JEFF AMBERG

Pictured Below
"Shotgun" house at 907 Greene Street in 1968

PHOTO COURTESY OF THE UNIVERSITY OF SOUTH CAROLINA, SOUTH CAROLINIANA LIBRARY: JOSEPH WINTERS COLLECTION

View of University Inn 2015, showing the Kirkland Apartments and the Black House which were incorporated into the design of the inn

PHOTO ©JEFF AMBERG

given fair market value for their homes. While the City and Columbia Housing Authority initiated the property acquisition with federal authorization, "the leadership of the City, the Housing Authority, and the university board of trustees were comprised of the 'Who's Who' of Columbia including many who had professional and business ties."[16]

The Wheeler Hill and Ward One neighborhoods were predominately African American. At the time the land acquisition program began in 1959 all of the southern states witnessed growing tension and struggles associated with the Civil Rights movement. At the time of the incursion into the Wheeler Hill and Ward One neighborhoods the University of South Carolina was still segregated, admitting only white students. The university admitted its first African-American students four years later in September of 1963.

The Columbia Housing Authority's acquisition of 37 acres of property for the university in the Wheeler Hill neighborhood required the clearance of over 200 existing single family homes and 40 businesses.[17] Most of the single-story wood frame homes were designed in the Southern tradition of "shotgun" houses. Many were rental properties and maintained poorly by their owners. "While some described the section as a slum area, to its residents it was a vibrant community, and many resented that their neighborhood was to be destroyed without their consent."[18] Conditions in the Ward One neighborhood to the west were similar to those in Wheeler Hill. Neighborhood resentment in Ward One was heightened when residents learned that their homes were being demolished for the construction of the university's basketball arena, the Coliseum, which has since been rendered obsolete by the university's new arena, the Colonial Life Center.

In contrast to the physical deterioration of buildings on Wheeler Hill and in Ward One, the University Hills neighborhood to the east was an attractive, tree-shaded, single-family middle-class residential neighborhood occupied by faculty, staff, and longtime residents of Columbia, a "walk to work" neighborhood for faculty and staff. University expansion into this neighborhood was particularly attractive for topographic reasons because it was generally at the same ground elevation as the historic core campus. The stated objective was to create another "Horseshoe" along the axis of an existing street, College Street. Lands to the south (Wheeler Hill) and west (Ward One) would have appeared much less attractive to the University administration because of the sharp fall in the topography and poor conditions of the properties. To the south the topography fell 100 feet in just four blocks from the historic campus core, and to the west the fall in topography was compounded by the need to cross one of the most heavily traveled streets in downtown Columbia: Assembly Street.

Property acquisition in University Hills was carried out on a negotiated one-by-one basis, resulting in a "checkered" pattern of university ownership. This had the effect of devaluing the intervening properties and making them more easily acquired. The university also superimposed into the University Hills neighborhood an 18-story residential tower, Capstone, among single family residences three blocks from the nearest

View of University Hills neighborhood on Pendleton Street in 2015

PHOTO: ©JEFF AMBERG

university facility on Gibbes Green. Two hulking parking structures were added nearby. All three structures dwarfed the adjoining single family residences and could be described as "neighborhood busters."

"The eastward extension of the campus and subsequent disruption of the historic residential neighborhood in the College Street area generated anger and protest among the area's residents, who included Carolina professors and students and some of Columbia's most prominent families. It permanently damaged a neighborhood critical to the long-term health of the university community."[19] When property owners continued to resist, "The Carolina Research and Development Foundation (CRDF) resorted to condemnation proceedings to secure their properties."[20] The goal of a second "Horseshoe" in the neighborhood has never been realized. The awkward space that remains features large institutional buildings on one side with a row of single family residences facing them across the remnant stub of College Street.

In response to the conflict that the campus expansion eastward generated, the university's board of trustees in 1975 modified the university's expansion plan, eliminating six blocks of Wheeler Hill to the south and one block of the proposed eastern expansion. Since the university's Development Foundation had already acquired and cleared the property in Wheeler Hill, the foundation placed the lots back onto the real estate market. The neighborhood today is a prototypical suburban neighborhood of beautiful gentrified single-family homes.

With the clearance of their properties the Wheeler Hill and Ward One neighborhoods had lost their voices. However, the residents of University Hills organized the University Hills Neighborhood Association and secured a historic district designation for their neighborhood. "In the post–World War II era we were fighting the mood of the times; out with the old and in with the new. The City, and University accused us of being elitist and standing in the way of progress. We finally got a handle on it in 2002. Our official position was; 'We can provide you with a stable neighborhood. We buy it and fix it up and it doesn't cost you a nickel. We finally got it together in 2002.'"[21]

When the University Foundation came to the University Hills Neighborhood Association in 2001 with the proposed inn on Pendleton Street—on property that it had acquired in the 1950s and 1960s—it ignited a firestorm of protest from neighborhood residents. The proposal coincided with the arrival of the university's new president, Andrew Sorensen, who arrived early to give a talk to a civic group in the spring of 2002 prior to taking office in July of that year. John Stucker reports that the incoming president was greeted by negative headlines in the local newspaper, such as "City to University: No Hotel."[22] His response upon taking office was "I was hired to do a lot of things at this University and building a hotel was not one of them."[23] President Sorensen instructed Rick Kelly, vice president for finance, and the university's community liaison, Shirley Mills, to "work it out."[24] This led to retaining the local architectural office of Boudreaux, Carter, and Hultstrand to develop a new concept for the inn. The unique design that followed, created by architects Chuck Hultstrand and Scott Lambert, has a neighborhood residential scale and incorporates the historic house and apartment building that were on the site. The design concept was met with unanimous praise by the University Hills Neighborhood Association.

After more than five decades, John Stucker reported in 2015 that the University Hills neighborhood and the university are in concert and jointly addressing the residual issues of code enforcement and public safety.

Conflict Resolution. The initiative of urban universities to expand in the post–World War era was coupled with the flight of the white middle class from the cities to the suburbs. As a defensive move, cities throughout the nation began redeveloping older and blighted urban neighborhoods under a federal redevelopment act. The urban universities that were considered the "crown jewels" of failing cities had the full support of their city's political and business establishment. Such was the case in Columbia with the city's redevelopment programs on Arsenal Hill and Ward One.

Multiple factors have contributed to the urban universities' conflicts with their host communities: (a) the struggle to accommodate the boom in student enrollment brought about by the GI Bill, (b) suburbanization with the flight of the middle class from the inner city, which effected change in the racial and economic composition of the neighborhoods bounding the urban universities, (c) the self- inflicted conflicts when urban universities expanded outward from traditional campus boundaries into adjoining established neighborhoods without understanding the depth of the socioeconomic issues at play therein, and (d) the immaturity of urban community master planning in the 1950s and 1960s.

Contemporary urban planning was birthed in the post–World War II period as the Harvard Graduate School of Design, along with other universities, broadened their planning curricula to include sociology, economics, and government, as well as physical planning and design. Interdisciplinary studios brought students together from the planning, landscape architecture, and architectural design programs. At the same time, two unique professional offices were founded by Harvard professors that had broad influence on professional practice throughout the country and abroad. Walter Gropius, professor of architecture at the Harvard Graduate School of Design, founded the Architect's Collaborative, and Hideo Sasaki, dean of the landscape department at the School of Design, founded Sasaki Associates. Both professional service firms featured an interdisciplinary approach to master planning and design. Also in the early 1960s the American Planning Association (APA) and the Society of College and University Planners (SCUP) were founded.

Jane Jacob's seminal work *The Death and Life of Great American Cities* had become required reading, giving students an understanding of the complexity and richness of the urban environment much in the same way that Rachel Carson's book *Silent Spring* launched the national environmental movement. By the late 1960s the newly minted planning professionals took wing and began to address the mistakes of urban renewal with a new understanding of urban planning. They developed a wide range of techniques for community engagement including the "charrette," town hall meetings, focus groups, traditional interview techniques, and today's web-based programs such as Sasaki's "My Campus."

As David C. Perry and Wim Wiewil noted in their case studies of urban universities in *The University as Urban Developer,* "The second factor influencing the university's community strategy has been the growth of knowledge in the community development field that is now established with a body of learning and literature. The mistakes of urban renewal would not be made today. The importance of neighborhood revitalization as opposed to land clearance is now apparent and community involvement is now a standard."[25]

Shirley Mills, the university's director of government and community relations, describes the current city/university relationship as "excellent." Shirley notes that as of 2015 the mayor is a graduate of the university and the city manager a graduate of the university's Honors College. Residual neighborhood problems are related to student residents, traffic, and student parking.

The University in Transition. The decade of the 1980s saw the University of South Carolina brought on to the international stage under the charismatic and visionary leadership of President James B. Holderman, whose tenure began September 11, 1977, and ended abruptly with his resignation in 1990. Assuming the presidency at age 41, Holderman had been the former executive director of the Illinois Board of Higher Education, and former vice president of the Eli Lilly Foundation. In the interview process for the Presidency, "[h]e charmed the daylights out of the Board" [Board of Trustees].[26]

"President Holderman's most conspicuous impact at Carolina was to raise the University of South Carolina's national and international profile in a program that he called 'windows to the world.'"[27] Through his personal network he brought an extraordinary succession of national and international figures to the university, including Presidents Regan and George H.W. Bush, Pope John Paul II, and celebrities such as Helen Hayes, Jimmy Stewart, Cicely Tyson, and Andrew Lloyd Webber. Lee Bussell, a graduate of and frequent consultant to the university, expressed a sentiment that is still widely held today when he said, "Jim Holderman brought an unbelievable vision to the University of South Carolina."[28]

President Holderman resigned from the university in 1990 following widespread negative publicity triggered by his administration's misuse of discretionary funds. President Holderman had convinced the board of trustees to allow him to have certain segments of revenue called a "discretionary fund." There was no fiscal oversight of the discretionary fund by the board of trustees. Events leading to his resignation began in 1985 with the revelation of Madame Jihan Sadat's salary and expenses of over $390,000 dollars for teaching one class of three hours each week. Madame Sadat was living in Washington, DC, after her husband, Egypt's third president, was assassinated in 1981. Charles Jeffcoat, the University's director of facilities at the time, recalls flying to Washington once a week to pick up Madame Sadat in the university's plane. Over the course of the next decade, the press revealed a series of expenditures from the president's "discretionary fund," including expensive gifts to visiting dignitaries and a student intern program in which students were selected privately and were recipients of gifts and expensive travel with the president. The board of trustees were further embarrassed when the promised availability of financing from donors for new buildings for the Swearingen Engineering Center and the Koger Arts Center proved to be false. The state legislature had to "bail out" the University. In the words of one University of South Carolina trustee serving in the latter part of the Holderman tenure, "It was clear you didn't ask questions about the budget. It was very frustrating." When the board of trustees in 1990 passed strict limits on discretionary spending, President Holderman resigned.

The trustees appointed Arthur K. Smith as interim president and shortly thereafter selected Dr. John Palms, a scientist, to replace him as president. Dr. Palms assumed his office in 1991. Thus began a new era at the University of South Carolina, one that would restore the moral and academic integrity of the university. ■

THE BICENTENNIAL MASTER PLAN DIRECTED GROWTH OF THE UNIVERSITY WEST TO THE VISTA REDEVELOPMENT AREA AND THE CONGAREE RIVER.

The Congaree River PHOTO ©JEFF AMBERG

Section III

A VISION FOR THE VISTA

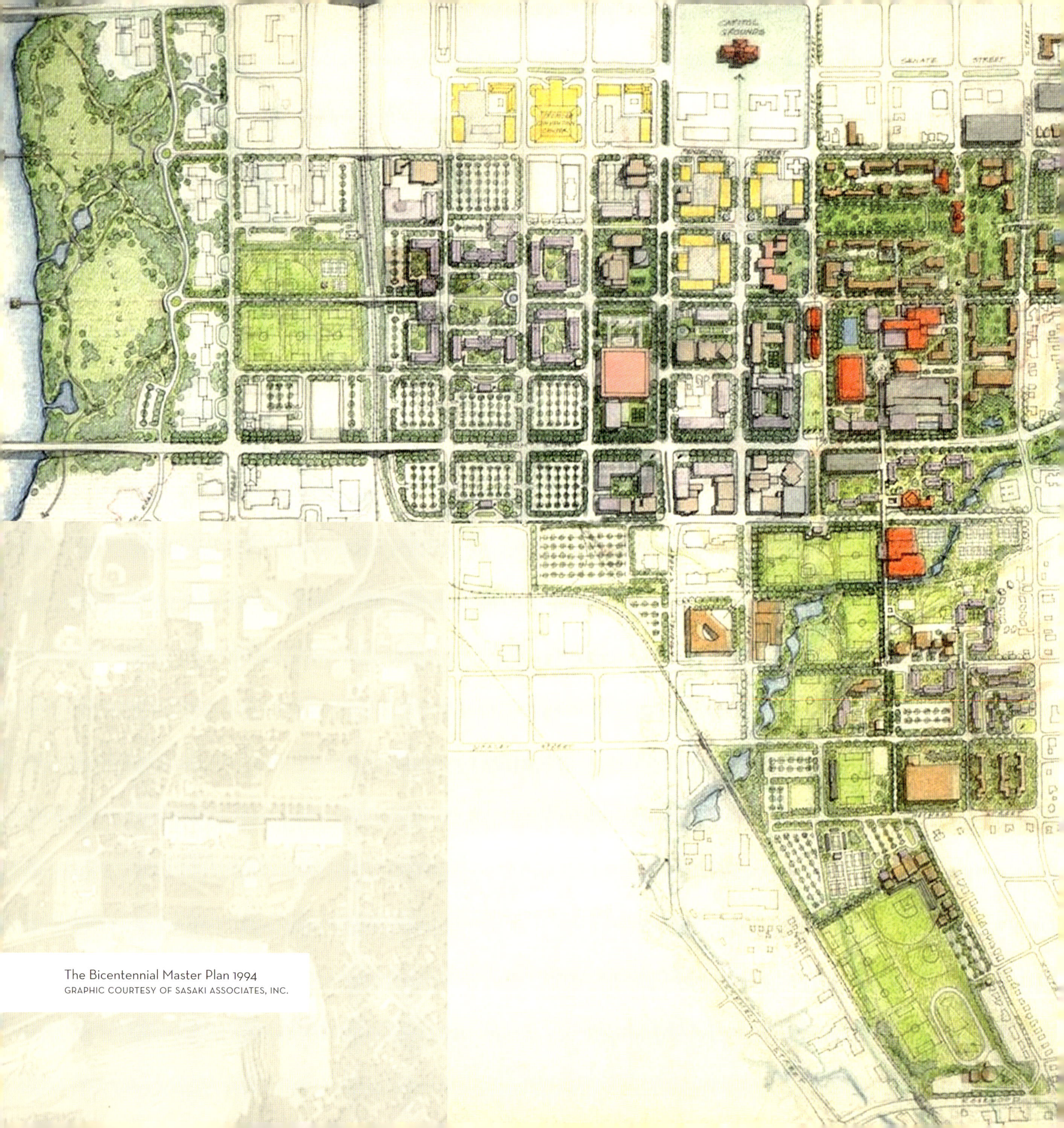

The Bicentennial Master Plan 1994
GRAPHIC COURTESY OF SASAKI ASSOCIATES, INC.

Chapter 6

The Bicentennial Master Plan

At the onset of his presidency at the University of South Carolina in 1991, Dr. John Palms and the trustees of the university launched a long-range strategic planning process that embraced both academic and physical planning dimensions.

The Pawleys Island Retreat. "We had to rebuild. So we planned for the future."[1] These were the words of the chairman of the university's board of trustees, Dr. C. Edward Floyd, who led the board and their new president on the trustees' first retreat at Litchfield on Pawleys Island in January of 1992.

Personally embarrassed by their failure of oversight and the public relations debacle that followed President Holderman's resignation, the trustees took the lead in seeking a "new beginning" at the Pawleys Island retreat. They had begun by selecting as president a distinguished scientist, who promised to restore the "moral and academic integrity" of the university. At the retreat, the trustees first affirmed the overriding goal of serving the citizens of South Carolina: "We are here to educate the people of South Carolina."[2] Then, they launched a strategic planning process to guide the academic and physical development of the campus. The retreat, hosted by several of the trustees who had second homes on the island, also gave them an opportunity to gain an appreciation of the persona and values of their fellow trustees in the relaxed island environment. This first retreat established a precedent for annual retreats by the university's board of trustees.

The trustee's retreat at Pawleys Isalnd laid the foundation for a renaissance in the development of the University of South Carolina campus. The last quarter-century has seen the maturation of the university's academic standing and a dramatic growth in academic and student life facilities on the campus. Student enrollment has grown from 27,600 students in the early 1990s to 35,000 students in the fall semester of 2014. Student population growth has been accompanied by improving SAT scores for entering freshmen, and the university has been able to maintain a student/teacher ratio of 18 to 1. Research expenditures have seen significant growth; the National Science Foundation reported in 2012 that the University of South Carolina ranked 96th among American research universities, with research expenditures of $214,901,000. Total research and sponsored awards totaled $250,100,000 in 2016.

From a physical development perspective, the campus has grown from 240 acres in the early '90s to 410 acres in 2010. In 2014 the university's Development Foundation acquired an additional 300 acres of land for the development of sorely needed playfields for student intramurals and club sports. New academic and research facilities have been built and the quality of student life facilities has been greatly enhanced.

The strategic master planning process launched by the trustees led directly to the development of the Bicentennial Master Plan and imbued the trustees and administration with a sustaining appreciation of the value of master planning. The last quarter-century at the university has seen a continuum of significant planning efforts.

Building a University Campus. Education has historically been one of the most highly held societal values in America. Throughout American history, the building of college and university campuses has had high priority and has been an avocation of community leadership from the time of the Puritans, who founded Harvard College in the 1600s, to great philanthropists like John D. Rockefeller Jr. founding the University of Chicago and Leland Stanford's parents' founding of Stanford University.

Building a university campus is a human endeavor that seems to draw the passion and genuine affection of its "builders," the men and women who are responsible for or volunteer for the care and nurturing of these institutions. Architects and master planners provide a two-dimensional plan for the development of the physical framework of a campus and a vision for its future. The "builders" bring its third dimension: the buildings and landscape. The "builders" skills, along with their personal likes and dislikes, have a profound impact upon the character of the physical environment of the campus.

Chief among the "builders" are university trustees along with university presidents and their administrations, donors, state and community public officials, dedicated alumni, friends, and residents of the host community.

Governing Boards of Trustees. At the University of South Carolina, the trustees have played a central leadership role in building their campus since the founding of South Carolina College in 1801. Historically, board members of the University of South Carolina have taken an active "hands-on" role in university policy and the physical development of the campus. At the founding of South Carolina College a select committee of the board of trustees rejected all the plans submitted in response to their design competition for the new college and drafted their own plan. In one of the university's darkest periods in 1990, capped by the resignation of President Holderman, the trustees took the initiative in restoring the integrity and academic standing of the University. Many of the trustees have served the university for several decades and the university has benefited from the continuity of their experience held over the course of four presidential administrations.

Boards of trustees' primary supervisory responsibility is fiduciary. The critical importance of this fiduciary responsibility was brought home to the trustees at the University of South Carolina when the presidency of James Holderman ended because of fiscal mismanagement. William Hubbard, who came on to the board near the end of James Holderman's presidency, said, "It was very frustrating. The financial data was so murky and unclear."[3] In the words of Herbert Adams, "We were not doing our job until we instituted the Standing Committee on Fiscal Oversight."[4]

In 2013 the Association of College Trustees and Alumni (ACTA) convened a group of policy-makers at the City University of New York to address the role of trustees in the current crisis in higher education. They reported:

1. "Shared governance cannot and must not be an excuse for board inaction, especially now, when America's preeminent role in higher education is threatened.
2. Leadership of higher education is out of balance. Too many trustees have seen their role narrowly defined as boosters, cheerleaders, and donors.
3. Trustees are fiduciaries for their institutions, but have a primary obligation to the taxpayers and students.
4. Trustees and administrators have, for the most part, done a good job of protecting the academic freedom of faculty, but they have often failed to guard the academic freedom of students.
5. Trustees cannot and should not expect participants in the multibillion-dollar industry of intercollegiate athletics to ensure academics remain a college's primary mission."[5]

The ACTA report went on to say, "Trustees must require high standards of themselves and ensure accountability to the families and taxpayers who support the colleges and universities that they govern. America's success as a global leader rides on the quality and accessibility of our nation's higher education institutions."[6]

The manner in which trustees of universities are selected has a strong influence on the character and culture of boards of trustees and their subsequent influence on the physical development of their campuses. Selection of trustees for public universities vary from state to state. In two-thirds of the states, the governor appoints the trustees. In Florida, for example, trustees are selected by the governor and the Board of Governors of the state university system. Each party appoints five trustees as per the constitution to staggered six-year terms. The faculty also appoints one representative (selected by the faculty senate), as does the student body, represented by the president of student government. The faculty and student representatives serve one year terms so they rotate often, resulting in a board of trustees comprised of 12 members.

In Georgia, the governor appoints the Board of Regents, which has jurisdiction over the Georgia system of public colleges and universities. While each of the Georgia colleges and universities have their own separate board or supporting foundation, the president of each institution is responsible to the chancellor of the Board of Regents. Changes in political leadership in those states where the governor appoints trustees can result in both frequent turnover in board membership and a lack of continuity and experience on the boards.

South Carolina faces the opposite situation. The selection process for trustees in South Carolina has resulted in the board of trustees serving very long terms and being dominated by lawyers and other professionals. While the governor is an ex-officio chair of the board, 16 members are elected by the General Assembly in joint session; 2 are appointed by the governor; one by the state superintendent of education; and one by the president of the Greater USC Alumni Association. As of 2014, four trustees had served over 20 years on the board, and one had served over 30 years. The South Carolina board is dominated by white males who graduated from the university. In 2014 the board had one African American and two women. The governor, Nikki Haley, did not reappoint the most prominent woman on the board, Darla Moore, in either of her two appointments—"One of the Governor's greatest mistakes," according to one prominent board member. At the University of South Carolina the selection process for trustees has also resulted in a close relationship to legislature and state politics. "Our Trustees are extremely engaged with politics."[(7)]

The system of trustee selection for public universities provides a direct avenue for the political leadership of states to influence the educational policies and development of their campuses. According to Chris Corr, prominent trustee of the University of Florida in Gainesville, "Typically the Governor is looking for people with demonstrated interest and experience in policy and the State of Florida as well as people that will put time into the role rather than just making an appearance at board meetings. Even though the Board of Governors selects five and the Governor appoints five, the Board consults with the Governor, so typically the sitting Governor has the greatest influence. Governor Scott's [the Governor of Florida in 2014] criteria has been mostly about: first, keeping tuition low and affordable for Florida families; and second policies that lead to students getting jobs. Governor Scott also is promoting a system that works like a 'system.' Meaning he views the whole system as working as one, with different universities focused on different things but all in synch in a way that make the whole better."[(8)]

The character of individual board members and the board culture that develops is an important influence on both policy and the physical development of campuses.

At the University of Florida, trustee Chris Corr also noted, "The character of the board members can vary widely as you would expect. I know at UF the board culture is about 'what's best for the institution' as opposed to any one personality on the board. The University comes first. This is discussed and celebrated often and I think that approach to the culture has served us well."[(9)]

The relationship of a university administration to its board of trustees is an equal challenge to the administration and the trustees. Corr, who is also senior vice president of Rayonier and president of Rayonier's real estate development subsidiary, spoke to this challenge: "I think the short answer is the same as any corporate board has with management is walking the line between management and governance. Every president (CEO) works with his board differently. Some embrace the board as a strategic resource, others want to engage them as little as possible. I think the biggest challenge is finding the right balance between micro managing and having enough information to make informed decisions. At the end of the day, the board will only know what management shares with it but the board has to be tough enough to provoke and pry but only doing it when there is good cause to do so, as opposed to making work with little return or value. If things are held close, bad things can happen like the situation with the football program at Penn State. These are the things that I worry about, how to have enough visibility so a tragic situations like the one at Penn State do not occur but not do the job of management of the university at the same time."[(10)]

A member of the University of South Carolina Administration characterized the administration/board relationship as follows: "Some trustees view the administration as not knowing what they are doing on project related activities, and some administrators view trustees as a necessary evil and too involved." A trustee of the University of South Carolina characterized one of the university's presidents as "not a good listener" and said of another president, "He is more responsive to the Board." The deliberate and slow pace of institutional decision making contrasts sharply with the background of many trustees, who with their typical executive business and legal backgrounds are more decisive in their decision making. Also, trustees are dependent upon data provided to them by university administrators, who by nature are protective of information that they control.

In 2014 William Hubbard, from the perspective of a trustee who has served over 20 years on the university's board of trustees, described the current relationship of the board with its president, Harris Pastides, and his administration, as the best: "Everybody at USC is on the same team . . . the best ever."[11]

The fiduciary responsibility of trustees is their greatest responsibility. In order to carry out this responsibility, trustees must have the appropriate information. When the information is lacking, the potential exists for fiscal mismanagement. A trustee of the University of South Carolina remarked about its budget during the decade of the 1980s: "When Holderman was President no one knew what was going on."

Boards of trustees typically work through a series of committees, such as "Buildings and Grounds" and "Finance." They interface with the university administration through the secretary of the board, who develops the agendas for their periodic meetings and retreats. Boards select a chairman, who plays a key role in the relationship between the board and the administration. University of South Carolina trustee Miles Loadholt, who has served as a trustee since 1996 and chaired the university's board from 2008 to 2012, described the role of chairman: "He speaks for the Board, coordinates the agenda, and organizes the meetings with the Secretary of the Board. The Board Chair is the first to 'get the call' of significant events impacting the University and makes the determination whether the rest of the Board should be informed."[12] The chair for the University of South Carolina board is elected by the members of the board for a four-year term. "It is a position that is actively sought by Board members."[13] The role of chairman of the board is the highest public service role in the state of South Carolina and is highly prized.

University of South Carolina Trustees. At the University of South Carolina, the four longest-serving and most influential members of the board of trustees comprise "a band of fraternity brothers" from Kappa Alpha Order, an organization that glorifies the chivalry of the Old South. Dr. C. Edward Floyd, a practicing surgeon, William Hubbard, a lawyer, Mark Buyck Jr., a lawyer, and Mack I Whittle Jr., a business executive, were all "KAs" as undergraduates at the university. Dr. Floyd and Mark Buyck Jr. were also roommates while at the university. All four fraternity brothers have served 20 or more years on the board.

Kappa Alpha Order, one of the South's historic fraternities, was founded in 1865 at Washington College, Virginia, at the conclusion of the Civil War. Robert E. Lee, who had assumed the presidency of Washington College at the war's end, is described as the fraternity's "Spiritual Founder" on its website. The KAs are known as "the gentlemen of the fraternity world," and "service" is one of their espoused principles—community service, volunteerism, and commitment to philanthropy.

The dedication, indeed passion, and sense of civic responsibility of the trustees of the University of South Carolina is an extraordinary asset in the building of the university. In response to an inquiry about his motivation for giving more than 30 years of service as a board member to the university, Dr. Floyd said, "I love the University."[14] Trustee Mack Whittle's response was "Love of the University and desire to make things better."[15]

Leadership for the Bicentennial Master Plan. Critical trustee leadership for the Bicentennial Master Plan was provided by the chairman of the board, William Floyd, and other dedicated trustees including William Hubbard, Mark Buyck, Herbert Adams, and Mack Whittle. Plan leadership within the administration was the responsibility of Dr. Palms, assisted by his chief executive assistant, Lyles Glenn, and director of facilities Charles Jeffcoat. The "bridge" between the trustees and the administration lies with the secretary to the board. Thomas Stepp played this pivotal role from 1978 until his retirement in 2011.

John Palms

ALL PORTRAITS COURTESY OF THE UNIVERSITY OF SOUTH CAROLINA DIVISION OFCOMMUNCATIONS, OTHER THAN THOSE NOTED

John Palms (1991-2002). Breaking a predilection for selecting internal candidates as president, a search committee chaired by trustee C. Mark Buyck Jr. recommended Dr. John Palms, provost at Emory University in Atlanta, for the presidency at the University of South Carolina to replace President Holderman and interim President Arthur K. Smith. Dr. Palms was a nuclear physicist with multiple degrees, including degrees from the Citadel in Charleston, South Carolina, and a Master of Science from Emory University in Atlanta, Georgia. Born in Rijswijk, Netherlands, Dr. Palms was an academician who told the university's selection committee, "I want to restore the moral authority of the institution and concentrate on its core values." [16]

Upon ascending to the presidency, Dr. Palms launched a restructuring of the management of the university. He carried out a program of thirty-minute interviews with the university's academic and administrative leadership, the vice presidents and deans, in order to become personally acquainted and to assess their interest and capabilities. Many were reassigned after the interview process.

"John Palms proved to be a great President who calmed things down at the University. In response to the scandal in athletics, for example, Dr. Palms personally went to California and recruited Mike McGee from the University of Southern California to serve as the University's new Athletic Director."[17] Trustee Mack Whittle described Dr. Palms as "The right man at the right time"[18] and trustee William Hubbard said, "Dr. Palms brought ethics and principle to the University. He started the cultural change. His administrative processes were first rate and totally transparent. The University has been on an upward trajectory since his selection as President in 1990."[19]

With his focus on rebuilding the institution's academic reputation, Dr. Palms launched the initiative for faculty research and set the goal for the university to become a Carnegie One institution. During his tenure he articulated a budgeting philosophy that advocated that money received from fundraising be channeled into USC's best programs, rather than spreading the funds evenly.

In successfully restoring the moral integrity and academic reputation of the university, Dr. Palms focus was necessarily internal. In 1999 the university's board of trustees commissioned a state-wide survey of the public and business communities to ascertain South Carolinians perception of the university. The findings showed that the public perceived the university as too insular and self centered, showing little regard to the rest of the state. The CEO of SCANA, South Carolina's public utility, famously remarked, "The University is a big dog asleep on the porch. It needs to get off the porch into the yard to play."[20]

The challenge to the university to assume a broader state-wide role was a consideration in the trustees' choice of Andrew Sorensen as the university's next president upon the retirement of President Palms in 2002.

C. Edward Floyd. Dr. Floyd assumed the chairmanship of the board of trustees in the crisis year of 1992 following the resignation of President Holderman. He was challenged to lead the university out of the public relations debacle that had festered for the five previous years. Dr. Floyd led the board of trustees to its first retreat at Litchfield on Pawleys Island, SC, to plan the university's future. "Since we knew that the rebuilding would take time we decided at the retreat to line up the next three guys to chair the Board in the future; William Hubbard [1996 to 2000], followed by Mack Whittle [2000 to 2004], and Herbert Adams [2004 to 2008]."[21]

Under Dr. Floyd and the chairs that followed, the board took a strong leadership role. At times the board disagreed with the university administration. The board, for example, refused to approve expansion of the Osborne administration building in

Pictured Left to Right
C. Edward Floyd
William Hubbard
Mark W. Buyck Jr.

the 1990s, denied the proposal to build a welcome center on what is now the site of the Strom Thurmond Wellness Center, and overcame the administration's reluctance to develop the Greek Village.

While the state's two other senior institutions, Clemson University and the College of Charleston, raised enrollment standards, which effectively reduced their enrollments, the USC Board adopted an opposite tack. Despite the reluctance of the faculty, administrators, and some board members, the board developed an enrollment philosophy of "we are here to educate the people of South Carolina" and welcomed all qualified students who meet the university's entrance requirements. This policy has led to a dramatic increase in enrollment, which has also been accompanied by slowly rising SAT scores.

William Hubbard. A soft-spoken lawyer, William Hubbard succeeded Dr. Floyd as board chair from 1996 to 2000, and has remained on the board of trustees to the present time, providing over 28 years of service to the university. Hubbard assumed the role of president of the American Bar Association for 2014-2015. A staunch supporter of master planning, Hubbard has strongly influenced the aesthetics and environmental quality of the campus while serving as board chair and as a member of the trustee's buildings and grounds committee. The buildings and grounds committee at the University of South Carolina oversees long-range planning and reviews proposed new projects prior to full board of trustees action. Hubbard's concern for the quality of the campus landscape and recognition of the need for shade in Columbia's hot climate has led him to play the role of "Johnny Appleseed" on the campus. He was seen on many occasions walking the campus with Ben Coonrod, the university's landscape architect, now retired, showing Ben locations on the campus where he felt additional shade trees could be planted.

Mark W. Buyck Jr. Mark W. Buyck Jr., a lawyer, was appointed to the board in 1987 and has more than 20 years of service with the board. Buyck chaired the selection committee that brought Dr. Palms to the university. As a member of the buildings and grounds committee of the trustees, Buyck's strong advocacy for master planning and a traditional style of architecture has had a profound impact on the quality of architectural design for new campus buildings. He believes the university's biggest challenges are the growth in enrollment, the declining state monetary support for the university, and the desire "to get down to the river" via the Innovista Master Plan.

Thomas Stepp. Thomas Stepp served as secretary to the board of trustees as well as the university's corporate secretary from 1987 to his retirement in 2011. He served under the last four presidents of the university and through multiple changes in the leadership of the board of trustees. In his role as secretary to the board of trustees he was the liaison between the administration and the board. The role of secretary to the board included drafting the agendas for board meetings, drafting motions, recording the official minutes of board meetings, and seeing that board members got the information they needed.

Pictured Left to Right
Thomas Stepp
Lyles Glenn
Charles Jeffcoat

Stepp engendered an extraordinary degree of confidence and trust from the board of trustees as well as the university administrations that he served. He was a quintessential diplomat in the essential "bridging" role between the administration and the trustees.

At one of Sasaki's periodic review sessions with the university's director of facilities, trustee William Hubbard encountered the Sasaki design team, who were on campus to present the concept plan for Foundation Square. Upon learning of the forthcoming presentation, Hubbard announced that he would attend. Since the proposed potentially controversial design concept had yet to be shown to anyone in the administration or to any trustee, the director of facilities immediately notified Stepp, who joined the presentation. After a PowerPoint presentation, a response to the design concept was sought from the attendees. Silence prevailed until Hubbard spoke up to say that he "loved" the idea, whereupon Stepp, with evident relief, stood up and exited the room.

In appreciation of his 25 years of service the board of trustees awarded Stepp an honorary degree upon his retirement.

Lyles Glenn. Lyles Glenn assumed the position of chief executive assistant to the president under President Dr. Palms. He said, "The campus was in a shambles when we began our work. Our first focus was to rebuild the administration, the University Foundations, and to develop a long range strategic master plan."[22] In 1992, at the direction of President Palms and the board of trustees to "improve planning," Glenn along with Charles Jeffcoat, director of facilities, initiated a search for a national planning and design consultant to develop a long-range strategic master plan for the campus. This led to the development of the University of South Carolina Bicentennial Master Plan published in 1994.

During his tenure one of Glenn's significant initiatives occurred when US Senator Fritz Hollings of South Carolina came to him and reported that the United States Department of Justice (DOJ) was "thinking about the development of a training facility (Advocacy Center) for its lawyers on a university campus." Hollings made clear to Glenn that he expected him "to make this happen" at the University of South Carolina.[23] Glenn made it happen, and the US DOJ established a training facility known as the Advocacy Center for its employees on the USC campus. While the anticipated programmatic synergy with the university's law school never materialized, the university was the beneficiary of a facility that brings lawyers from all over the United States to its campus. Mr. Glenn assumed the role of vice president and chief operating officer of the university in 1999 and served until his departure in 2002.

Charles Jeffcoat. Charles Jeffcoat came to the university in 1988 as director of facilities. Jeffcoat bridged the last two years of the Holderman presidency and served through the presidency of Andrew Sorensen. He was assisted by three key associates, affectionately referred to as "Charlie's Angels"—Stacie Davenport, Lisa Jerald, and Donna Collins—who helped him grow and develop the facilities' operation in response to the growth of the university.

When he arrived in 1988 the university lacked a campus master plan. Jeffcoat recalled his frustrations in addressing facility decisions and noted that decisions were often based upon who had the money or who was the strongest dean.

Jeffcoat directed the planners and designers in the development of the most significant and comprehensive master planning effort ever undertaken by the University of South Carolina: the Bicentennial Master Plan. The Bicentennial Master Plan dramatically reordered the direction of growth of the campus and established a series of sustainable campus design principles which still govern campus development today. Jeffcoat retired in 2008.

The Need for Planning. "Charles Jeffcoat the Director of Facilities had told us that the campus grounds and facilities were being neglected and recommended that we prepare a comprehensive campus master plan."[(24)] Jeffcoat had recognized the need for a campus master plan upon his arrival at the university in 1988. Student enrollment was growing, student life facilities had been badly neglected, campus grounds were in poor condition, and campus green spaces were being paved for surface parking lots. Decisions regarding the need for new space and the use of existing space lacked an analytical foundation.

With the support of the trustees and vice president of facilities, Pete Denton, who made the funding available, Jeffcoat launched the national search for a campus master planner, leading to the selection of Sasaki Associates Inc., who associated with the local Columbia architectural firm of Boudreaux, Hulstrand and Carter Ltd., Swygert Crowder Consulting Engineers, and the space management firm of Paulien Associates of Denver, Colorado. Sasaki's work with colleges and universities throughout the United States and the firm's work with Mayor Joseph Riley of Charleston, SC, on the master plan of downtown historic district and the design of the Waterfront Park were cited as factors in the selection process.

"When we decided to do the master plan we then got somebody 'damn good.' You [Sasaki] were our guiding light."[(25)]

A quarter-century of intensive master planning and design for the campus has followed the preparation and publication of the Bicentennial Master Plan in 1994. While multiple architects and engineers have carried out project design work within the framework of the master plan, the university has maintained a long-term relationship with the campus planner it selected in 1992.

Rick Kelly, who came to the university in 2000, well after the Bicentennial Master Plan was being implemented, spoke to this relationship when he said, "When I came to the University the one constant of the Trustees was their reliance on Sasaki. At the Trustee's Buildings and Grounds Committee meetings the inevitable question would be . . . 'What does Sasaki think about this?'"[(26)] Fred Delk, executive director of the Columbia Development Corporation, said, "Sasaki served as a 'bridge' in the town/gown relationship between the City and the University."[(27)]

The Planning Process. The planning process that was initiated for the Bicentennial Master Plan followed the work of a "futures committee," chaired by Dr. Jerry Odom. Under the direction of Lyles Glenn, executive vice president for administration, the planning work that followed was designed to focus on four principal objectives set forth by the futures committee:

1. "To respond to the issues and a set of priority actions and projects for both short term and long term needs of the campus."

2. "To establish a long-range vision for the physical development of the campus that would provide a framework for siting of capital projects and provide a constructive role with surrounding neighborhoods."

3. "To undertake a rigorous assessment of the utilization of existing space on campus and to develop a set of space planning standards for the management of building space."

4. "To develop a computerized system of building conditions and building information for space management."[(28)]

The planners initiated a contemporary, interdisciplinary campus master planning process for the Bicentennial Master Plan that included broad engagement with the university community. The process was driven by the goals and objectives set forth by the futures committee and under the purview of a master plan committee. A rigorous analysis of existing physical conditions and space use was followed by an exploration of plan alternatives, leading to the development of the Master Plan. The neglect of the campus grounds, illustrated in a presentation to the trustees by an image of a large over-flowing trash dumpster sitting astride a principal campus pedestrian pathway, made a lasting impression upon the trustees.

The master plan committee for the Bicentennial Plan was composed of university faculty, staff, and administration, and student representatives. The committee included Dr. R. W. "Peter" Denton, vice president for business and finance; Dr. John J. Duffy, vice provost and executive dean for regional campuses and continuing education; Dr. Walter B. Edgar, director of southern studies; Charles G. Jeffcoat, director of facilities management and university architect; Dr. James C. Moeser, vice president for academic affairs and provost; Dennis A. Pruitt, vice president for student affairs and dean of students; Dr. David H. Rembert, professor of biology and associate dean of the College of Science and Mathematics; Dr. James H. Rex, vice president for university advancement; Thomas L. Stepp, secretary of the board of trustees; Dr. George Terry, vice provost and dean of libraries and information systems; Tom Young, student body president 1992–93; and Carl Solomon, student body president '93–94. The master planning was carried out by an interdisciplinary planning and design team composed of professional planners, architects, landscape architects, engineers, and space managers. The planning team first confirmed the objectives established by the futures committee and goals of the master plan committee. Particular attention was given to an analysis of the university's use of its existing building space and its methods for managing space. A comprehensive program statement was derived from existing and projected facility needs, including academia, research, student services and housing, recreation, campus open space, traffic and parking, and campus utilities.

The facilities development program was informed by an extensive interview process carried out with students, government officials, and university faculty, staff, and administration. Following preparation of the program statement, a series of alternative plan strategies were developed with the master plan committee. A preferred plan alternative was drawn from the alternative concepts, which served as the foundation for the Bicentennial Master Plan.

The amount of space, management of its use, and the character of space at a university is a principal component of a university's capital budget and annual operating costs. The "silos" that tend to develop around the separate academic units at a university can lead to the "privatization" of office and teaching spaces. When this has resulted in lower overall space utilization, it then leads to increased capital and operating costs. Competition among academic units and the "personalization" of space through a poorly managed building programming and design process—or a process dominated by an academic or architectural personality—can lead to a building that is inefficient and obsolete to succeeding users. The University System of Georgia, for example, was burdened by the design of a series of round buildings, fashionable in the 1970s. Their interior trapezoidal shapes proved inefficient from the onset and defy efforts at renovation for contemporary office or teaching use today.

At the University of South Carolina, Sasaki's space management consultant, Dan Paulien of Paulien Associates, carried out the first comprehensive assessment of building space use at the university, utilizing national space standards from the Society of International College and University Planners. The space analysis revealed urgent needs for additional space and the need for central management of classroom space. In the early 1990s the individual academic units at the university had priority access to the classrooms in buildings assigned to their colleges and schools. Unassigned hours in classrooms were pooled and scheduled by hand on spreadsheets in the registrar's office.

The Facilities Program. In the fall of 1993, the University of South Carolina accommodated some 27,600 students on the Columbia campus—16,250 undergraduates and 11,350 graduate students. In the early 1990s USC projected a relatively modest growth of 1–2% each year for the forthcoming decade, resulting in an additional 4,000 students by the end of the decade. Analysis of the academic programs revealed significant deficiencies for research space in the College of Science and Mathematics, office and teaching spaces in the School of Public Health and the College of Humanities and Social Sciences, and "back" office space for administrative services. Critical deficiencies were also identified in student life facilities, including student housing, campus meeting and social spaces, dining facilities, and indoor and outdoor recreation facilities.

Student housing at the university was in particularly poor physical condition in the '90s, which, coupled with restrictive parietal rules at the time, created a very unattractive environment for on-campus student living. In the late 1980s a South Carolina state legislator, a chairman of the state's house education committee, and a trustee, attempted to superimpose a parietal rule prohibiting opposite sex visitation in on-campus student residences. The *Atlanta Journal Constitution* satirized the University of South Carolina as the "Virgin Vault."[29] The university's parietal rules and the poor condition of much of the existing student housing resulted in a lack of demand for on-campus housing. University administrators were very reluctant to consider additional new student housing. Although the housing program for the Bicentennial Plan identified the need for an additional 2,500 beds of on-campus student housing, the vice president of student affairs declared at the time that he did not see any new student housing on the campus for the foreseeable future. However, following the goal set forth by the trustees at their Pawleys Island retreat to "build

DEVELOPMENT PROGRAM FOR THE BICENTENIAL MASTER PLAN

PRIORITY NEEDS 1994

ACADEMIC ADMINISTRATIVE		
APPLIED PROFESSIONAL SERVICES	RELOCATE	
JOURNALISM AND MASS COMMUNICATIONS	RELOCATE	
HUMANITIES AND SOCIAL SCIENCES	28,000	ASF
SCIENCE AND MATHEMATICS	135,000	ASF
PUBLIC HEALTH	18,000	ASF
LIBRARIES AND COLLECTIONS	196,000	ASF
ADMINISTRATION	50,000	ASF
ADVOCACY CENTER	260,000	ASF
STUDENT LIFE		
HOUSING	2,000–2,500	BEDS
SERVICES	40,000	ASF
RECREATION-OUTDOOR	41	ACRES
RECREATION-INDOOR	150,000	ASF
PARKING	1,500–2,000	SPACES
CAMPUS ENVIRONMENT		
CAMPUS GATEWAY, PEDESTRIAN CIRCULATION AND OPEN SPACE		
VARSITY ATHLETICS		
INDOOR PRACTICE FACILITY, ROOST IMPROVEMENTS, PRACTICE FIELDS, STADIUM IMPROVEMENTS		

Pictured Above from the Top
View to Swearingen Engineering Center and Main Street showing 100-foot fall in typography from the Horseshoe

View of Assembly Street showing 6 lanes of moving traffic with parking on curbside and the center median

PHOTOS ©JEFF AMBERG

things to attract students," parietal rules were modified, which has led to the development of hundreds of new and renovated housing units on the campus.

The Bicentennial Master Plan outlined a comprehensive implementation program and capital budget to achieve its programmatic goals. New facilities supported academic studies, housing, varsity athletics, deferred maintenance, campus environmental improvements, and parking. The total estimated capital costs of the proposed facility program for the Bicentennial Plan was $425 million for new facilities and deferred maintenance. Chuck Hultstrand recalls the "shocked" expressions during the final presentation of the plan when the $425 million capital budget for proposed academic, administrative, student life, parking, varsity athletic facilities, and green space improvements were presented to the trustees. Dr. Floyd, board chair, also recalled the trustees' "sticker shock" and expressed his wonder in having accomplished the entire program within a decade.

Planning Challenges. At the beginning of the 1990s, the university's greatest need was strong organizing principles for the redevelopment and expansion of the campus. Significant physical development factors confronted the planning and design team in accommodating the facilities program on the existing campus: first, reconciling the development program with the city of Columbia's historic street grid; second, addressing the topographic pattern of hills and valleys, and third, reconciling the university's growth with its adjoining residential neighborhoods.

City streets, such as Assembly Street with its 150-foot wide right-of-way, six lanes of high-speed traffic, and parking on both sides, as well as along a center island in the street, were particularly challenging to students crossing between class changes. The university had already placed its arena, the Coliseum, its first academic facility, the Koger Center of the Performing Arts, the School of Music and the Moore School of Business on the west side of Assembly Street.

Topographically the historic Horseshoe sits at the highest point of the campus, with campus facilities to the south 100 feet "downhill." The Swearingen Engineering Center, for example, sits over 100 feet downhill from the Horseshoe. While the university had already undertaken a reconciliation process with the University Hills neighborhood at the onset of the planning, and the trustees had stopped further university incursion into Wheeler Hill, the university's neighbors were still wary of university initiatives.

Planning Principles. A series of organizing principles evolved to guide development of the Bicentennial Master Plan. First, the plan directed future growth of the campus west toward the Vista redevelopment area and the Congaree River, away from the University Hills and Wheeler Hill neighborhoods. Second, the plan called for maximizing the efficient use of existing campus lands and building space. Major reinvestment and completion was recommended for previously developed but unfinished areas such as South Campus. Third, the plan embraced the distinctive planning and design principles inherent in the Horseshoe and recommended extending these principles to the remainder of the campus. Fourth, the plan acknowledged the historic street grid of the city and discouraged the university from attempting to close streets, but proposed that public streets embedded in the campus be redesigned as "shared streets" with enhanced pedestrian safety and amenities.

Design Principles. In its growth spurt in the post–World War II period, the university had sought a new modern campus by focusing on buildings designed by the leading architects of that period, including the Architects' Collaborative (TAC), Skidmore, Owings, and Merrill, and Edward Durrell Stone. Each architect produced modern buildings. However, the focus was on individual building design at the expense of their relationship to the larger campus. American campus design is distinguished by its design composition of buildings and open space. The open landscape spaces serve as the connective tissue between buildings. At the University of South Carolina campus, the environmental quality of the "connective tissue" of the campus had been steadily deteriorating, a condition compounded by the paving of green space for surface parking.

In 1992 the design team pointed to the Horseshoe with its beautifully proportioned interior green framed by classical historic buildings as the prototypical model of campus design. The interior green provided safe and attractive interior pedestrian movement between buildings while the buildings were accessible to vehicles from the surrounding frame of public streets.

Extending the spatial, landscape, and architectural design qualities of the historic Horseshoe to the remainder of the university campus became the central urban design concept for the Bicentennial Master Plan.

View of College Street Promenade

PHOTOS COURTESY OF KEITH MCGRAW

Campus diagrams

GRAPHICS COURTESY OF SASAKI ASSOCIATES, INC.

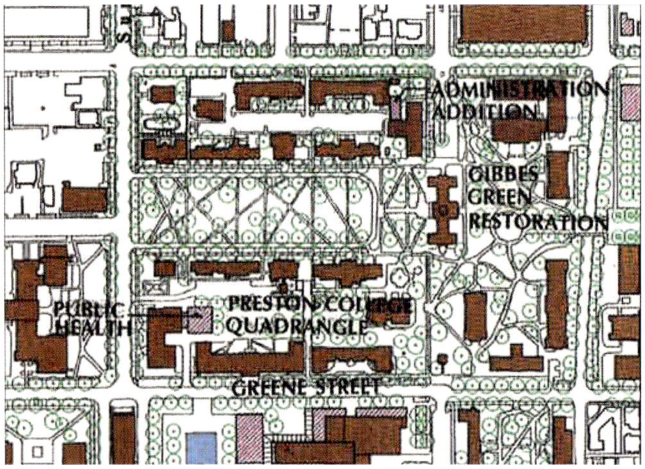

The Horseshoe

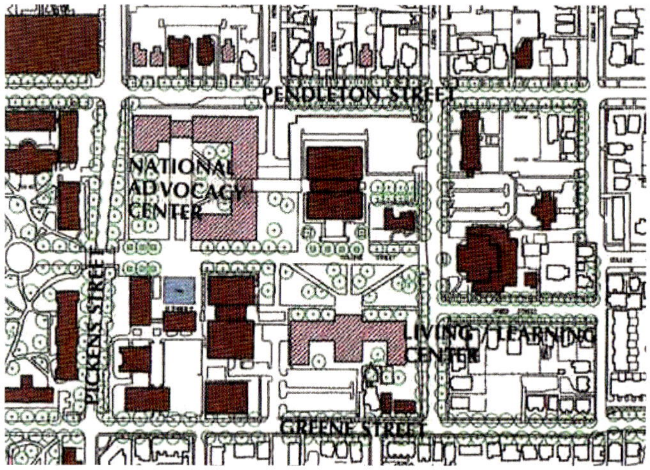

College St. Promenade

Land Use. The land use element of the Bicentennial Master Plan defined seven campus districts with specific recommendations for facility and environmental improvements for each: The Horseshoe, the College Street Promenade, Central Campus District, Science District, South Campus District, the Varsity Campus District, and the Assembly and South Main Streets Districts. Most of the recommendations of the Bicentennial Master Plan have been implemented. The plans are outlined below.

The process of restoration of the historic buildings and landscape of the Horseshoe had already been undertaken. The plan recommended a similar restoration of landscape and buildings on Gibbes Green and the relocation of back-of-house administrative office functions from the academic core to the periphery of the campus in order to maintain a compact pedestrian academic core and to remove the parking requirements of these administrative facilities.

To implement this recommendation, the university purchased an office building at 1600 Hampton Street, five blocks from the Horseshoe, and has consolidated many of its back-of-house functions at that location. Buildings fronting Gibbes Green have been restored and the interior landscaped green underwent extensive renovation in 2015.

The 1960s concept of creating a campus quadrangle terminating in Capstone along College Street (the College Street Promenade) had never been fully realized. A row of small houses remained on the south side of the street. The Bicentennial Plan recommended that the existing houses be moved a block away to vacant lots on the north side of Pendleton Street. The move of the houses was designed to repair fabric of the neighborhood street, where the university had acquired and demolished houses for the proposed University Inn. Relocation of the houses was designed to provide a site for a proposed new Living/Learning Center.

While the concept of the College Street Promenade has not been implemented, the "Inn at USC" has filled the vacant lots on Pendleton Street with a unique design that has restored the residential character of Pendleton Street.

The Bicentennial Plan envisioned major redevelopment of the core campus as the university's "town center," incorporating expanded food service, retail, and meeting spaces at Russell House (the existing student center), a new student fitness center, and a university inn with hospitality and conferencing facilities supported by a new 1,000-car parking structure. Student dinning and services facilities in Russell House have been improved. The University Inn was placed on Pendleton Street, where it bears a direct relationship to the Advocacy Center of the Department of Justice. The proposed site for the student fitness center on Blossom Street proved to be too small, leading to the current location of the Strom Thurmond Wellness Center at the intersection of Assembly and Blossom Streets.

The plan's recommendation for the expansion of science facilities has been implemented with the development of the 260,000 square-foot Graduate Science Research Center. Removal of the "veiled block" dormitories on the site later permitted development of the university's new Honors College.

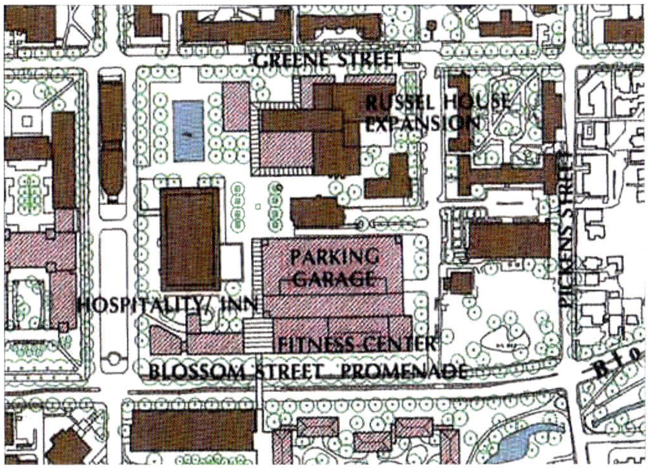

Central Campus

A comprehensive redevelopment of South Campus was recommended for expansion of student housing and recreation facilities. The plan also envisioned redevelopment of Rocky Branch Creek as a linear park, and the renovation of the historic Booker T. Washington High School auditorium as a center for community activity and cultural exchange. The plan anticipated the eventual removal of the existing Blatt Physical Education Center (which lay in the flood plain of Rocky Branch Creek) with completion of the proposed new fitness center.

Booker T. Washington High School has been renovated and three new student housing complexes have been developed. As of 2015 preliminary planning was underway for a comprehensive redevelopment of South Campus for mixed-use housing.

Despite the lack of enthusiasm of the university's staff for new housing on campus, the introduction of the new suite-style housing for the East Housing Quad, designed by Sasaki and Boudreau, Carter, and Hultstrand, proved immensely popular with the students and was quickly followed by architect Robert A. M. Stern's design of the South Quad and later the West Quad. The infamous "veiled block" dormitories were demolished and a systematic renovation program was initiated for other existing student housing on the campus. The veiled block dormitories were structures completely covered with a screens of pierced tiles which limited outside views from the windows and became a nesting place for a variety of wildlife.

To accommodate the programmatic needs of varsity athletics, the plan recommended redevelopment of the existing varsity athletic facilities at the Roost and the acquisition of adjoining property for varsity field expansion. Under the leadership of athletic director Eric Hyman, a comprehensive athletics master plan was carried out, leading to the development of the Athletics Village and construction of new varsity athletic venues. The Colonial Life Center, a multipurpose arena for basketball and other public events located in the Vista redevelopment area, has replaced most of the functions of the existing Coliseum.

By the 1990s the west side of Assembly Street was home to a series of semi-public facilities, including the university's performing arts facility, the Koger Center, and the School of Music. The Bicentennial Master Plan recommended redesign of both Assembly and South Main Streets to improve the quality of their pedestrian environment by reducing the number of travel lanes, and improvements to pedestrian safety and landscape. The university, at its initiative, has redeveloped four blocks of Assembly Street from Blossom to Pendleton Streets. Trustee William Hubbard, who took a personal interest in the redevelopment of Assembly Street, tells the story of working with the State Department of Public Works, who rejected the university's landscape architect's preferred species of street tree, a native oak, for fear of falling acorns damaging passing automobiles.

Transportation. "A University is a series of individual faculty entrepreneurs held together by a common grievance over parking," said the late Clark Kerr, president of the University of California system from 1958 to 1967.[30] The demand for parking in the post–World War II period has been, perhaps, the most destructive force to the environmental quality of the traditional American campus. It is a manifestation of the familiar 1960s song, "They paved paradise and put up a parking lot."

Parking space remains one of the most volatile facility issues on American campuses. The goals of the parking and vehicular circulation element of the Bicentennial Master Plan were twofold. While providing convenient parking for visitors, faculty, staff, and commuter students, the primary goal was to restore the quality of the campus landscape. A parking methodology

View of the University of South Carolina campus in 2006

PHOTO COURTESY OF SOUTH CAROLINIANA LIBRARY

was developed that assessed parking demand for each campus district. The Master Plan provided needed faculty and staff parking for each district within reasonable walking distances of their offices and teaching facilities. The plan recommendation that administrative functions not requiring interface with students be moved off the core campus was part of the strategy to reduce parking demand in the academic core. The university purchase of 1600 Hampton Street, five blocks from the core campus, removed hundreds of cars from the core campus.

While the University of South Carolina campus had been spared the worst of "suburbanization," it had not been immune to the parking disease. Small surface parking lots had been "tucked" into formerly green spaces on the historic core campus and two hulking parking structures, the Pendleton and Senate Street garages, were built in the adjoining single-family residential neighborhood.

When trying to solve the campus parking problem at Cornell University in Ithaca, New York, Ronald G. Ehrenberg, long time administrator, shared his frustration when he wrote; "Faculty members believe that they have the inalienable right to park right next to their office and be able to leave campus and return during the day whenever they want to."[31] As campus green spaces were paved to accommodate cars on traditionally pedestrian campuses and distances between academic facilities lengthened to accommodate parking lots, universities across the country not only saw a decline in the beauty and environmental quality of their campuses, but an increasing loss of the efficiency of use of academic facilities. Utilization of academic space becomes increasingly inefficient with a lengthening class change interval. A five-minute change in the "class change interval" results in the loss of one class over the course of a day. The suburban "spread" of campuses has added to the capital requirements for new buildings, extended the maintenance of grounds, and stretched the operating costs of campus bus systems.

The Bicentennial Master Plan resisted the demands for "parking at the front door" and instead recommended "greening" of the campus and restoration of campus landscapes that had been paved. This included, for example, removal of the old science annex buildings and surface parking behind the President's House to provide a site for an addition to the Health Science Building and a new green quadrangle. In the spring of 1994 it was pointed out to the director of facilities, Charles Jeffcoat, that the small 40-car surface parking area that intruded between Russell House and the reflecting pool in front of Thomas Cooper Library could easily be removed. Derrick Huggins recalled the chairman of the board of trustees, William Hubbard, saying to Jeffcoat, "I want that parking lot removed before my tenure as Chairman is up."[32] That fall Jeffcoat reported that between the summer and fall quarter, when students and faculty were gone, and "under the cover of darkness," he had his work crew remove the asphalt parking lot and replace it with sod. The managers of the student union now report that the resulting green space has become one of the most popular outdoor spaces on the campus for student activities.

The Bicentennial Master Plan did not attempt to alter the historic street grid of the City. Columbia's historic town plan had served the university as a de facto campus master plan, providing both direction and an orthogonal order to the incremental growth of the campus. The disarray of the campus below Heyward Street, the southern limit of the historic planned city, with its industrial character and confused pattern of land use and vehicular circulation, is evidence of the value of Columbia's historic street grid in guiding the development of the city and the university campus.

A Vision for the Twenty-First Century. The Bicentennial Master Plan accommodated the ten-year projected facility needs of the university within the confines of the existing campus grounds. However, conscious of the long life of institutions and the trustees' goal that the university be able to welcome all qualified student applicants from a growing state, the Bicentennial Plan set forth a vision for the future of the campus beyond the ten-year planning horizon.

A "Futures Plan" was crafted illustrating future growth of the campus westward through the Vista redevelopment area to the banks of the Congaree River. At the time of the development of the Bicentennial Plan in 1990, the Vista area was dominated by vacant properties, surface parking lots, an abandoned steel mill, abandoned rail lines, and small commercial structures. Redevelopment of the Vista was focused on the redevelopment of the historic mercantile buildings along the Gervais Street corridor. Under the city's redevelopment program, derelict facilities in the area were gradually being cleared and the historic street grid was being restored. A single active railroad corridor remained in the Vista after the city consolidated the railroads passing through the city in 1982. The remaining rail line splits the area along a north-south axis and imposes a challenging physical barrier for development between the campus and the Congaree River.

Don Olson, Sasaki principal and project designer for the Bicentennial Master Plan, was a gifted artist in addition to being a Harvard-educated landscape architect and urban designer. He handcrafted the beautiful illustrations of the Bicentennial Plan and the Futures Plan; computer graphics were in their early stages of development in the early 1990s and very limiting in their design expression.

The Futures Plan illustrated a mixed-use urban district of academic, housing, research, and private development west of Assembly Street, organized along an extension of Greene Street. The existing Greene Street has its origin in Five Points, a student entertainment node east of the campus, and traverses the existing campus to the Vista, where it abruptly ends at the rail line. The Futures Plan envisioned Greene Street as a landscaped pedestrian promenade, reaching from the academic heart of the existing campus westward, crossing Assembly Street, bridging the rail line, and terminating in a proposed waterfront park on the Congaree River. It was anticipated that the Futures Plan would be carried out in partnership with the city's redevelopment agency and private development partners. Jim Doolin, Sasaki's project planner for the Bicentennial Master Plan, said his enduring memory of his role in the development of the plan was that "[w]e reached for a larger civic vision for the University campus that engaged with its host community and broke the mold of a traditional self-contained inward focused campus."[33]

The Futures Plan developed as part of the Bicentennial Master Plan in the early 1990s was the precursor of the Innovista Master Plan, developed in 2006.

Building the Plan. The university board of trustees enthusiastically endorsed the Bicentennial Master Plan. In the words of Dr. Floyd, chairman of the board, "It is important that the University's buildings and campus grounds reflect the quality of the University of South Carolina's academic programs. With the Bicentennial Master Plan we will not only refine the University's appearance, we will build a more supportive and nurturing environment for today's students and for generations to come."[34] Trustee William Hubbard described the Bicentennial Master Plan as "[a] world class plan that enabled us to see the University campus in a completely different way."[35]

Heeding the analysis and recommendations of the Master Plan, President Palms (later followed by President Sorensen) with the enthusiastic support of the board of trustees launched a vigorous implementation program. Over the next decade, new building facilities rectified the academic as well as student life deficiencies identified in the Master Plan. The university's Futures Plan, which led to the location of the City/County Convention Center and the Convention Center Hotel following development of the Colonial Life Center, was a testament to the power of envisioning the future beyond the typical ten-year planning horizon. ■

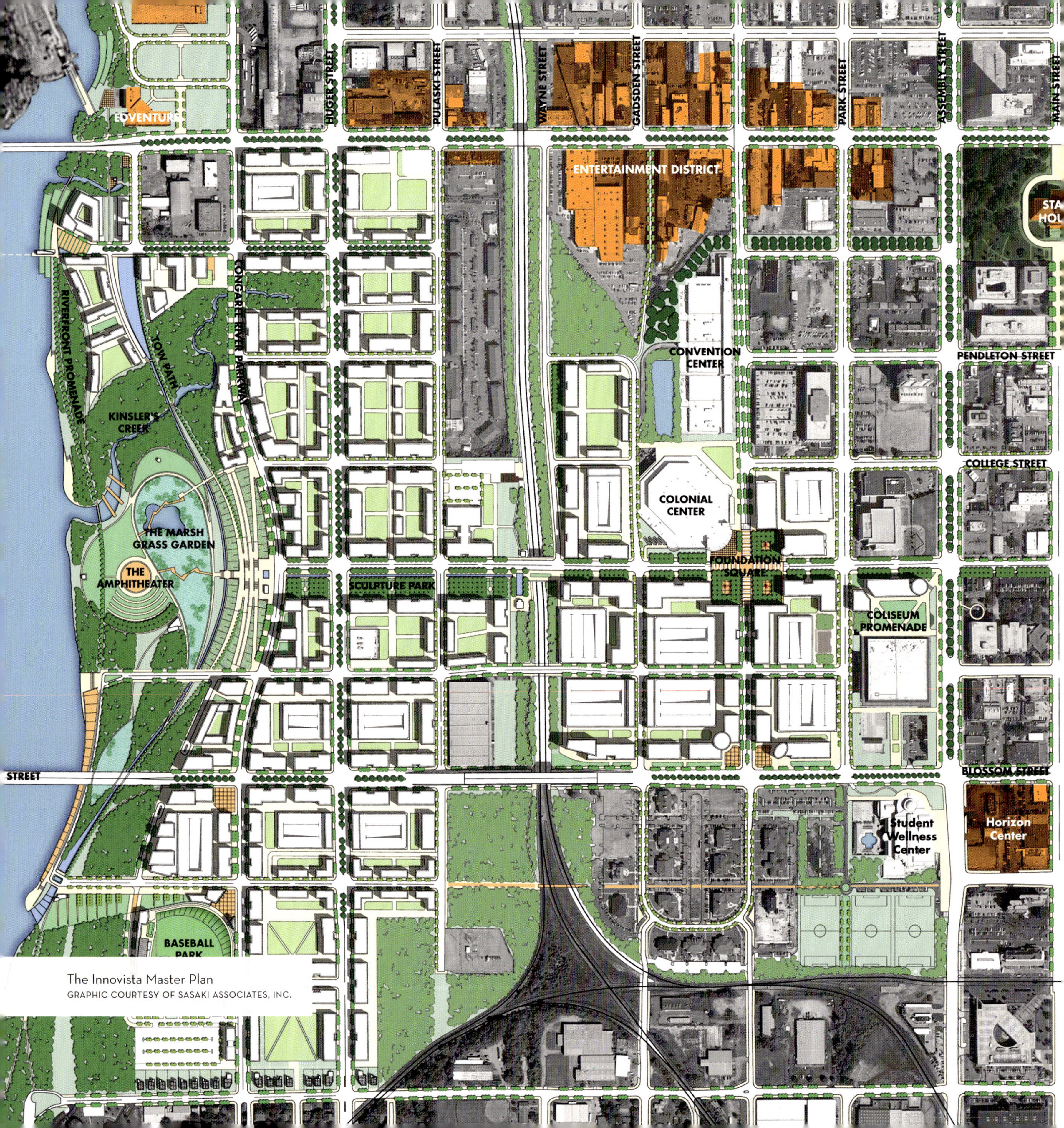

The Innovista Master Plan
GRAPHIC COURTESY OF SASAKI ASSOCIATES, INC.

Chapter 7

A Decade of Planning

At the turn of the twenty-first century, the University of South Carolina launched a second period of intensive master planning and design for the campus under the leadership of its new president, Andrew Sorensen. President Sorensen's vice president of business, Rick Kelly, was given the responsibility to direct the planning and design program. Charles Jeffcoat, director of facilities and planning, later succeeded by Thomas Quasney, managed the work of the planners and designers. The relationship of President Sorensen and Rick Kelly was such that Rick was given the lead role in directing what was perhaps the most dynamic and far-reaching period of master planning and design in the university's history.

The "decade of planning" included the site selection and planning for a new baseball park on the Congaree River, a master plan to consolidate disparate varsity athletic functions into an "Athletics Village," architectural and landscape design guidelines to guide the development of new campus facilities, and the master plan for Innovista, a university research park designed as a new urban mixed-use neighborhood containing university facilities along with private development. In 2010 the university completed a comprehensive update of its master plan.

University Leadership in the Decade of Planning. In addition to President Sorensen, Rick Kelly, and Charles Jeffcoat, the key university leadership for the decade of planning included Mack Whittle, who served as chairman of the board of trustees from 2000 to 2004, trustee Herbert Adams, who served as chairman from 2004 to 2008, and Dr. Jerry Odom, an executive officer of the University Development Foundation. Dennis Pruitt, vice president of student affairs, vice provost, and dean of students, oversaw an extraordinary expansion of student support facilities, including student dining, housing, and recreation facilities. Eric Hyman initiated a comprehensive upgrading of the university's varsity athletics facilities. Shirley Mills, the university's director of government and community relations and legislative liaison, provided critical communication with the city and the state legislature during this decade of university growth. Thomas Quasney assumed the role of director of facilities and planning from Charles Jeffcoat in 2007.

Andrew Sorensen

President Andrew Sorensen (2002–2008). With the goal of moving to a more assertive state-wide role, the trustees selected Andrew Sorensen, who was serving as president of the University of Alabama at the time, as the University of South Carolina's next president. With his focus on research, President Sorensen quickly moved the university "off the porch" and back outside the brick walls of the campus with his vision for the development of a university research park, Innovista. He conceived the research park as a way of developing another source of income for the university in the face of rapidly declining state support, and as a way of translating the university's research activities into economic development and job creation for the state. President Sorensen launched the university into a leadership role in the city of Columbia as well as the state of South Carolina.

Small in physical stature, Sorensen had an outgoing and exuberant personality. An ordained minister, he was a man who joined the university's marching band to play trombone at halftime during football games and enjoyed riding his bicycle around the campus. He was considered "a very smart guy" and direct in confronting issues, a characteristic that did not "sit well" with some of the trustees. According to trustee Herbert Adams, President Sorensen brought a much-needed "can do" attitude to the university. President Sorensen resigned in 2008 and suffered an untimely death in 2011.

Rick Kelly. Rick Kelly, vice president for business, was a dominating personality within the university administration, directing the master planning and design work of the planners, urban designers, and project designers from the time he arrived at the university in May of 2000 until his retirement in 2009. Kelly came to the university from the State of South Carolina's Budget and Control Board. The State Budget and Control Board, which controls the disposition of the state's public funds, is considered the most powerful agency in South Carolina. Rick served the board from 1981 to 2000 and was the board's executive director for two and a half years before coming to the university. With this experience he brought to the university not only an intimate knowledge of the workings of the state legislature and the Budget and Control Board but a personal relationship with its members. He also brought his associate from the board, Helen Ziegler, daughter of a state senator, to the university as associate vice president of business affairs to assist him on special projects.

Kelly found a home at the University of South Carolina. Beyond his responsibilities as vice president for finance, Rick was passionate about the condition of "his" campus's buildings and grounds. While giving a guided tour of the Horseshoe he described the health and care that the century-old oak trees on the greensward of the Horseshoe were receiving, and spoke fondly of what he described as one of the oldest and largest crepe myrtle trees in the state of South Carolina.

Pictured Left to Right
Mack Whittle
Herbert Adams
Dennis Pruitt

Campus planning under Kelly's direction gathered a head of steam during President Sorensen's tenure. President Sorensen was said to have given Kelly "free reign." He authorized Sasaki's planners and designers to carry out multiple district-planning studies, including Innovista, the site plan for the new baseball park, the Athletic Facilities Master Plan, and a manual, "University of South Carolina Design Guidelines," governing the development of new campus facilities. Kelly was responsible for overseeing hundreds of millions of dollars in new academic and student life facilities in a period of time that saw a dramatic improvement in the quality of the campus environment and student life.

Mack Whittle. Mack Whittle, chairman of the board from 2000 through 2004, confirmed the trustees' goal "to admit as many qualified South Carolinians as possible." In responding to a question about the relationship with the trustees and the administration, he said, "In addition to its fiduciary responsibilities, I believe it is the responsibility of the Trustees to hold the Administration accountable for its strategic plan and the metrics associated with the SAT scores of entering freshmen, faculty/staff ratios, and graduation rates."[1] Whittle was especially proud of the university's improving academic reputation.

Herbert Adams. Elected to the board of trustees in 1984, Herbert Adams served on the board for 28 years, until 2012, at which time he stood down from re-election. He served as chairman during the decade of planning from 2004 to 2008. Adams was impacted by the crisis that grew from President Holderman's misuse of his discretionary funds and ultimate resignation. Recognizing the board's lack of proper attention to finances, he took the lead in instituting a standing committee of the board for fiscal oversight. The new committee developed a strong fiscal policy of internal guidelines and audits. During his time at the university, as a student Adams worked three or four part-time jobs to pay for his education. In response to an inquiry about the longevity of his 28 years of service, Herbert Adams echoed the sentiments of other long-serving trustees in his love of the University of South Carolina. "The University provided me with a degree and a livelihood."[2]

Dr. Dennis Pruitt. Dennis Pruitt, vice president for student affairs, vice provost, and dean of students at the University of South Carolina, is one of the university's longest-serving senior administrators. As vice president of student affairs Dr. Pruitt oversees housing, health services, student-engagement initiatives, campus recreation, Greek life, and Russell House, the University's student union. In the "decade of planning" Dr. Pruitt oversaw an extraordinary improvement in the quality of student life facilities, including student housing, dining, and recreation facilities.

When the newly inaugurated President Palms began his interview program of the university's vice presidents, he caught Dr. Pruitt off guard. "After preparing reams of material and attempting to anticipate every question," said Dr. Pruitt, President Palms asked him a single question; "Do you really like working with students?" He responded, "I love working with students, the good the bad and the indifferent."[3] His

Pictured Left to Right
Dr. Jerry Odom
Eric Hyman
Shirley Mills

response more than satisfied the new president and Dr. Pruitt remains the university's vice president for student affairs as of 2015.

Dr. Jerry Odom. Dr. Jerry Odom has served the University of South Carolina for many years in multiple ways. Starting in 1969 as an assistant professor of chemistry, Jerry assumed the chair of the chemistry department in 1986, became executive vice president for academic affairs, provost in 1997, and executive director of the University Development Foundation in 2006. A distinguished professor, Dr. Odom found himself in the middle of the Innovista controversy when, as executive director of the University Development Foundation, the university asked him to help them out by having his foundation pay the termination fee to the real estate developer whose contract the university had terminated. The foundation agreed to pay the fee. "The University asked if we would consider helping them out of a jam. Our sole mission is to help the University out in any way."(4)

Eric Hyman. Eric Hyman came to the University of South Carolina as athletic director from Texas Christian University in 2005, with a reputation as an "architect of championship programs, an advocate for athlete's academic success and as a skilled administrator." Under his tenure from 2005 to 2012, athletics launched a $200 million capital fundraising program, which has dramatically transformed a collection of old and obsolete varsity athletic facilities at the university. The university's state-of-the-art baseball stadium opened in 2009 and NCAA national championships for the baseball team followed in 2010 and 2011. His crowning achievement has been the development of an Athletics Village—the Dodie Anderson Athletic Enrichment Center—together with an athletics office facility, which brings all the university's coaches together for the first time. The Athletics Village frames a new landscape quadrangle, dubbed the "Little Horseshoe" in reference to the university's historic quadrangle.

Shirley Mills. Shirley Mills has served the University of South Carolina as director of government and community relations and legislative liaison since 1993. Shirley has found her distinctive educational background in theatre to be an asset in her work. "While I never worked in theatre, theatre proved to be very helpful in my work of developing community relationships."(5)

Mills's role placed her at the forefront of resolving town/gown issues with the university's neighbors. The university's relationship with the city and its neighbors had reached a new low in the 1990s with the university's proposal to build an inn in the adjoining University Hills neighborhood. The proposal, as described previously, entailed tearing down historic residences and constructing a building whose size and character was considered incompatible with the single-family neighborhood in which it was to be placed. The height of the firestorm of protest coincided with the arrival of incoming President Andrew Sorensen. Upon President Sorensen's arrival, Shirley was given the responsibility to "fix" the problem. Fix it she did. Shirley initiated a contemporary community engagement process with the University Hills neighborhood and the city that led to the development of a distinctive inn that gained broad acceptance by the neighborhood. The community engagement process Shirley initiated is held as a model for town/gown relationships in Columbia. The successful resolution of the conflict over the inn represented a major turning point in the university's relationship with its neighbors and the city of Columbia. "Doing the right thing and being transparent"[6] has served to guide Shirley's two decades of work with the university's neighbors, the city of Columbia, and the South Carolina Legislature.

Thomas Quasney. Thomas Quasney, a USC graduate in mechanical engineering with an MBA from Florida State, succeeded Mr. Joe Rogers as director of facilities and planning. Prior to coming to the university, Quasney had served in the United States Air Force for 26 years as an operational engineer under the senior general responsible for Air Force operations throughout the United States. Recruited in 2007 by Rick Kelley and Helen Ziegler, Quasney said, "I was excited to return to the University because I was so grateful for my USC education that allowed me to be an engineer and an officer in the US Air Force. While in the service whenever I returned to the states and had the opportunity I would visit and walk the campus reminiscing about my time as a student at the University."[7]

During his tenure Quasney oversaw the development of the Honors College, two student residences, and the Moore School of Business. Tom left the university in October 2012, and is now director of operations for Fluor, one of the world's largest publicly-traded engineering and project management companies.

Upon President Sorensen's arrival, Shirley was given the responsibility to "fix" the problem. Fix it she did. Shirley initiated a contemporary community engagement process with the University Hills neighborhood and the city that led to the development of a distinctive inn that gained broad acceptance by the neighborhood.

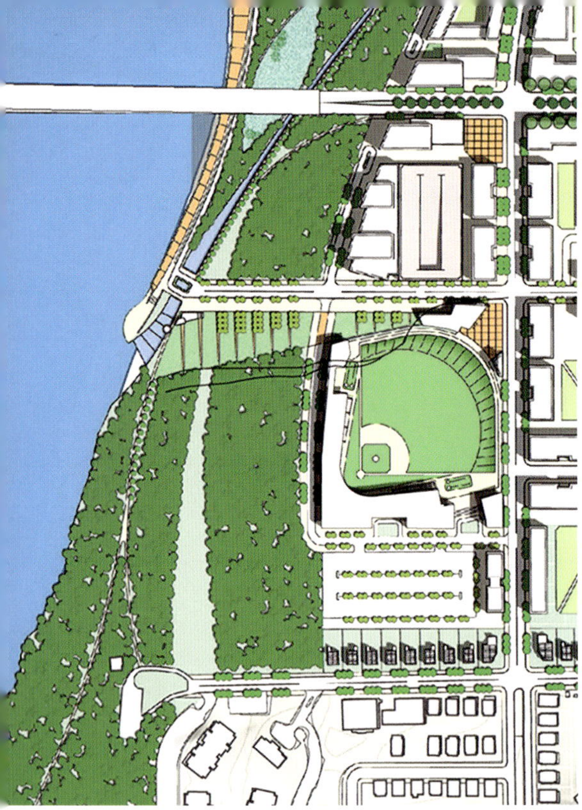

The new baseball park on the Congaree River

GRAPHIC COURTESY OF SASAKI ASSOCIATES, INC.

IMAGE COURTESY OF BLUE COLLAR STUDIO

The New Baseball Park. The "decade of planning" began with the university's search for a location for a baseball park to house its championship baseball team. After a fruitless search for a site within campus land holdings and the expenditure of several million dollars for preliminary drawings of a park on the site of a storm-water detention pit behind the Colonial Center, Charles Thompson "stepped up to the plate" and "astonished" Rick Kelly by offering to sell 35 acres of land on the river for the ballpark. An avid baseball fan, Thompson had lamented the loss of the city's semi-professional team, the Capital City Bombers, and also "wanted to see some development activity on his waterfront land."[8] Thompson's offer was accepted and the University Development Foundation purchased the site. The facility was located on the bluff overlooking the river, with the field and spectator facilities oriented to a view of the university and the dome of the state capitol in the distance.

The site plan for the ballpark designed it as an integral part of the urban fabric. An urban mixed-use development was illustrated on the north side of the stadium. A row of single-family houses was illustrated to the south of the proposed stadium on Catawba Street, facing the existing historic millhouses across the street.

In the course of Sasaki's preparation of the site development plan for the baseball facility, an amusing discourse occurred during the final work session with the university's baseball coach, Ray Tanner, now the university's athletic director. Sasaki's project designer, Igor Andersen, European-born and educated, had just completed a presentation of the site design plan, extolling the virtues of its urban design characteristics with the ballpark views from the grandstand to the university campus and the dome of the state capitol. The orientation of the field also featured a distinctive spectator entry from center field. Upon conclusion of his presentation Ray Tanner asked Igor where the "bullpen" and "batters eye" were located on the preliminary site plan, whereupon Igor Andersen turned to his colleague and whispered; "What is a boule pen, batter's eye?" HOK, a leading stadium designer, was selected as the project design architect and provided the appropriate location for both.

The Greek Village. Shortly after the University of South Carolina joined the Southeastern Conference (SEC), the trustees, along with vice president of student affairs, Dennis Pruitt, and other administrative officials, visited other SEC campuses. The visits included a tour of each institution's Greek housing facilities. After the tours the trustees concluded that to successfully compete with their counterparts in the conference the University of South Carolina had to address the long simmering issue of Greek housing on its campus. At the time most of the fraternities and sororities were housed in university facilities on campus—the fraternities in the McBryde Quadrangle and the sororities in South Tower. A few were located in nearby residential neighborhoods. Despite the caution expressed by the SEC institutions that were visited—"Think twice before you build Greek housing"[(9)] —the strong fraternal tradition of the trustees prevailed and the "Greek Village" was developed. One of the streets in the university's Greek Village is named Buyck Way after trustee Mark W. Buyck Jr., a strong proponent for the Greek system.

Efforts to find a location for a "Greek village" in prior years had proved particularly vexing. A series of alternative locations had been explored, including the Benson School site on Pickens Street, the parking lot at Bates House on Whaley Street, and property on south Assembly Street. The Benson School site and parking lot at Bates House failed because of strong objections from adjoining neighbors. The property on south Assembly Street was not considered suitable because of its location and environmental concerns. The present location of the Greek Village on Blossom Street is isolated from any adjoining neighborhoods. According to vice president Dennis Pruitt, problems associated with the present location have been limited to the fraternity brothers throwing various objects at passing freight trains on the adjoining rail line.

Only six to eight Greek chapters were anticipated to have sufficient financial resources to build new "houses," thus the strong demand for building sites for the Greek chapters surprised the university. The university leases the building sites for a nominal amount. The university also forfeited their food plans to the Greek chapters, which enabled the chapters to develop financially feasible plans. However, none of the racial minority fraternities have yet been able to develop financially feasible plans that would enable them to build in the Greek Village. By 2015, more than 20 houses had been constructed and strong demand exists for additional building sites.

The Greek program has served an important function in student life on the USC campus and is considered a national model by other institutions considering similar programs. Dr. Pruitt reports that an unexpected positive benefit has been the enthusiasm of fraternal alumni in contributing to the development of their chapters and renewing their relationship of giving to the university. The Greek Village and its program have been extremely successful, according to Dr. Pruitt, and comprised more than 4,500 total members in 2015.

However, many in the university community hold conflicting views of the Greek Village. By its nature the Greek program produces housing that is segregated by sex, race, and economic standing. The inability of the minority fraternities and sororities to participate because of financial constraints raises serious questions of social equity. The site location of the "Greek Village" on Blossom Street, one of the principal gateways to the University, with its opulent "southern-style mansions," also conveys an elitist message in a state and an institution that continue to struggle with their social history.

"Southern style" mansions of the Greek Village

IMAGE COURTESY OF KEITH MCGRAW

Pictured Right
Site development plan of the Athletic Village

GRAPHICS COURTESY OF SASAKI ASSOCIATES, INC.

Facing Page
Proposed entry to the Athletic Village and the "Little Horseshoe"

GRAPHICS COURTESY OF SASAKI ASSOCIATES, INC.

View of the Athletic Village from the pedestrian promenade which provides spectator access to the sports fields

IMAGE COURTESY OF KEITH MCGRAW

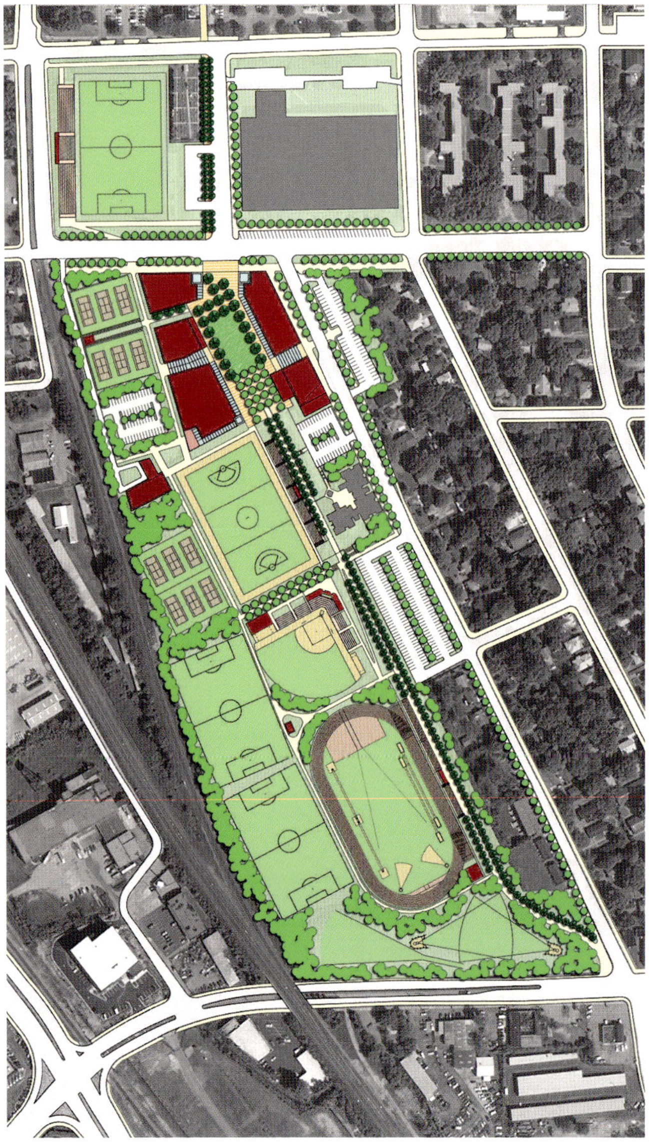

The Athletics Village. Over the decades varsity athletic facilities at the university had been scattered across the southern part of the campus. Traditional varsity sports such as track, baseball, and soccer, along with some dedicated athletics housing, were located nearest the campus at the "Roost." Coaches were housed farther away in one of the 1970s-style infamous round buildings called, appropriately enough, "The Roundhouse." William Brice Stadium for football and its coaches' offices are located still farther away, adjacent to the state fairgrounds in a semi-industrial setting. The planning process for the Bicentennial Master Plan had identified new programmatic needs for both men and women's varsity sports in 1994.

Under the leadership of Athletic Director Eric Hyman, the university launched the development of an athletics facilities master plan. Trey Sasser, an engineer, along with architect Bill Winkler and Igor Andersen of Sasaki, developed a comprehensive program of facility needs for varsity athletics from which the concept of an "Athletics Village" emerged. The "Village" concept consolidated athletics offices, training, and academic support facilities in one location. Eric Hyman, with the support of the trustees, gave first priority to the development of an "academic enrichment center" in the village, which provides academic support to the university's athletes.

The site development master plan for the Athletic Village features a new landscaped quadrangle as its centerpiece. Dubbed the "Little Horseshoe," the quadrangle is framed by the athletic offices and academic support facilities. A long pedestrian promenade reaches outward from the new quadrangle, providing spectator access to the adjoining field sports venues for track, softball, lacrosse, and tennis.

USC Athletics Village

EMERGENCY

View of Harper and Elliott Colleges showing how classically designed designed buildings of the antebellum era frame the university's historic horseshoe

IMAGE PROVIDED BY THE AUTHOR

Design Guidelines. New buildings and their architectural styles at the University of South Carolina, and indeed on American campuses throughout the country, continue to provoke emotional debate. The traditional styles of Jefferson's neo-classical University of Virginia, the collegiate gothic of the Universities of Notre Dame and Florida, and the Italian hill-town style at the University of Colorado evoke "university campus" to alumni and prospective students. The University of South Carolina's Horseshoe, where classically designed buildings of the Federal style enclose a beautifully landscaped quadrangle, evokes a palpable emotional response from the University's alumni and first-time visitors to the university.

Historically the development of architectural styles has been a direct response to the culture of the place, the building materials that were available, and the building technologies of the times. At the University of South Carolina, brick, stucco, and paint were the building materials available to the first architects and builders on the Horseshoe. The first architects, designing in the Federal style of the antebellum period, utilized pattern books featuring classical facades and building elements to guide the architectural expression of the early buildings.

The buildings framing the Horseshoe are beautifully proportioned and simply designed. They can be considered "fabric" buildings whose architectural style is secondary to their site location. Rather than standing out they frame the landscape of the Horseshoe. The only building on the Horseshoe that makes a singular architectural statement is the South Caroliniana Library, with the over-scaled columns of its portico. The addition of the portico to the library was a reflection of the importance and "landmark" status of the library.

Since the middle of the twentieth century the architectural profession has passed through a series of short-lived love affairs with neo-traditional, international, modernist, brutalist, post-modern, and other styles thought to be fashionable in their times. In the last several decades computer-aided design technology and an unlimited palette of building materials has allowed the architectural profession complete freedom of expression in designing new building forms. Many universities, including Harvard, the University of Cincinnati, and the Massachusetts Institute of Technology, have sought the "best and the brightest" of today's architectural profession for their new buildings. The results have been mixed and some institutions have been saddled with buildings that are unusable for today's curricula and teaching methods. Buildings considered fashionable at the time of their design are ugly by today's standards. Today almost all American university campuses are burdened with the "fashionable mistakes" of the post–World War II period.

Nowhere has the architectural design debate between historians and the modernists been more intense than at the University of Virginia. It was brought to a head in the spring of 2006 over the proposed design of a new complex called "South Lawn" adjacent to the original Jeffersonian grounds. The university had accepted the resignation of the acclaimed New York architect James Polshek after four years of alternative design solutions had been rejected by the university's board of visitors and had replaced him with the California firm of Moore, Ruble, Yudell. While the trustees were frightened that they would get a glass box, some students and faculty at the School of Architecture accused the administration of turning the university into a "theme park of nostalgia, an assemblage of mediocre, slavishly neo-classical buildings."[10] The new scheme that was finally approved by the board of visitors echoed Thomas Jefferson's great Lawn and featured two rows of red brick pavilions joined by colonnades fronting a landscaped quadrangle.

Werner Sensbach, director of facilities planning and administration at the University of Virginia from 1965 to 1991, provided a beautiful and poetic description of the unique characteristics of American campus design and campus buildings: "Good campus architecture is necessarily subordinate and integral. New structures should be thoughtful, artful, and handsome but fitting and modest." He went on to say, "New campus buildings should be subordinate to the campus spaces in which they participate and campus spaces should be thought of as outdoor rooms, in which buildings are the walls, lawns, and walkways the floor and trees and sky the ceiling. Each space should be considered a place of destination as well as a space to pass through."[11] Achieving the desired result begins with the selection of the architect, which can be a challenging task in itself. Architects throughout the decades have been greatly influenced by successive stylistic periods, from the classical to today's exercises in computer-driven sculptural forms. Schools of architecture are offering a range of training for architects. The Harvard Graduate School of Design is noted for its leadership in modernism. The schools of architecture at the Universities of Miami and Notre Dame offer its students a background in New Urbanism and historic architectural vernaculars. Many architectural practices are noted for a particular design style. The selection of architect Robert Stern will assure the design of a classical building with elements of Greek revival, as with Stern's Advocacy Center and South Quad on the University of South Carolina's campus. Selection of architect Frank Gehry will assure a DE constructivist building, such as his Stata Center at the Massachusetts Institute of Technology (MIT) in Cambridge, Massachusetts. The late Pietro Belluschi, former dean of architecture and planning at MIT, advised that when you select one of the leading architectural practitioners, you know beforehand what you are going to get. If you retain them and do not like their design, you will have to take the pen out of their hands.

In the post–World War II period the University of South Carolina selected architects of national reputation to work with local architectural professionals to design its new building facilities. The most significant architectural designs of the period on the campus include Edward Durell Stone's Thomas Cooper Library, and Skidmore Owings and Merrill's Swearingen Engineering Center. These buildings bring a sustaining aesthetic and will continue to contribute to the design quality of the campus in the decades ahead. Other buildings of that era, such as the veil-block dormitories have already been removed and replaced with other new facilities.

The restoration of the historic buildings framing the Horseshoe brought with it a renewed appreciation of the classical architectural vernacular. The efforts in the 1990s at the University of South Carolina to impose a Greek Revival style of architecture on new buildings has had mixed results. While Robert Stern's Advocacy Center is admired, the formal and "heavy" institutional character of his South Quad student residence complex seems more appropriate for a public courthouse.

Architects designing buildings at the university should look to the qualities of the historic buildings that frame the Horseshoe. These buildings are designed with restrained ornamentation. Their beauty lies in their human scale, their beautiful proportions, the scale relationship of window openings to building mass, and the warm colors of the stucco finishes.

The design process for new buildings on the USC campus had grown increasingly contentious and subject to personal tastes—of their proponents, members of the buildings and grounds committee of the trustees, and donors of buildings—as well as the "fashion brand" of the project architects. Influential members of the trustees' buildings and grounds

View of South Quad Student Housing by architect Robert Stern

IMAGE COURTESY OF KEITH MCGRAW

committee responsible for reviewing new projects, led by Mark W. Buyck Jr., a passionate devotee of the Greek revival style of architecture, and William Hubbard, a great admirer of Thomas Jefferson's classical University of Virginia, sought a more orderly process, as well as a more "timeless" style of architecture for the campus. To defuse controversy and to help bring order to the project design process, a manual of design guidelines for project designers, the "University of South Carolina Design Guidelines," was published in 2008.

The underlying thesis of the Design Guidelines is the importance of utilizing the spatial and architectural design principles of the Horseshoe to guide the design of new buildings and the spatial development of the campus.

The Design Guidelines skirt the subject of architectural style, focusing instead upon the underlying framework of streets, landscaped greens, pedestrian connections, and universal architectural design approaches to building orientation, scale, proportions, and building massing. Werner Sensbach, former director of facilities planning and administration at the University of Virginia, argues that "University leaders must insist that the architects they hire design on a warm human scale. Scale, not style, is the essential element in good campus design." [12]

The objective of the Design Guidelines for the university was to bring order to the process of facility planning and design and to provide guidance to the project planners and architects. A principal recommendation of the guidelines was a recommendation for the university to form a "Design Review Committee" with outside professional design membership. The university instituted a design review committee in 2009; it reviews the architects' projects at a schematic and design development phase of work before the final review of the completed design. A second major recommendation called for the university to retain a university architect on staff. In response the university has retained Derek Gruner, whose professional architectural design skill and soft-spoken communication style has brought much-needed order to the design review process

Thomas Cooper Library designed by Edward Durell Stone

IMAGE COURTESY OF KEITH MCGRAW

The Design Guidelines for the University of South Carolina are organized around recommendations on "Guiding Principles," "Best Practices," "Space Types," and "Special Districts."

"Guiding Principles" focuses on the framing foundational elements of streets and greens. The guidelines confirmed the value associated with the historic street grid of the city of Columbia, but also recommended a refinement of the street grid into a hierarchical system of street types, differentiating between vehicular and pedestrian uses. Boulevards and avenues were designated primarily for vehicular use, while streets traversing the campus were designated as pedestrian-primary streets, with vehicular travel as their secondary use.

"Best Practices" details landscape and architectural strategies. For example, in response to the university's hot climatic conditions the landscape strategies emphasized the importance of green spaces, tree planting for shade, and the sustainable management of water. Architectural strategies emphasized building massing and proportions, building orientation in response to climate, façade composition and articulation, and contemporary sustainable strategies. Open spaces such as the Horseshoe have played a critical role in defining the identity and experience of the USC campus. "Space Types" categorizes the landscape forms and their function in the development of the campus.

Special districts in the University Master Plan, such as the proposed Foundation Square and the Athletics Village, received detailed design guidelines. As an example, the design guidelines for the Athletics Village illustrate the specific site location, building massing, and landscape architectural guidelines for the complex of buildings and sports fields. The guidelines anticipate that the architectural design of the building elements will be phased over a number of years and designed by different architects. The guidelines illustrate the intended building massing of the Athletics Village with its focus on an interior green quadrangle, including details such as building heights and building corners that would benefit from special architectural expression, the principal pedestrian access points into the complex, the general location of building entries from the interior green, and service entries from the outside frame of streets. The guidelines also provide three-dimensional drawings illustrating the building massing in relationship to surface grades, the conceptual character of the interior quadrangle, and the proposed linear promenade designed to provide spectators access to all the field venues.

Design guidelines, however, do not address the influence that a donor can have in the selection of building sites and the selection of architects, or the ego and competitive nature of internationally famous architects. President Harris Pastides articulated the challenges in managing the new building process in his address at the dedication of the new Moore

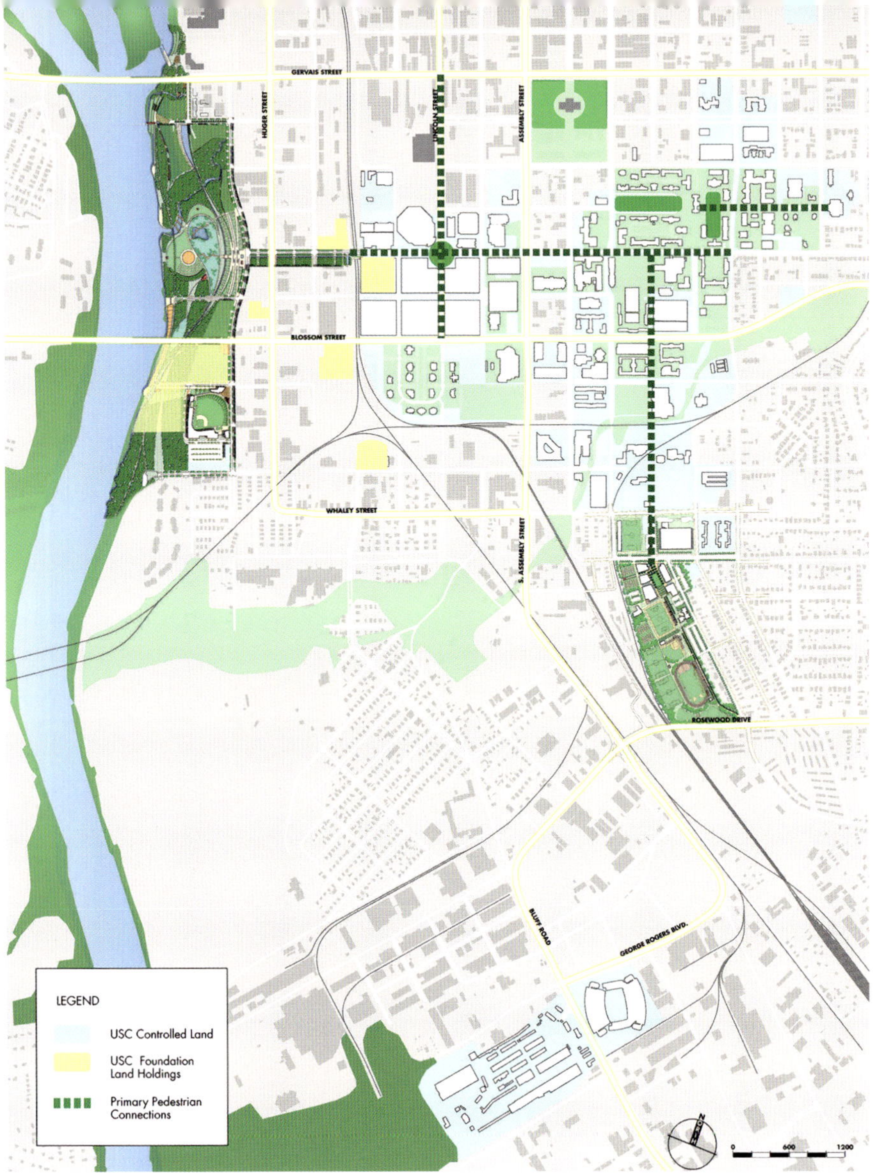

The "Guiding Principles" of the university's Design Guidelines focus upon the primary foundational elements of greens and their connective tissue of pedestrian-friendly streets and pedestrian promenades

ALL GRAPHICS COURTESY OF SASAKI ASSOCIATES, INC.

School of Business when he said: "The challenges confronting a university in managing the process of building new facilities from site selection, to selection of architects, and the design of buildings is well illustrated by the University of South Carolina's new Moore School of Business."[13]

Trustee Darla Moore, a generous donor to the university, had pledged and contributed over 65 million dollars for the school's academic and research programs. Upon her appointment to the board of trustees of the university she brought her personal interest in architecture and landscape architecture to the university. Her role in the selection of the architect for the university's new School of Business illustrated the significant impact that donors can have on the physical development of a campus.

The selection of architects for public work in the state of South Carolina is rigorously controlled through state-mandated procedures that require public notice, followed by a short-listing of architects for an interview. Interviews are carried out by a committee appointed by the university and chaired by the state engineer. Committee members utilize a "score card," ranking each firm interviewed with scores of 1 to 10 on seven different categories.

For major commissions such as the proposed new business school, nationally prominent architects typically team with local South Carolina architects. Moore made it known that she wished to have Rafael Viñoly, an internationally famous architect, design the building. Given her well known preference of architect for the design of the proposed building, other architects, both locally and nationally, were hesitant to apply. However, given assurances of an equitable process under the state statutes, a notable list of national architects teamed with local architectural firms was assembled—including Rafael Viñoly. Five teams of architects were "shortlisted" for interviews, including Viñoly. Twenty-four hours before the interviews, the architectural teams were notified that Darla Moore had expressed interest in "listening to" the interviews. Out of courtesy her request was granted by the university.

Upon completion of interviews for a typical state-funded project, such as the Business School, committee discussion typically follows, along with a tallying of the score cards. The selection of the architect is typically made shortly thereafter. In this case, the competing firms received e-mails week after week notifying them that no decision had been made. More than two months had passed when, in an unprecedented action, it was announced that the procurement had been cancelled. Shortly thereafter an announcement was made that Rafael Viñoly would design the School of Business. South Carolina law permits the donor to select the architect if the donor pays the architectural fee.

In recognition of her long standing support of the university and the School of Business, the university has named the new facility "The Darla Moore School of Business."

Perspective view of Athletics Village

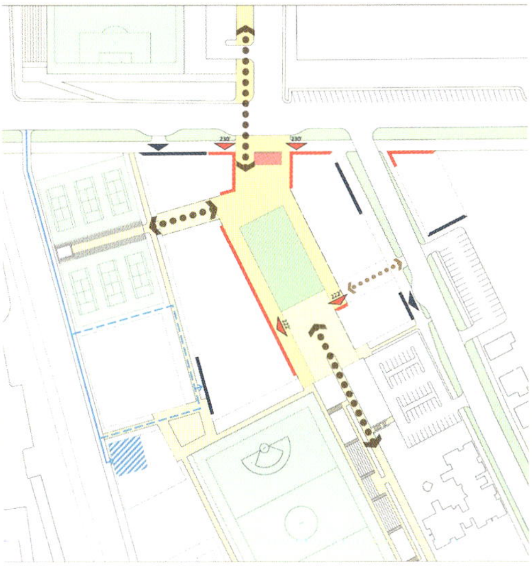

Design Guidelines for points of entry and special facade treatments

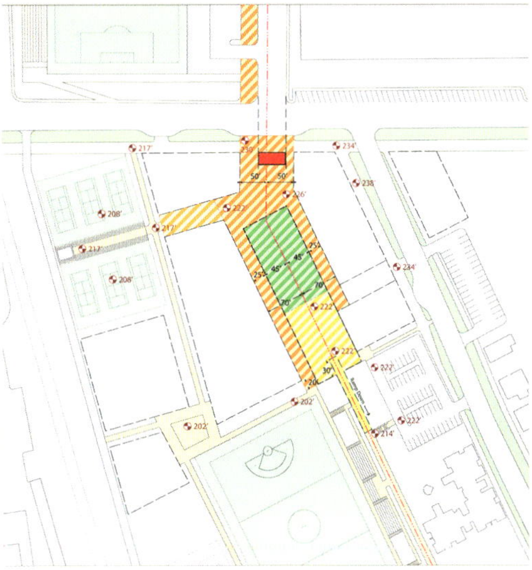

Design Guidelines for surface treatments of open spaces

Design Guidelines for building locations

THE
LIBRARY
No Limits

Pictured Left
The Darla Moore School of Business designed by architect Rafael Viñoly and dedicated in 2014

Facing Page
The historic South Caroliniana Library designed by architect Robert Mills in 1890

IMAGES COURTESY OF KEITH MCGRAW

In his remarks at the dedication of the new Moore School of Business, President Pastides sought to defuse the controversy around Rafael Viñoly's contemporary architectural design for the new building:

"In the nineteenth century we were influenced by one of America's first native-born architects, Robert Mills. A friend of Thomas Jefferson, Mills was only 21 when he submitted a design for Rutledge College (1802), our first building. The board of trustees were not enamored with his first design and assigned a second architect to work with him. Mills went on to design the Washington Monument, the Treasury Building, and Charleston's Historic district. He also designed our South Caroliniana Library, which was completed in 1840.

Today, we celebrate another leap of faith. I'm delighted that a relationship between an architect of great skill and vision, Rafael Viñoly, and a client with enduring faith and an uncompromising belief in excellence, Darla Moore and her university, found each other and created this new landmark.

The Caroliniana was revolutionary for its time and it is notable as the first free-standing academic library building in the United States. Mills also designed the Maxcy Monument, still at the center of the Horseshoe. During the middle of the twentieth century, Edward Durell Stone, surely one of the nation's most influential but not, necessarily, revered architects, introduced another memorable design to Carolina. This came in the form of a provocative rendering for a new library that was to be named after the university's second president. Stone had already made a name for himself with exceptional commissions like the Museum of Modern Art in New York, the US Embassy in Delhi, Stanford University's Medical Center, and also, by the way, Mepkin Abbey, formerly known as Mepkin Plantation, home of American magazine magnate Henry R. Luce of New York.

Mid-Century Modern, the Thomas Cooper Library design looked nothing like the buildings on the Horseshoe. As you might imagine, there was push back. "Too modern!" they said. "Doesn't blend in!" they said. "Fire him," said others."[14]

The American university campus is unique, rooted in western European traditions but distinct in its spatial form and character. Each campus is a reflection of its physical setting, the culture and associated values of its region, and bears the imprint of its "builders." Too often a university campus is thought of in terms of buildings alone. The uniqueness of the American campus lies in its composition of buildings and open space, so beautifully illustrated in the Horseshoe. Much like the Bayeux Tapestry in Normandy, France, the American university campus is a tapestry woven by many hands over many years. The American university campus asks each generation of architects and planners to realize that they are but one of countless weavers of a single tapestry that is expected to endure for decades into the future. ■

Colombia achieved international promeneance in the nineteenth century with a series of technological innovations in its mills located in the area now being planned as Innovista

IMAGE COURTESY OF USC CREATIVE SERVICES, INC.

Chapter 8

Setting the Stage for Innovista

In 2004, President Sorensen and Dr. Harris Pastides, vice president of research who would go on to serve as president of the university, developed a concept for a research park for the university. The concept was designed to exploit the university's initiatives in alternative energy, nanotechnology, biomedical science, and environmental science, and to develop another source of income for the university.

A seven-block site of university-controlled land (currently being utilized for surface parking) in the Vista redevelopment area adjacent to the campus was selected for the research park. Coincidently, the area was part of the historic mill district of Columbia where the world's first electric powered cotton mills in the early nineteenth century had gained worldwide attention.

University Research Parks. The concept of a research park for the University of South Carolina had as its backdrop a history of universities seeking to focus their research activities and exploit their applications for commercial use. University research parks had their genesis as far back as 1862 when the United States Congress, during the Civil War, passed the Morrill Land Grant Act. The act granted federal land to each state to be sold to finance new public universities. The purpose of the act was explained as follows: "Without excluding other scientific and classical studies and including military tactic to teach such branches of learning as are related to agriculture and the mechanic arts in such manner as the legislatures of the states may respectively prescribe in order to promote the liberal and practical education of the industrial classes in several pursuits and professions in life." [1]

The act granted 30,000 acres of federal land per each member of Congress a state had as of 1860. The proceeds of their sales were to be utilized to fund the new institutions. While the act, signed by Abraham Lincoln in the midst of the Civil War, excluded states in rebellion against the union from receiving the benefits, it was extended to the southern states, including South Carolina, after the war. South Carolina had been the first state to secede from the Union on December 20, 1860.

The great universities founded by the act's public land grant, including Clemson University in South Carolina, revolutionized American agriculture in the twentieth century through their agricultural research programs and remain leaders today in advancing research across a broad range of disciplines. The Morrill Land Grant Act was the country's recognition of the value of a broad-based system of education for its peoples and the research and economic development role of public colleges and universities in carrying out that mission.

The Georgia Institute of Technology in Atlanta can be considered the forerunner of the urban university research park movement; it began applying its engineering research programs in the 1930s to the creation of new applications and products. The post–World War II period saw renewed interest in applied research, beginning with Stanford University's research park and followed most notably by the Research Triangle Park in North Carolina, the Princeton Forrestal Center at Princeton University, and the Massachusetts Institute of Technology's (MIT) Tech Square and University Park.

Since the mid-1930s, Georgia Tech has created hundreds of new companies. Stanford's applied research has fueled the technology boom in Silicon Valley and MIT, in partnership with Harvard University and the teaching hospitals in Boston, MA, has birthed the biotechnology boom in the Boston metropolitan area. The impetus and goals for the establishment of these research parks vary widely and in unexpected ways.

President Sorensen and other university and state officials visited North Carolina State's Centennial Park prior to development of the research park concept for the University of South Carolina. With the exception of Georgia Tech's and MIT's research parks, all of the previously mentioned research parks, including Centennial Park, were developed as traditional "suburban" office parks. Centennial Park at North Carolina State University also provided for the expansion of the university's academic facilities. MIT's Tech Square consisted of a complex of three urban high rise buildings in the Kendall Square area of Cambridge, Massachusetts. Its University Park was developed as a state-of-the-art, high density, mixed-use urban research park with a full range of urban land uses in addition to research facilities.

MIT's University Park served as the precedent for the University of South Carolina's research park.

The Georgia Tech Research Institute. The Georgia Tech Research Institute (GTRI) in Atlanta is a research park and applied research arm of the Georgia Institute of Technology. Founded in the midst of the Great Depression by the Georgia General Assembly, it was patterned after the state's successful agricultural experiment stations. In 1933, President Sanford of the University of Georgia proposed that a "technical research activity" be established at Georgia Tech in order to boost the state's struggling economy in the midst of the Great Depression.[2] Originally designed to create jobs in the depression era of the 1930s, GTRI in 2014 employed around 1,765 people, and is involved in approximately $305 million in research annually for more than 200 clients in industry and government.[3]

By the late 1930s, the GTRI's research activities were producing marketable technology. A non-profit entity, the Industrial Development Council, was formed in order to allow it to contract work outside the state budget process. The council, now known as the Georgia Tech Research Corporation, serves as the sole contracting agent for Georgia Tech faculty and its academic units, and is manager of the intellectual property that results from the university's research. In addition to having its

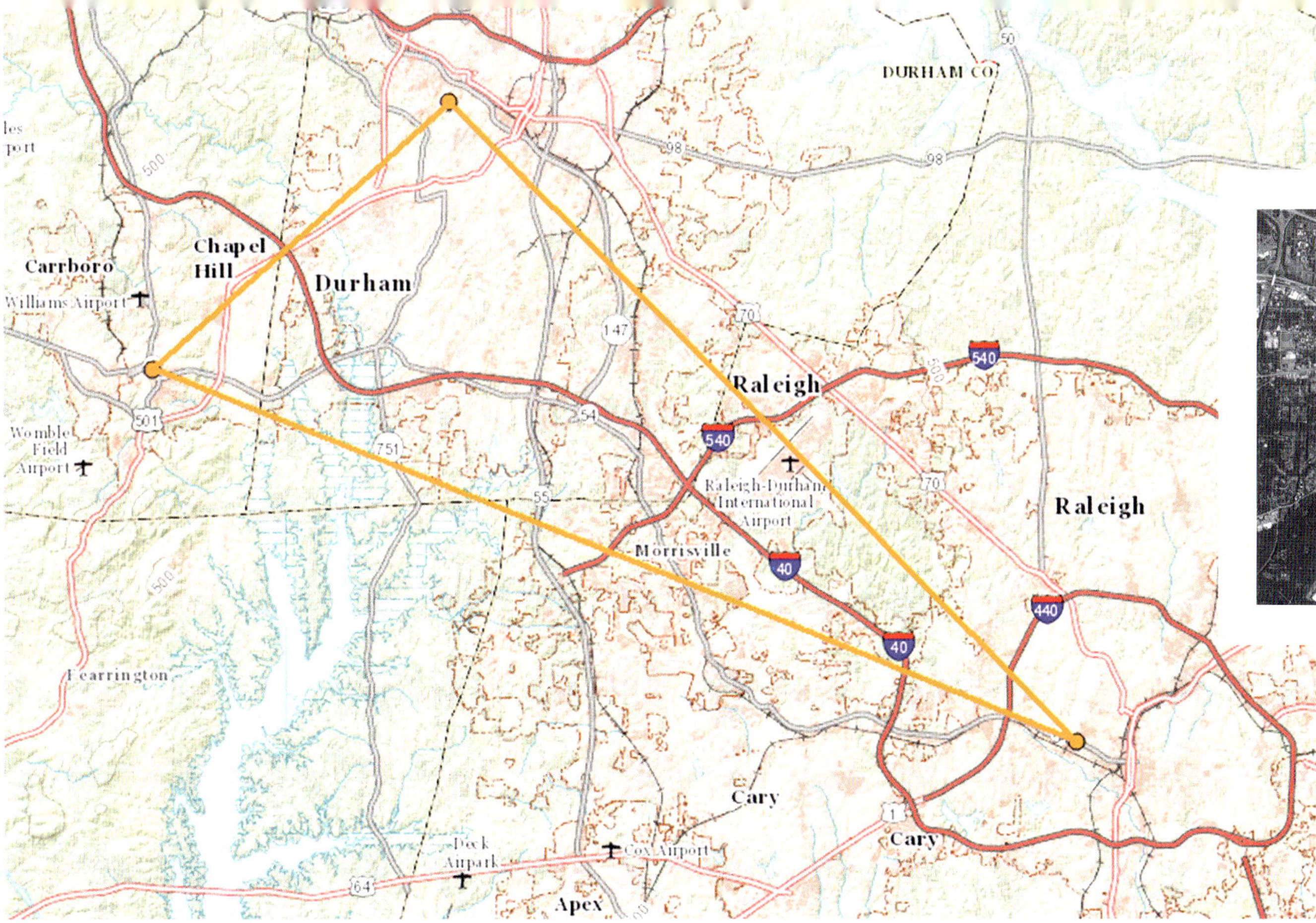

Pictured Left
A map of the Research Triangle
PHOTO COURTESY OF WIKIPEDIA

own staff of researchers, the Georgia Tech faculty is actively engaged with GTRI. The 1952–53 Annual Report noted that "66 faculty in 15 schools were performing research."[4] The National Science Foundation's higher education research and development survey of higher education r&d expenditures in 2012 ranked Georgia Tech 25th among American universities and colleges with expenditures of $688,905,000 for research and development.

The Research Triangle. The founding of the Research Triangle Park in North Carolina in the 1950s was motivated by the presence of three research universities in close proximity, social concerns about the standard of living in the region, and the state's inability to retain their "best and brightest" students upon their graduation. The state estimated that two-thirds of the graduates from nearby Duke University, the University of North Carolina, and North Carolina State University left the state after graduation because of the lack of professional job opportunities. Also, during that time period, North Carolina's per capita income was two-thirds the national average. In 1955 Governor Luther Hodges created the Research Triangle Development Council to test the idea of a research park and to develop the concept.

The council established three initial goals: first, "To attract industrial research laboratories and facilities;" second, "To increase employment opportunities for citizens of the state;" and third, "To increase the per capita income of the citizens of the state."[5] In response to the skepticism of the universities, the council created a not-for-profit "Research Institute" to serve as an intermediary between the universities and the private research corporations. The council also set about assembling a large rural site with thousands of acres available for the research park. For the first decade, the state government and private businesses played a principal role in the support and development of the Research Triangle Park. The park struggled early on but reached a turning point in 1965 when Governor Terry Sanford announced that the federal National Institute for Environmental Health Sciences would be placed in the park.

From a physical perspective, the park developed as a classic suburban business park, subdivided into large lots for freestanding office buildings and surface parking. By 2007 the Research Triangle Park encompassed almost 7,000 acres of land, 20 million square feet of buildings, and 157 firms employing 39,000 people.[6]

Princeton University's Princeton Forrestal Center is a precedent setting mixed-use corporate office, research, retail and residential community

IMAGE COURTESY OF SASAKI ASSOCIATES, INC. LANDSLIDES

The Princeton Forrestal Center. In the early 1970s, Princeton University, anticipating uncontrolled suburban growth around its campus in the city of Princeton in central New Jersey, developed the concept of a mixed-use office and research park on some 1,600 acres of its land adjacent to the main campus. In the words of its long-time development partner, Robert Wolfe of Picus Associates, the university's initial concern was "to maintain and upgrade the quality of life in the region and to utilize the Forrestal Center as a means to influence the shape and pattern of development in central New Jersey."(7) The Princeton Forrestal Center's mission statement on its website states: "Princeton University's mission in planning and developing the Princeton Forrestal Center was to protect and enhance the quality of life in the region as Central New Jersey grew, and to provide a reasonable financial return on its investment." It did this by implementing a master plan that protected the land's natural systems, required high-quality design, and tried to anticipate the expanding mobility and infrastructure requirements of the region.

Lawrence Rockefeller, a Princeton trustee and an avowed environmentalist, had long been concerned about the quality of the suburban development encroaching upon the Princeton campus. Rockefeller championed the cause of environmental sustainability and "quality of place" for the Princeton region. The concept of the Princeton Forrestal Center emerged from his leadership. He was appointed chair of a subcommittee of the board of trustees to address the issue.

Robert Wolfe, who had joined the Princeton University staff as assistant treasurer from 1974 to 1976 under treasurer Paul Firstenberg, became the Forrestal Center's first employee when the project was authorized by the trustees in 1975. Shortly thereafter he became a partner with K.S. Sweet of Philadelphia, whom the university initially retained as its real estate development partner. Wolfe formed Picus Associates to replace Sweet Associates as the managing partner of the Princeton Forrestal Center. Sasaki Associates, and the market analyst firm Hammer Siler George Associates of Washington,

View of the Village Square in the Princeton Forrestal Village, a lifestyle retail village in the Princeton Forrestal Center

IMAGE COURTESY OF SASAKI ASSOCIATES, INC.

DC, were retained by Princeton University to prepare the Master Plan for the proposed research park

At the onset of planning for the research park the campus of Princeton University was nestled in a bucolic rural environment adjacent to Lake Carnegie and the historic Delaware and Raritan Canal. Princeton, New Jersey, is a classically beautiful college town. The university held 1,200 acres of land adjacent to the campus astride US Route 1. The property was undeveloped except for two laboratory facilities: the Plasma Physics Lab and Particle Accelerator of the original Forrestal campus of Rockefeller University. In addition to concerns about suburban development encroaching from both north and south along the US Route 1 corridor, Lawrence Rockefeller was particularly anxious to preserve a large old growth beech forest on the 1,200-acre site.

In the post-WWII period the prototypical suburban office park was characterized by single-use one- to three-story office buildings surrounded by surface parking. Princeton's development partner, Robert Wolfe, along with the Sasaki planners and Hammer Siler George Associates, developed a precedent-setting concept for a new mixed-use community containing corporate office facilities, research labs, retail, and residential land uses. The master plan for the center included a lifestyle retail center, Forrestal Village, which was developed with retail, restaurants, a hotel, health club, apartments, assisted living, and daycare uses to service and support the office and research employees. The objective of the mixed-use concept was to address the isolation of the single-use office parks typical of the time by providing on-site supporting services. The mixed-use concept was also designed to retain employees on site, thereby mitigating the traffic impacts on US Route 1, which serviced the research park.

Site and architectural design controls were established, along with a design review committee to ensure the quality of development. The old growth beech forest was preserved in the master plan and utilized as part of a unique comprehensive storm water management system for the research park.

While a primary initial objective of the Princeton trustees was to address their concerns about maintaining the quality of the environment in central New Jersey, a secondary objective was to create an income stream for the university's endowment. The university also planned to foster a partnership between academia and the private sector.

The university took a long-term view in devising the plan and in working through the real estate development process that followed. First, it leased the land rather than selling it outright. Initial leases were $35,000 per acre for 50-year pre-paid leases. By 1986 the pre-paid land leases averaged $200,000 to $250,000 per acre. Second, in order to limit its risk, the university limited its role to that of land developer—developing the plan and constructing the infrastructure rather than engaging in speculative building. It also declined to be an equity or joint venture partner in any of the buildings.

"With a great plan in place which had been approved by Plainsboro Township, the Township in which the Center was located, and with implementation of quality projects underway such as the Johnson Foundation national headquarters, the essential goal of the Trustees had been realized. A transaction with Merrill Lynch assured the financial success of the Center."[8]

By 2014 the Forrestal Center had grown to 2,200 acres containing 7 million square feet of corporate office and research space: 1,300 hotel rooms, 800 homes in single-family, townhouse, and condominium configurations. Major corporate tenants included Bristol-Myers Squibb, Siemens, and IBM. Additional acreage was purchased that allowed for the development of the lifestyle commercial center, the Forrestal Village. In 2014 approval was received to add 400 apartment units to the Forrestal Village.

Significantly, the development of the Princeton Forrestal Center also addressed the perennial institutional problem of Princeton University's tax-free status. The Princeton Forrestal Center in 2014 contributed a total assessed real estate value of $1.4 billion dollars to the tax base of the Plainsboro and South Brunswick townships in New Jersey where the research park is located.

In response to an inquiry about the relationship of the university's academic programs and research activities to the Forrestal Center, Robert Wolfe reports, "The University has never been willing to get programmatically involved. They have not viewed the Forrestal Center as part of its academic mission and has never participated programmatically in the development of the Forrestal Center. There are no academic programs assigned to the Center and effectively no research activities. The old Forrestal campus with the particle accelerator and the plasma physics lab was often referred to as the garage of the engineering school."[9]

In order to maintain a pedestrian campus, Princeton is currently moving some of its back-of-house functions, such as a high-density library storage facility and university data center, off the core campus to the Forrestal Center. Only 10% of the market-rate housing within the Forrestal Center is occupied by university faculty and staff. A retirement community in the center houses many alumni but it is not restricted to graduates of Princeton.

In 1987 the university purchased the adjacent 500-acre Princeton Nurseries property, despite the lack of enthusiasm for the purchase by its development partner, Picus. Three hundred acres of the property were in the adjoining township of Brunswick, which proceeded to rezone the property for offices and single-family housing. In response to the anticipated traffic impact, the Forrestal Center developed a full-grade separated interchange at the research park's principal gateway on US Route 1. Given the extreme controversy that the size of the project generated, university president Harold Shapiro put the entire project on the shelf in 1988, much to the annoyance of the township of Brunswick. The collapse of the real estate market and the recession that followed in the decade of the '90s has left the property languishing. Today 200 acres of the property have been set aside for permanent open space adjacent to the historic Delaware and Raritan Canal. Some 250 acres are now zoned for 2.9 million square feet of office space, which "makes no sense at all" according to Wolfe, who added: "We need to convert it into a mixed use project."[10]

After forty years Princeton University feels that it has more than achieved its original objectives and wants to end its role as a local real estate land developer. Robert Wolfe points out the center's contribution to the university's endowment was significant when the university's endowment in the 1970s was $500 million. In 2014 Princeton's endowment was $22 billion and the Forrestal Center's contribution to the university's endowment is but a footnote.

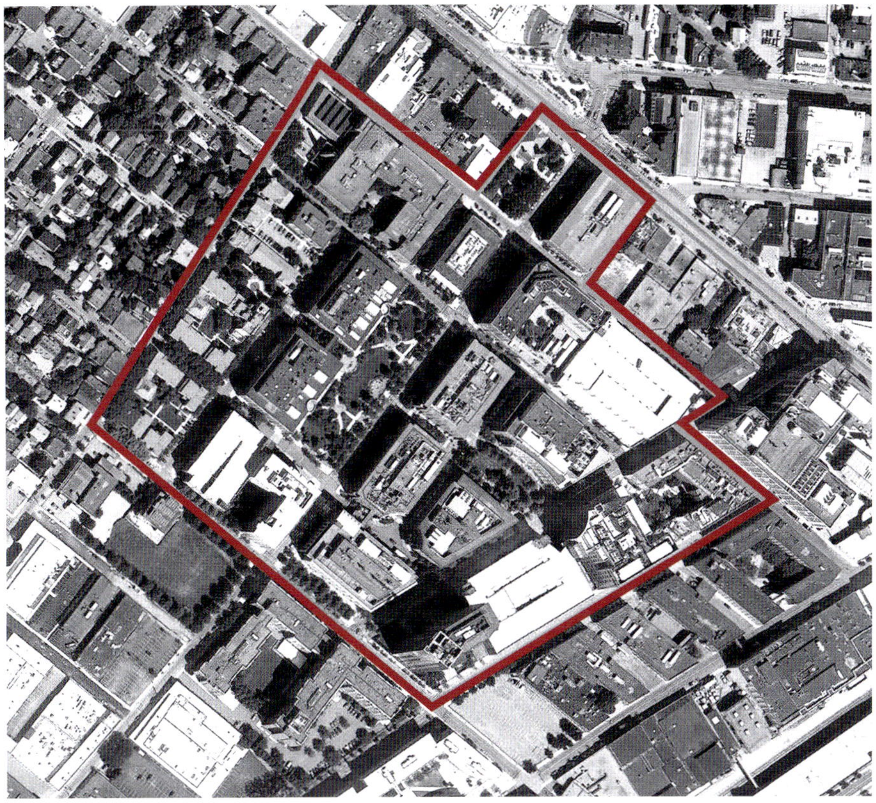

Aerial view of MIT's "University Park" in Cambridge, MA, showing dense urban configuration

IMAGE COURTESY OF SASAKI ASSOCIATES, INC.

As Princeton's development partner, Robert Wolfe summarized two primary pitfalls in the university/real estate developer relationship. First, "[t]he biggest challenge is that a major university and major corporations are totally different beasts. Universities don't understand corporations and have to learn that they can't treat corporations like a University professor in the engineering school."[11] Mr. Wolfe points out that part of his role has been to serve as a translator between the two parties. Second, "how the university sets itself up to be a real estate developer is critical. It is not like setting up a new academic department."[12] Wolfe went on to say, "Given the success of the Princeton Forrestal Center, Princeton University clearly has 'set itself up' properly with a clear vision and goals for what it hoped to accomplish, a strong master plan with a unique development concept, and an experienced real estate development partner."[13]

University Park at the Massachusetts Institute of Technology. Since the early 1970s the Massachusetts Institute of Technology (MIT) in Cambridge, Massachusetts, has launched two urban research projects—Tech Square and University Park—as outlets for its applied research, to capitalize on the related real estate opportunities, and to address the deteriorated neighborhoods that flanked its campus. Its first venture in the early 1970s was the development of an urban research park, Tech Square, as a private adjunct to its research activities and as an attempt to "kick start" the redevelopment of a deteriorating semi-industrial area, Kendall Square, on the east side of its campus. The project, comprised of three office/research buildings, has subsequently been sold. However, by 2015 the Kendall Square area was the heart of the burgeoning biotechnology boom in Massachusetts.

Also in the 1970s, MIT acquired the 27-acre Simplex industrial property on the west side of the campus in the Cambridgeport district of the city of Cambridge, the bulk of which was Simplex Wire and Cable. Simplex moved its operations out of the city in 1970. The buildings on the site were demolished over the ensuing fifteen years. The property lay vacant and had become increasingly derelict for over a decade with a depressing impact on both the university and its Cambridgeport neighbors. Under increasing internal pressure and external pressure from the City of Cambridge, MIT instituted a preliminary planning process with the city for the development of a mixed-use urban research park to be called University Park. MIT launched a national search for a real estate development partner and from forty-five separate proposals MIT selected Forrest City Enterprises of Cleveland, Ohio, in 1982 as its development partner.

Four years of intensive planning followed Forrest City's selection. The goal was to reconcile MIT's interests with those of the neighborhood, the City of Cambridge, and the realities of the real estate market. Final planning and zoning approval was reached in 1988. Forrest City was given 20 years to complete development of the project. The business arrangement at University Park has MIT retaining ownership of the land. Each building within the complex sits on a 75-year ground lease. MIT has a participating interest in the ground lease and the rent structure. Forrest City developed and continues to manage the

MIT's University Park is an urban mixed-use office and biotechnology research park which has incorporated a hotel, housing, retail uses, including a grocery store and public parks in the new urban neighborhood

IMAGE COURTESY OF SASAKI ASSOCIATES, INC.

property. All development on site, including a public park, was privately financed by Forrest City. The company estimates that it has invested $50 million in infrastructure in University Park. Public cost sharing with the City of Cambridge was reached for the bordering streets. The City of Cambridge also receives real estate taxes from the developed property in University Park at the prevailing tax rates in the city.

By 2005 University Park at MIT had been fully developed, with 10 state-of-the-art office and biotechnology buildings, 674 units of mixed-income housing, a 210-room hotel and conference center, a 50,000 square-foot grocery store, and another 55,000 square feet of commercial space including restaurants, retail, a health club, a childcare center, and structured parking for 2,700 cars. One additional parcel has since been added to the campus, and a 250,000 square-foot research facility with street-level retail will open there in 2016. A distinguishing feature of the site is a beautiful urban park as the center focus of the project.

MIT's first goal was to protect the integrity of its campus by introducing quality urban development on a decrepit site on the west side of its campus as it had done in Kendall Square on the east side of its campus. Second, the university hoped to further support the emerging research activities around the MIT campus and, third, create an income stream for its endowment. MIT has no academic or research activities on the property. The housing on the site is a combination of market rate and subsidized affordable rental units, with no designated MIT student or faculty housing.

The City of Cambridge's goals were to remove the blighting effect of the abandoned industrial site, to secure market rate and affordable housing for the Cambridgeport community, to introduce a public park to this part of the city, and to enhance the city's tax base. According to Gayle Farris, 25-year former CEO of Forrest City Enterprises Sciences and Technology Group, the City of Cambridge and the local neighborhoods did not want an expansion of the MIT campus, and thus used the required rezoning to achieve its goals of private taxpaying commercial development, mixed-income housing, and a limit to the amount of retail use.

Peter Calkins, who now leads Forrest City's Science+Technology Group and over a 22-year span helped to develop most of University Park, believes the original development agreement was skillfully done and provided Forrest City with great flexibility at the onset of the project when the market feasibility was still uncertain. He points out, for example, that the development agreement called for MIT to carry the land (for a fairly modest carry fee) until each individual component was ready to be developed. Forrest City committed to taking down the first parcel within five years, but thereafter had full flexibility to take down parcels as market conditions enabled them to. Forrest City established a master developer account to carry the costs of planning and shared infrastructure, which was then allocated out to each individual building as they were developed.

In the early 1980s, Forrest City Enterprises made the corporate decision to focus on complex urban mixed-use real estate development projects that required public/private partnerships. "University Park at MIT represented the perfect opportunity to engage in such a project with the added incentive of partnering with MIT, which already had a strong track record launching technology companies. We felt that we couldn't go wrong being in the path of development that was beginning to emerge in Cambridge."[14] Forrest City's decision back in 1982 has borne fruit as MIT and Cambridge have become the center of the nation's biotech boom. By 2014, MIT's research activities, along with those of Harvard and the other research universities and teaching hospitals in the Boston metropolitan area, had led to the rapid development of the biotechnology industry in the greater Boston area. The Boston Globe reports, "Where we used to be simply the Hub of Biotech, we have suddenly turned into the hub of the [Big] Pharma Universe transforming from merely a research capital to a center of corporate expansion and development."[15] Independently and though acquisition, major pharmaceutical companies such as GlaxoSmithKline, Merck, Serono, Sanofi, Millennium, and Novartis have established very significant research and corporate development centers in Cambridge and Boston. The entrepreneurial start-up culture continues to thrive as well.

While Forrest City has developed other university research facilities, including the Illinois Science + Technology Park and the Translational Research Lab at the University of Pennsylvania, it considers University Park at MIT its premier accomplishment. Calkins reports, "It has been a very fulfilling relationship. The project has done very well for us financially and we consider University Park at MIT one of the company's most successful projects. MIT is very happy."[16]

Goals of University Research Parks. The primary goal of the State of North Carolina in the development of the Research Triangle Park was economic development and job creation. North Carolina State University in Raleigh had the dual goals for its Centennial Research Park of seeking land for expansion of the campus as well as economic development. The Georgia Tech Research Institute is the clearest expression of creating an entity for technology transfer from the applied research of an academic institution.

A surprising finding in the development of university research parks is the lack, in several notable ventures, of any academic programmatic relationship between the research park and the founding institution, as is the case with the Princeton Forrestal Center and MIT's University Park. Both have been developed as real estate ventures.

A significant "take away" from Princeton University's and MIT's experience with their research parks is the

The significant "take away" from Princeton University's and MIT's experience with their research parks is their understanding that the quality of the physical environment of their host communities impacts their ability to carry out their academic mission.

understanding that the quality of the physical environment of their host communities impacts their ability to carry out their academic mission.

The University as a Real Estate Developer. Universities bring distinctive assets to real estate development. From a marketing perspective, universities bring a stable and long term demand. They can also bring a special cachet with respect to their host communities as places to live and work. The amenities of a university, such as the arts and sports, enrich the lives of residents in the communities in which they reside. Princeton, New Jersey, and Oxford, Mississippi, are quintessential "college towns" not only because they are the locations of great universities; they are beautiful places to live and work. Cambridge, Massachusetts, has become a "college town" for those seeking an urban environment.

In the world of real estate development, universities also bring a different mindset and values than a prototypical real estate developer. Universities, for example, bring a slower, risk-adverse decision making process to real estate development and a long-term view to financial goals and the quality of development. A real estate developer is willing to take risk, can make decisions quickly, and more typically has a short-term view of real estate. If, for example, a university has had long-term ownership of the land that is to be developed, the land's low financial basis allows a university to be more patient with respect to real estate market demand. This is in contrast to the typical real estate developer, who often has recently purchased the asset and needs to realize an early return on his or her investment. A university, by not having to maximize profits over a short term, can weather the volatile cycles to which real estate is susceptible. By 1986 the Princeton Forrestal Center, for example, had survived two major real estate recessions. "The University's ability to weather them stems from its long-term approach as well as the prudence in phasing expenditures."[17]

Universities also have legal limitations in developing real estate. Their non-profit legal status requires them to operate through third parties such as development foundations or not-for-profit community organizations. The University of South Carolina, for example, partnered with the Columbia Housing Authority in the post–World War II period in acquiring property in Wheeler Hill and Ward One. In a partnership relationship, a university's long term view of real estate and the slower, risk-adverse, institutional decision making process can place them in conflict with their development partners' understanding of market conditions and more dynamic operating style. For example, an institution's desire for institutional grade construction of student housing in a public/private venture, resulting in higher rental rates than "stick built" construction, may conflict with the development partner's obligation to ensure long term occupancy of the building.

The University of South Carolina's public/private venture with Holder Properties for the construction of its new mixed-use student residence complex in Innovista required the developer to utilize an institutional class of construction—steel structure with masonry exterior—in contrast to the competing "stick built" housing projects that proliferate around the university's campus. University vice president Dennis Pruitt estimates that the quality of construction will add $400 to $700 per semester to student room rates, entailing some risk for both the developer and the university. However, the university sought an institutional grade of construction because it will eventually assume ownership of the property under the terms of its land lease with the developer.

The university system of Georgia has developed a contrarian view for its portfolio of student housing at the 34 colleges and universities in its system. National housing developer Corbious is buying the system's portfolio from nine institutions and will assume responsibility for the provision of housing at those institutions for 65 years. Alan Travis, director of planning for the Georgia Board of Regents, says that the board of regents expects to demolish some of its other housing if it is not worth keeping once the typical 20-year bonded indebtedness is retired.

Universities that have successfully engaged in real estate activities have learned the importance of first setting goals and priorities. In the development of research parks, is the goal job creation (such as at the North Carolina Research Triangle Park), research and technology transfer (as at the Georgia Tech Research Institute), or environmental stewardship and quality of place (as at MIT and Princeton)? The development process will have somewhat different requirements depending upon the institution's goals. Second, is there a real estate market to support the proposed development project? At universities that are experiencing an increase in enrollment, there is likely to be a strong housing market demand. Such is the case in Columbia as of 2015 with the continued growth of USC. For a university research park that anticipates private partners, there is a relationship between the university's annual research expenditures and its ability to attract private partners. Third, a high-quality master plan is needed, one which is capable of being phased and implemented over a long period of time. A high-quality plan can be self-marketing and allow a university the flexibility to survive the vagaries and cycles of the real estate market. Fourth, public engagement is essential for a public university in an urban setting such as the University of South Carolina. Fifth, a university venturing into the real estate business requires an experienced real estate development partner at its side. ■

THE PARTNERSHIP ENVISIONED A NEW MIXED-USE LIVEWORK URBAN NEIGHBORHOOD FOR COLUMBIA CONTAINING UNIVERSITY FACILITIES ALONG WITH PRIVATE HOUSING, OFFICE, RETAIL, PARKS AND RECREATION FACILITIES.

115TH YEAR, NO. 110 | SOUTH CAROLINA'S LARGEST NEW

USC, C

plan to

Bigger Columbia may
or may not be better

Subtract spring, a bouquet of cherry, redbud and dog wood blossoms, and Columbia seems almost neutral: No too big, not so small. Not too busy, not so dull. Not a Charleston-like jewel. Not a Charlotte-like drab. Not an Atlanta-like urban.

As any Southerner might explain, Columbia is middlin', a middlin' in a its meanings.

In this pleasantly middlin' town, change comes slowly. Dreams of re-design — tearing down the Central rectional Institution, constructing Fi Park, nurturing the Vista, reviving

he State

Thursday, April 20, 2006

COPYRIGHT © 2006 | COLUMBIA, S.C. | CAPITAL FINAL ++

thestate.com

EXCLUSIVE | BUILDINGOURCITY

ignards unveiling einvent downtown

Condos, retail would ring park, campus

EY FEATURES

epresentatives from USC, ard Associates and a community ing team will present details of proposal at 3:30 p.m. today at State Museum auditorium. It includes plans for:

- 0 new residences
- **erfront park** ringed by condo- iums and shops
- **105 million** price tag
- **ee-lined** Greene Street connect- USC to the river
- ...**$875 million** in private

By JAMES T. HAMMOND and C. GRANT JACKSON
jhammond@thestate.com
gjackson@thestate.com

USC today will unveil a sweeping plan for its research campus and 500 acres of the city center that includes a major new riverfront park and 3,000 new residences that school planners hope will attract researchers and students seeking an urban lifestyle.

The densely built, walkable downtown will have as its crown jewel a riverfront park — the largest in the city — with two footpaths, a marsh with boardwalks, a grassy amphitheater and, near

USC'S MASTER PLAN

USC and the Guignard family have announced a proposal that could transform downtown Columbia. A large undeveloped Guignard tract along the Congaree River would become a public park with an amphitheater, restored marshland and extensions of the Three Rivers Greenway and the Columbia Canal.

PHOTO © The State
April 20, 2006

Section IV

INNOVISTA: A NEW PARTNERSHIP

IBM serves as a principal tenant in the University's new office and research building.

IMAGE PROVIDED BY THE AUTHOR

Chapter 9

A Research Park for the University of South Carolina

"Our vision, and I do mean our vision for the research campus is that it becomes a magnet for attracting the brightest minds and most innovative companies in the world to USC, Columbia and to South Carolina."

These were the words of President Sorensen in describing the original concept for a university research park at the University of South Carolina in an address to his faculty in December of 2004.[1]

The Concept. Conceived at a time when other university research parks were enjoying great success and when federal research dollars were plentiful, the University of South Carolina's concept in designing Innovista was to translate its research initiatives in alternative energy, nanotechnology, biomedical science, and environmental science into economic development and job creation. The initial concept was to develop a research park as an extension of its academic research program, self-contained, on university property, and wholly controlled by the university.

Rick Kelly was directed to initiate a closely held internal planning process for an urban university research park adjacent to the core campus. A pre-liminary draft plan was prepared for seven blocks of university-controlled land between Park and Gadsen Streets in the Vista redevelopment area.

At the onset, the planning envisioned a mixed-use urban research park with street fronted multi-story buildings at urban densities of development. The MIT "University Park" was viewed as a precedent for the USC research park.

While the master planning was underway for a research park on university-held land, the university's planners, Sasaki Associates, were simultaneously working with Guignard heir Charles Thompson. Charles was manager of Guignard Associates, the limited liability corporation (LLC) that held 93 acres of the family's property holdings along the east bank of the Congaree River adjacent to the campus. Charles had sold 35 acres of the waterfront land to the university's development foundation the previous year for a new baseball park. He had separately retained Sasaki to help develop a master plan for the remainder of the family's waterfront land. Charles envisioned a mixed-use real estate project on his property fronting a waterfront park along the shoreline of the Congaree River.

A Team of Partners. In a meeting with President Sorensen and Rick Kelley in 2005, John Lumpkin, special advisor to President Sorensen, suggested that the university partner with the Guignard family, the largest land owner in the Vista, in order to plan the entire area between Assembly Street and the Congaree River. Coincidently, this was the area for which Sasaki had developed a conceptual "Futures Plan" as part of the Bicentennial Master Plan.

Charles Thompson

Charles Thompson, manager of the Guignard property, agreed to a partnership for the planning. The partnership envisioned a new mixed-use live/work urban neighborhood for Columbia, containing university facilities along with private housing, office, retail, parks, and recreation facilities: a "live, work, play community." President Sorensen articulated the goals of the concept, later branded "Innovista"—"By creating a vibrant, knowledge-based community, we become a powerful engine for creating high-paying jobs and raising per-capita income throughout our state."[2] Columbia's alternative press, the *Free Times,* interpreted the concept as "a distinctive urban district that is a center for innovation and contemporary living."[3]

The development of the plan for the university's research park brought forth new leadership from both within and outside the university community. In addition to President Sorensen and Charles Thompson, key members of the new partnership team included board chairmen Herbert Adams and Miles Loadholt, whose chairmanships spanned 2004 to 2012, Harris Pastides, dean of the Arnold School of Public Health, John Lumpkin, lawyer and special advisor to the president, Lee Bussell, alumnus and president of a prestigious public affairs firm in Columbia, and Bill Boyd, prominent Columbia lawyer.

Charles Thompson. Grandson of Jane Bruce Guignard, Thompson heads "Thompson Associates," a real estate management firm in Columbia. The Guignard family's waterfront land on the Congaree River in Innovista was among the properties that he managed. A passionate historian and environmentalist, Charlie has brought high-quality environmentally sustainable development principles to his projects and the properties that he manages. His real estate development philosophy is illustrated in the Village Commons project that he is developing on the east bank of the Congaree River in the adjoining city of Caycee. The master plan for the proposed mixed-use village incorporates a village square along with sites for residential and commercial facilities. A distinctive feature of the plan is the preservation of historic brick kilns from the family's nineteenth-century brick-making business.

John Lumpkin. John Lumpkin, a Magnum Cum Laude graduate of Princeton with a law degree from the University of South Carolina, was characterized by local newspaper the *State* as the number one business leader in Columbia.[4] Along with William Boyd, Lumpkin has been Columbia's primary citizen leader and advocate for the Innovista project. William Boyd, who served as chairman of the Waterfront

Pictured Left to Right
Bill Boyd
John Lumpkin
Lee Bussell

Steering Committee, described him as a "bulldog when he gets his teeth into a project like Innovista."[5] His advocacy for Innovista stayed the course through the recent "Great Recession." He was a key player in getting a portion of the recently approved penny sales tax in Richland County allocated to fund infrastructure improvements in Innovista.

Lumpkin, a confidant of President Sorensen and Rick Kelly, has served as a bridge to the mayor and city council for the implementation of Innovista. Shortly after the public announcement of the Innovista project, the university appointed him as its interim director of Innovista. Lumpkin took the initiative in the development of the Waterfront Steering Team, which became the public face of the Innovista project. He has single-handedly pursued funding for the infrastructure development of Innovista, and along with Lee Bussell helped to arrange briefing sessions in Washington, DC, with the state's congressional delegation, managed meetings with the Army Corp of Engineers for the riverfront, and led the negotiations with the city, county, and school board for the development of a tax increment finance district (TIF) for Innovista.

Bill Boyd. William "Bill" Boyd, a quintessential Southern gentleman, is considered one of Columbia's elder statesman. A lawyer who built one of Columbia's most successful law firms—Haynsworth, Sinkler and Boyd—Boyd assumed chairmanship of a citizens committee, the "Waterfront Steering Team," for the Innovista project. The Waterfront Steering Team was composed of 22 of Columbia's leading citizens and property owners and was designed to be the public face of the project. After assuming the role of chair, Boyd estimated that he and members of the Waterfront Steering Committee made more than 50 presentations of the project. In inquiring why he had accepted such a time-consuming assignment, Boyd responded first in a humorous vein—"A lapse of judgment on my part"—but went on to say, "It was a great opportunity for the City. A magical idea. Something they ought to do. The venture of the University, City and Guignard Family made it so appealing. It was something that I wanted to be a part of."[6]

Lee Bussell. Lee Bussell, a 1970 USC graduate of the College of Journalism, is the CEO of Chernoff Newman, the most prominent public affairs firm in South Carolina. A firm that provides professional services in branding, strategy, public relations, and media, Chernoff Newman has played a central role in the development and implementation of the Innovista concept. The *State* describes Lee as a "leader to create a knowledge-based economy."[7] Prior to the public announcement of the Innovista project at the State Museum on April 20, 2006, Lee orchestrated a series of important confidential briefings with the media, including the *State* newspaper with wide distribution throughout the state of South Carolina. The front page coverage in the *State* that followed the public presentation described the master plan for Innovista as a "transformative vision for Columbia."[8] Lee Bussell authored the brand name for the proposed research park, "Innovista," which is derived from the words "innovation" and "vista."

EDVENTURE
ERVAIS STREET
HUGER STREET
PULASKI STREET
WAYNE STREET
GADSDEN STREET
PARK STREET
ENTERTAINMENT DISTRICT
RIVERFRONT PROMENADE
CONGAREE RIVER PARKWAY
TOW PATH
KINSLER'S CREEK
CONVENTION CENTER
COLONIAL CENTER
CONGAREE RIVER
THE MARSH GRASS GARDEN
THE AMPHITHEATER
SCULPTURE PARK
FOUNDATION SQUARE
COLISEUM PROMENADE
BLOSSOM STREET
Student Wellness Center
BASEBALL PARK

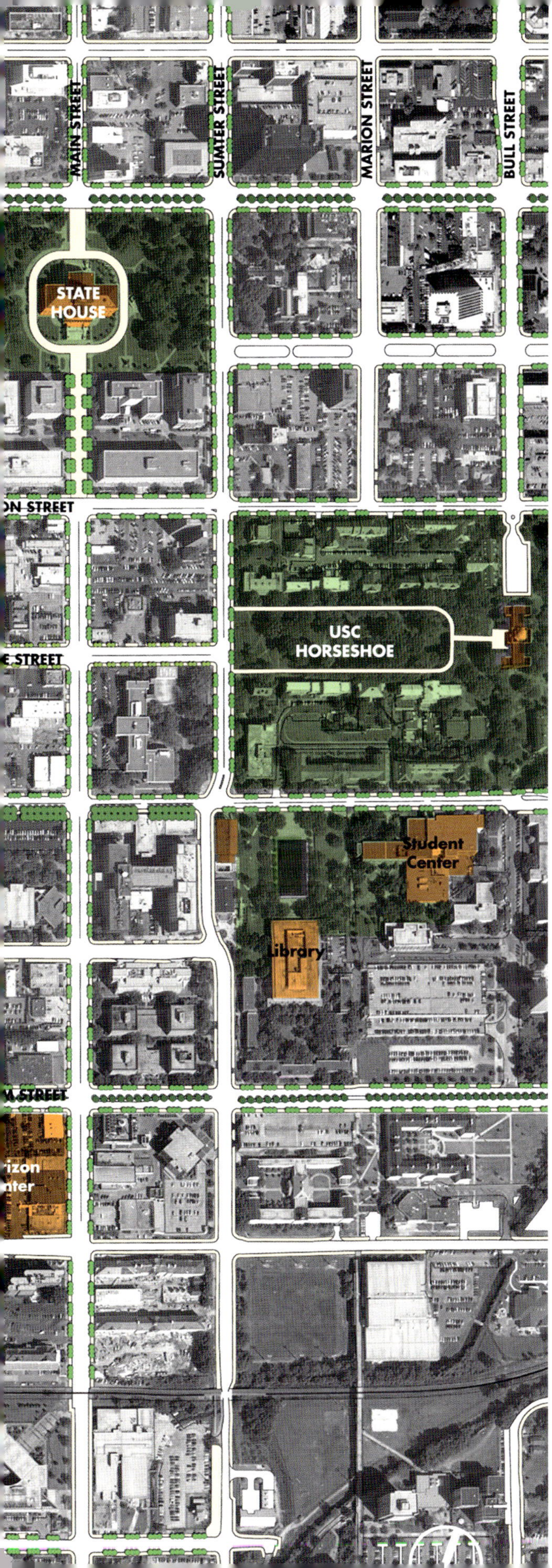

The Innovista concept of a new urban live/work district, with its proposed mix of university facilities with private development, was a radical transformation of the initial concept of a university research park. It placed the university into a leadership role in Columbia and the state, and suggested a new form of "urban campus" for the university. It also launched the university into the complexities and politics of urban real estate development in the city of Columbia. In their enthusiasm for the vision of the Innovista Master Plan, it is unlikely that either the administration of the university or the trustees were fully cognizant of the demands that carrying this plan out would place upon the university.

The Innovista concept under President Sorensen's leadership dramatically moved the university back outside the "brick walls" of the campus. Innovista provided President Sorensen with a means to forge a partnership with the city and the university a means to address its obligations to the state.

Pictured Above
View of the existing Colonial Life Arena in the heart of Innovista

PHOTO COURTESY OF USC CREAIVE SERVICES

Pictured Left
The Innovista Master Plan showing potential new mixed-use development and the Congaree Regional Waterfront Park in relationship to the Horseshoe, Statehouse and Vista entertainment districts IMAGE COURTESY OF SASAKI ASSOCIATES, INC.

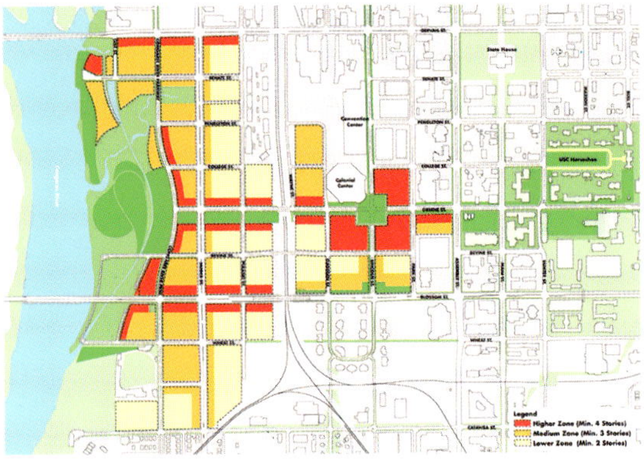

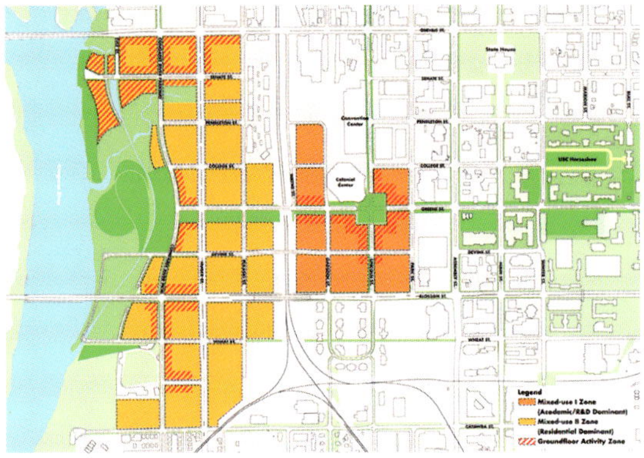

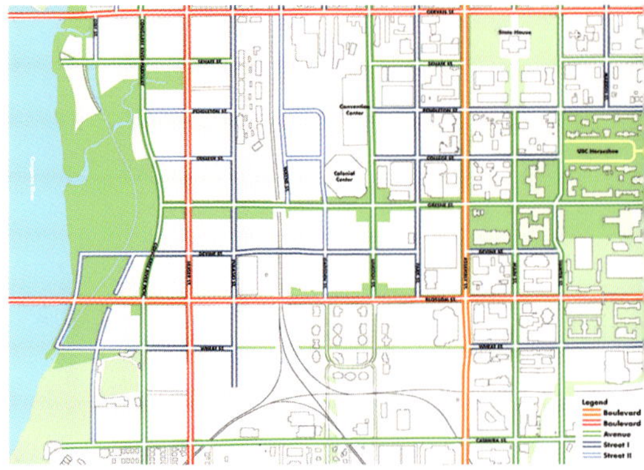

Plan of Innovista illustrating in red the intended location of higher street fronted buildings with active mixed uses at street level

Innovista Land Use Plan illustrating private residential dominant mixed use toward the river-front and university dominate mixed use adjacent to the existing campus

Plan of Innovista Streets and Pedestrian Ways illustrating the hierarchial sysem of pedestrian primary streets (green) and streets designated primarily for traffic and service. (red and blue)

IMAGE COURTESY OF SASAKI ASSOCIATES, INC.

The university was stepping into a leadership role at a time when the traditional business leadership of the city was on the wane. Historically, leadership in Columbia had been carried out by the heads of a select group of Columbia business leaders known as "the Big 8" who worked together in addressing community problems. The "Big 8," which included major banks and insurance companies such as the Colonial Life and Accident Insurance Co., had promoted among other projects the "City Beautiful" movement in Columbia in the post–World War II period, which ushered in the city's first redevelopment projects, including Wheeler Hill and Ward One. However, by 2005 almost all the "Big 8" had been purchased by big out-of-state companies whose absentee ownership was focused on the bottom line.[(9)]

The Planning Area. The new university/Guignard partnership retained Sasaki to prepare the master plan for Innovista: the 500-acre area located between Assembly Street and the Congaree River to the west, Gervais Street to the north, and Whaley Street to the south, an area similar to that embraced by the "Futures Plan" in the Bicentennial Plan developed 15 years earlier.

In 2006 the existing area contained some small offices and apartments, light industrial buildings, warehouses, surface parking lots, and significant amounts of vacant land. The city's consolidated rail line split the planning area along a north/south axis and presented a formidable physical barrier to bringing the university campus, downtown, and the State Capitol complex to the Congaree riverfront.

The planning area totaled approximately 400 acres excluding the roads' and railroads' rights-of-way. The university controlled 97 acres, 24% of the site. Guignard Associates' land on the riverfront totaled approximately 72 acres, or 18% of the site.[(12)] The remaining land in the study area, which totaled approximately 229 acres or 58% of the site, was held by over 100 other owners, including the state, city, and private owners.

The Planning Process. The initial master planning for the new partnership was a closely held planning and design process, internal within the university and the Guignard interests. Rick Kelly, John Lumpkin, Charles Thompson, Lee Bussell, and—from time to time—President Sorensen participated in the review and development of the Master Plan. The board chairs received periodic briefings. The new partnership was surprised by the design team's initial concept for a new mixed-use urban neighborhood stretching from Assembly Street to the river. However, President Sorensen, Rick Kelly, Charles Thompson, Lee Bussell, and John Lumpkin recognized the promise of the vision and its potential benefit to the university and the city of Columbia. The design team was authorized to fully develop the concept.

The Innovista Master Plan. The Master Plan for Innovista places university facilities, private housing, commercial uses, and office development in an urban district within the framework of the city of Columbia's historic street grid. The plan is designed to create a distinctive urban district that is a center for innovation and contemporary living within walking distance of the university, State Capitol complex, and downtown.

Three principal features distinguished the Innovista Master Plan: first, the proposed urban character and the intensity of mixed land use; second, a restoration of the historic Columbia street grid along with a repurposing of the use and character of the streets; and third, a unique urban landscape plan. The Innovista Master Plan is distinguished by its proposed landscaped public open spaces: the Greene Street Promenade, Foundation Square, a Sculpture Park, and the Congaree Regional Waterfront Park.

Land Use. The land use plan for Innovista assumed urban densities at a floor area ratio (FAR) of 2.0, anticipating four- and six-story street fronted buildings with parking structures internal to the city blocks. The large 400 foot square blocks of the planned city of Columbia permit vehicular parking to be located in parking structures within the center of the blocks. The overall building capacity of the planning area at a FAR of 2.0 has the potential to yield as much as 11 million square feet of mixed-use university and private development.[10]

Patrick Phillips, who was at that time president of Economic Research Associates (ERA) of Washington, DC, carried out a comprehensive economic analysis of the Innovista plan. ERA assessed the growth trends in the Columbia metropolitan statistical area, researched trends for the downtown, and generated a market profile for the office, retail, residential, and hotel markets. Within the context of the market analysis, the study concluded that Innovista had the market potential to develop 2.3 million gross square feet of office, 850,000 gross square feet of retail development, and 2,390 residential units by the university and private developers over 15 years. Furthermore, the market study estimated that the university share of the development potential would be 1.2 million square feet of the office development and 690 dormitory rooms, apartments, and condominium units for students.[11]

Streets and Pedestrian Ways. The pedestrian and vehicular circulation element of the Innovista plan was designed to support the land use concept of a new pedestrian-friendly mixed-use urban neighborhood and to tame Columbia's addiction to the automobile. Where industrial and railroad uses had obliterated the historic street plan of John Gabriel Guignard, the vehicular element of the Innovista Master Plan restores them and extends the street grid to a new parkway on the bluff above the Congaree River. The proposed parkway resolves the relationship of the historic gridded street plan to the hilly topography and curve of the river. The plan also repurposes the use of the streets by designating some streets primarily for pedestrians and others for vehicular service and travel.

Igor Andersen, Sasaki's urban designer for Innovista, redefined the street grid into a unique hierarchical system of boulevards, pedestrian-friendly avenues, and local streets serving the proposed live/work Innovista community. The vehicular circulation plan categorizes streets as "A" or "B" streets to differentiate streets that are primarily for pedestrians and bicycles and streets that are more typical streets for vehicles and service. The "A" streets are planned to receive enhanced pedestrian and bicycle features. "A" streets feature broad tree-shaded sidewalks with dedicated bike ways. The design guidelines mandate active commercial and residential uses at street level in adjoining buildings. Vehicular traffic is typically limited to two lanes on the "A" streets, with no curbside parking. The more typical "B" streets are designed to carry traffic and service vehicles, have two to four travel lanes, and allow some curbside parking. The barrier presented by the existing rail line will be overcome by a new viaduct on Greene Street.

The cost of extending, restoring, and repurposing the historic street grid, the Greene Street Viaduct over the railroad, and the Williams Street Parkway in the Innovista Plan was estimated to be $42.7 million in 2006.[12]

Parking. Freestanding parking structures are a dominating feature in downtown Columbia and on the university campus. The size and bulk of the existing parking structures, their industrial architectural character, and the blank facades at street level have weighed heavily against the development of an attractive, pedestrian-friendly urban environment. The Innovista Master Plan places all parking structures internal to the blocks, framed with commercial or residential buildings. The large 400-foot dimensions of the blocks in Columbia's historic street grid allow for the internal parking structures shown in the Innovista plan.

Special Precincts. Four special precincts were identified within the framework of the Innovista Master Plan. Three-dimensional master site development plans were prepared for each. The special precincts mark an important gateway, two riverfront landing locations, and Foundation Square in the heart of the new neighborhood. Special land use, open space, and building massing were prescribed in the Master Plan for these precincts. One precinct, the Blossom Street gateway on the east bank of the Congaree River, is one of the principal entries to the city and the university campus. At the point where the Blossom Street bridge traverses the Congaree River and the proposed Congaree Regional Waterfront Park below, mixed-use development parcels are designated on either side of the street. Special land use and building massing conditions are illustrated in the plan for the Lincoln Street Gateway at Blossom Street, which is the principal gateway to Innovista, the Colonial Center, and the city's convention center. A third special precinct was identified for the Senate Street Landing—one of two locations that will provide public vehicular access directly to the riverbank and the only location that has development parcels directly on the Congaree River. The fourth special precinct, Foundation Square, lies at the heart of Innovista.

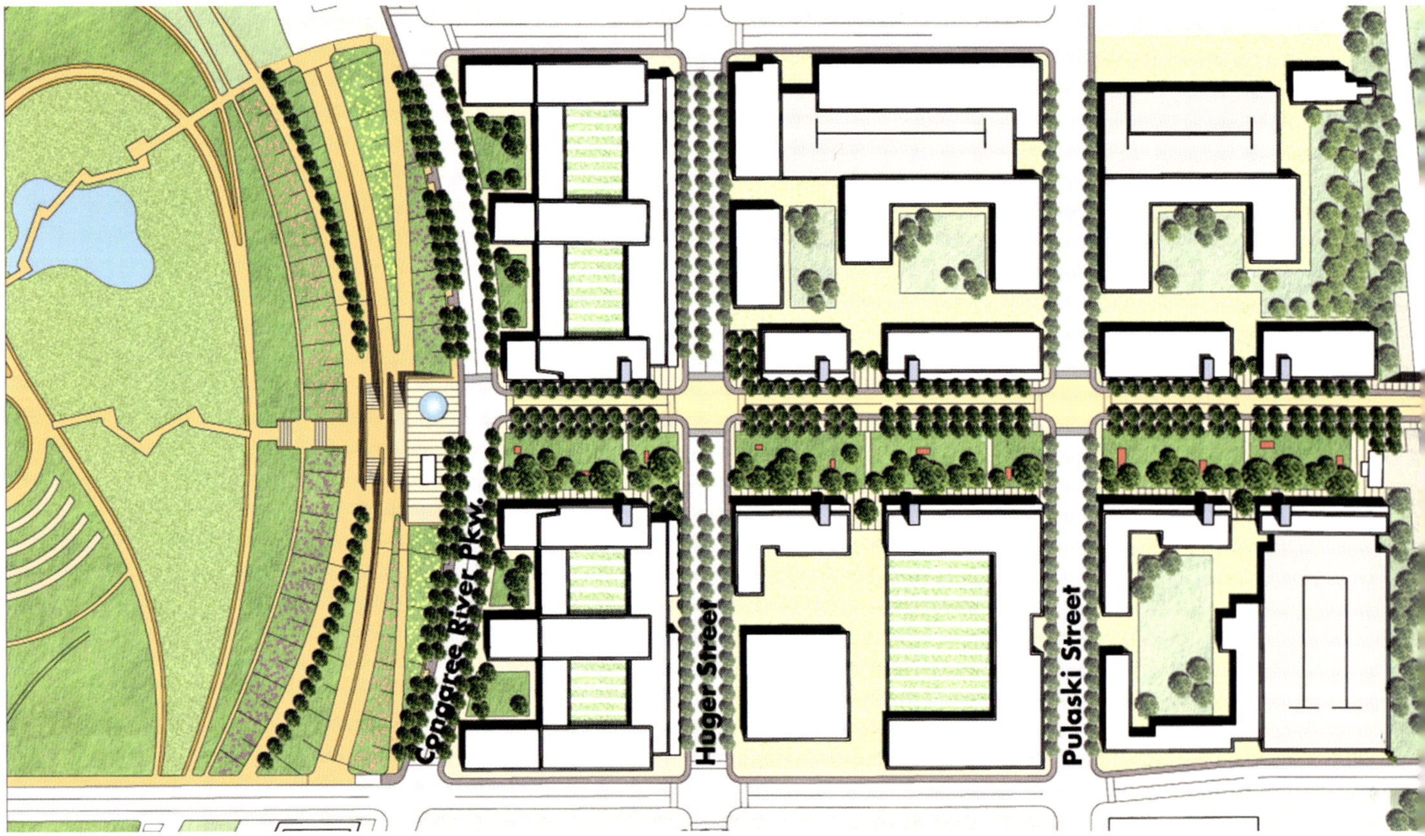

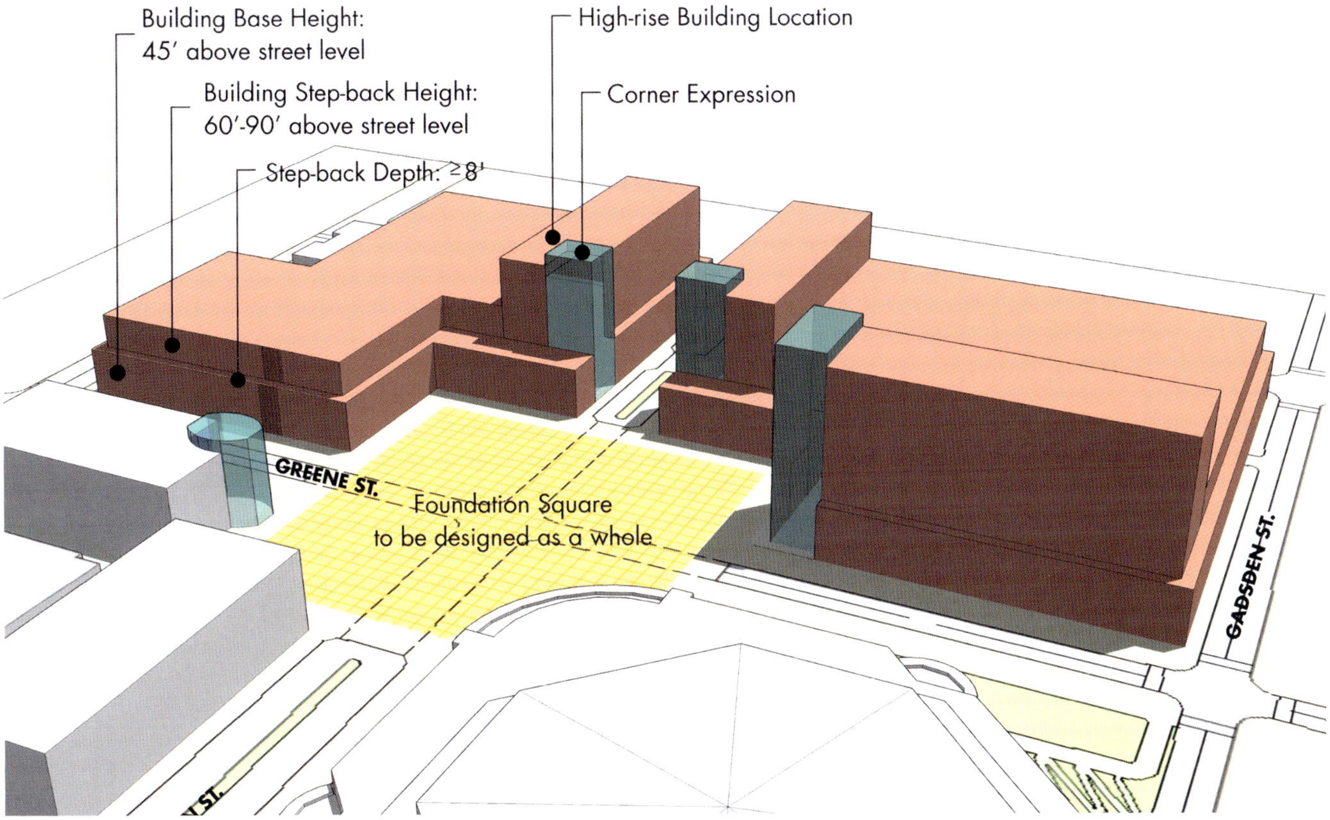

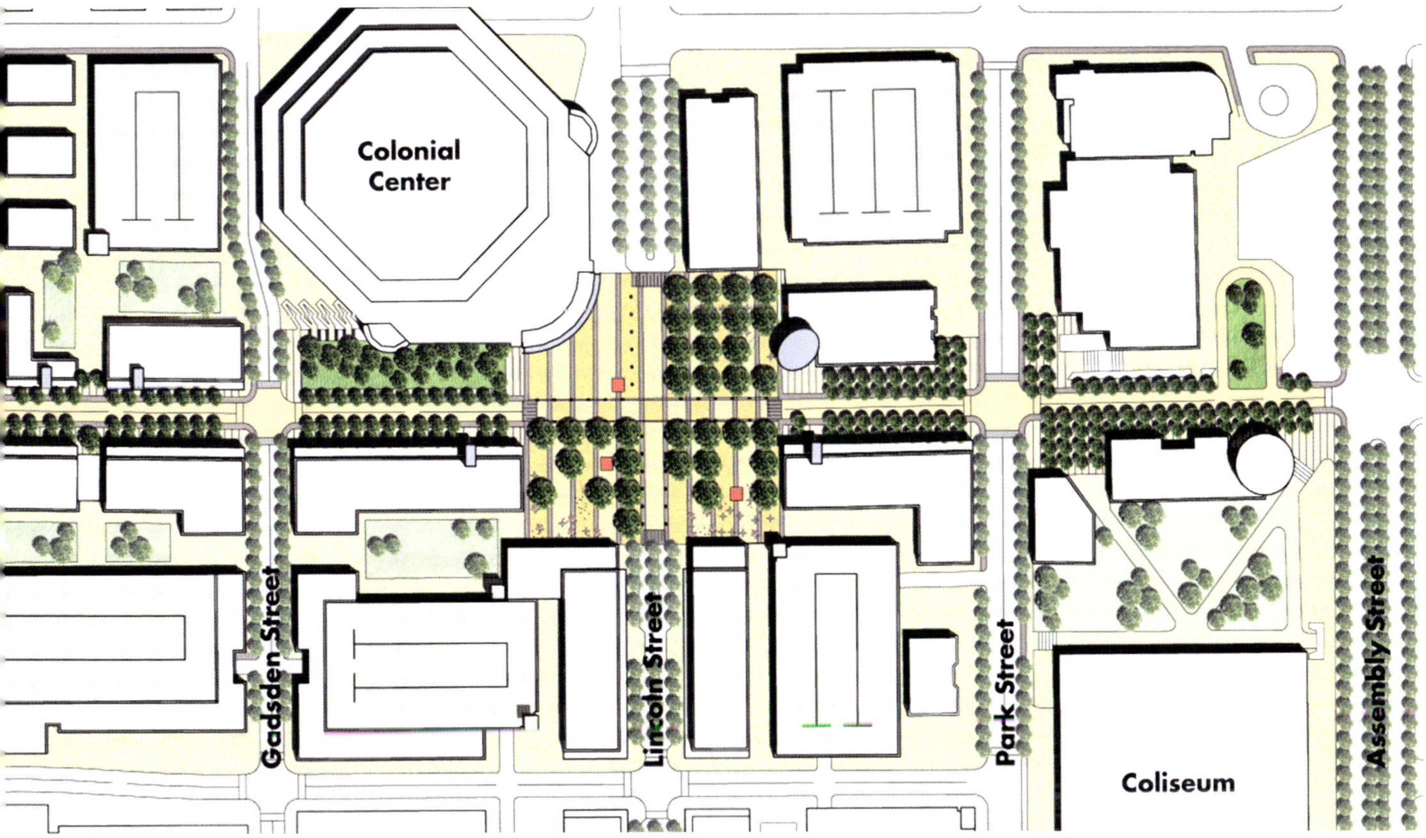

Plan and three-dimensional design guidelines for Foundation Square and the Green Street Promenade, special precincts in Innovista.

IMAGE COURTESY OF SASAKI ASSOCIATES, INC.

View of the Sculpture Park in the Greene Street Promenade looking west to the Congaree River in the background

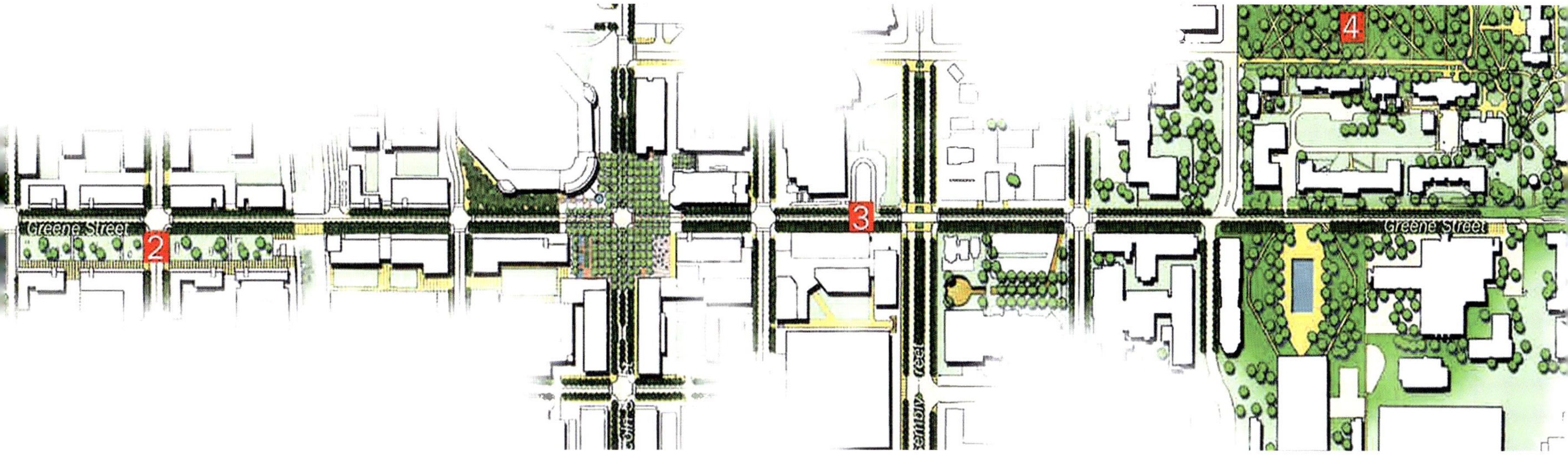

The Greene Street Promenade. The Greene Street Promenade is designed as a special street for pedestrians and bicycles linking the existing university campus to the proposed Congaree Regional Waterfront Park on the river. The street encapsulates the existing Greene Street right-of-way as a shared street for both pedestrians and vehicles and proceeds west from the historic academic core at the Horseshoe and Thomas Cooper Library to the Congaree River. The Greene Street Promenade incorporates a series of public landscape elements, including an urban square, "Foundation Square," at the Colonial Life Center, and a three-block-long "Sculpture Park" before terminating in the Congaree Regional Waterfront Park on the river. A new viaduct, the proposed Greene Street Viaduct, will bridge the barrier of the existing railroad tracks. One of the viaduct's distinguishing features is that it is illustrated as a raised fill platform rather than a typical bridge. In this way, it will carry the Greene Street design concept seamlessly across the railroad cut.

Plan of the Green Street Promenade designed to connect the academic heart of the university through Innovista to the Congaree River.

IMAGES COURTESY OF SASAKI ASSOCIATES, INC.

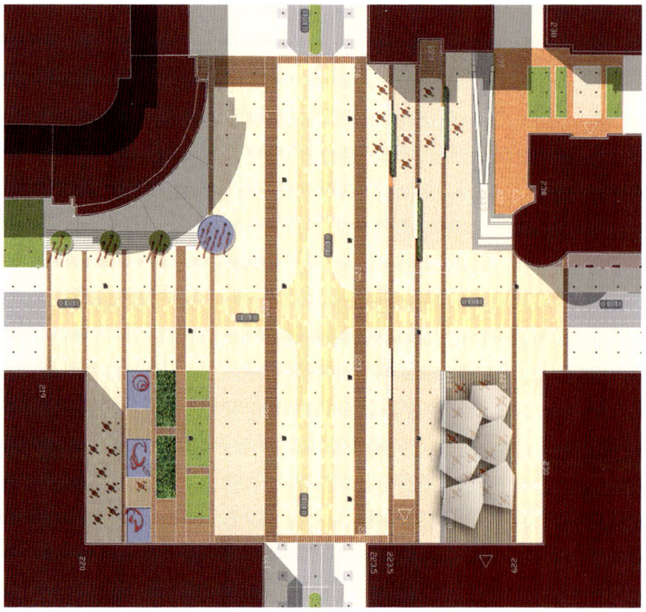

Pictured Right
Plan of Foundation Square showing a canopy of trees and special paved surface of the square

IMAGES COURTESY OF SASAKI ASSOCIATES, INC.

Foundation Square. Foundation Square is located at the crossroads of Innovista at the intersection of Greene and Lincoln Streets. The university's existing Discovery One research building and a proposed university building will frame two quadrants of the square. The existing 18,000-seat Colonial Life Arena frames a third quadrant. The fourth quadrant remains a key site for a mixed-use building, such as a hotel. Foundation Square is where the university and city meet by bringing together academic, research, business, entertainment, and commercial uses.

The design concept for Foundation Square creates a vibrant city square featuring a canopy of shade trees surrounded by active commercial buildings. The square itself is designed as a continuously paved surface across the two existing streets and adjoining sidewalks in the form of a "raised tablet." The design permits ease of pedestrian movement across the space while still allowing vehicle passage within the street's rights-of-way. Innovista's design guidelines call for active commercial uses, including outdoor dining at sidewalk level, in the buildings framing the square. The Colonial Life Arena that fronts the square is expected to be a major contributor to activity in the square. Foundation Square is designed to be closed to vehicular through-traffic for major events in the arena and on festival occasions.

The Sculpture Park. The proposed Sculpture Park is an 80-foot-wide linear park paralleling Greene Street for three blocks from the Greene Street Viaduct to its termination at the Congaree Regional Waterfront Park. The linear Sculpture Park is designed to enhance the pedestrian experience along the promenade to the waterfront park and to provide a location for large scale public sculpture. Multi-story residential buildings are anticipated to front the Sculpture Park along Greene Street.

Pictured Above
View of Foundation Square with Colonial Life Arena in the background showing cafes and shops in the buildngs framing the square

IMAGE COURTESY OF SASAKI ASSOCIATES, INC.

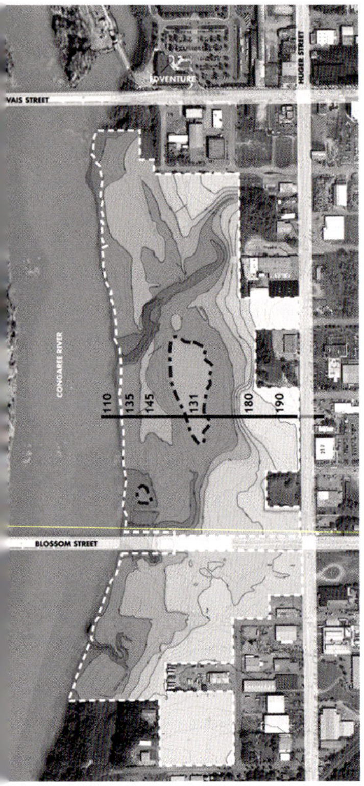

Pictured Above
Planning area for mixed-use development and the waterfront park showing 80' drop in grade

Pictured Right
Conceptual design plan for the Congaree Regional Waterfront Park showing restored freshwater marsh, amphitheater, remnant of the Columbia Canal and restored woodlands

IMAGES COURTESY OF SASAKI ASSOCIATES, INC.

The Congaree Regional Waterfront Park. The proposed Congaree Regional Waterfront Park was described as the "crown jewel" of the Innovista Master Plan by the *State*. The proposed waterfront park, long a dream of Charles Thompson, is located in the low-lying lands along the east bank of the Congaree River. The proposed park is designed to celebrate the city's industrial heritage and riverside location, and will complete the region's existing 12-mile-long linear trail system along the Broad, Saluda, and Congaree Rivers.

Today the site of the park consists of second growth woods, open meadows, and a freshwater marsh, which was created by construction of the historic Columbia Canal. Much of the proposed park site is located within the 100-year flood plain under the jurisdiction of the Army Corps of Engineers, and part of of the site is in the floodway. A sharp topographic break marks a divide between the proposed intensive mixed-use urban development of Innovista and the site for the park, which lays some 80 feet below. The park site contains a remnant of the historic Columbia Canal, along with several other sites of historic cultural significance. Erosion occurs along the river's edge at the north end of the site and along Kinsler's Creek, a drainage channel that carries storm water from downtown and the Vista to the Congaree River. The existing park site also serves as a utility corridor, holding Columbia's principal trunk sewer line along with a major power line. The visual impact of the power line and the trunk sewer, which sit above existing grades at the south end of the park, presents significant challenges to the landscape design of the park. Historically the site of the park had been cleared of its vegetation, used for grazing, and mined for brick-making and construction of the Columbia Canal.

In the tradition of great American urban parks, the design concept celebrates the site's distinctive natural and historic features and introduces public areas for recreation. The preliminary design calls for the restoration of the existing natural landscape, including the freshwater marsh and creeks. In acknowledgement of the waterfront's historic and cultural elements, some of which are on or are eligible for the

View of the Congaree Regional Waterfront Park looking back to mixed-use development on the bluff overlooking the Congaree River

From Right
View of waterfront promenade with Gervais Street Bridge in the background

View of the Congaree National Regional Waterfront park with Congaree River in background showing proposed meadow with ampitheatre, and freshwater marsh

IMAGES COURTESY OF SASAKI ASSOCIATES, INC.

National Register of Historic Places, the landscape design concept incorporates the remnants of the quarries, sawmills, brickworks, and the historic Columbia Canal and towpath.

The proposed park is organized around a central open space at the termination of the Greene Street Promenade. The central open space encompasses a restored freshwater marsh and a large amphitheater. Public landings on the river are illustrated on the north and south ends of the proposed park. On the north end of the park, higher ground permits the development of a mixed-use plaza branded "Senate Street Landing" at the terminus of Senate Street, which features restaurants and other supporting commercial facilities. Senate Street Landing is proposed to have a more formal landscape, including an urban parapet along the river's edge to curb existing erosion along the riverbank. At the south end of the park near the university's new baseball park, the conceptual design of Wheat Street Landing provides public access to the water via a stepped terrace. A proposed new parkway, Williams Street, atop the bluff receives Columbia's historic street grid and provides continuous public access to the park.

The conceptual landscape design of the proposed Congaree Regional Waterfront Park has not been without controversy. "At the risk of sounding flip, I see it [the park] as an Albrecht Speer, Nuremburg style, public space. It ain't natural or human—it's monumental and looks like the mall at Washington D.C. rather than the banks of the Congaree River," said Bob Guild, then president of the nearby Grandby Neighborhood Association.(13)

The conceptual design of the proposed park assumed that public process would be part of the project design once funding was obtained for design and construction. Changes to the design concept are expected to occur at that time.

Sasaki's Stuart Dawson, designer of Charleston's award-winning Waterfront Park, and urban designer Igor Andersen, who developed the conceptual design for the proposed park, described the design as a response to the distinctive characteristics of the Congaree River—the natural conditions of the site, its historic features, and the anticipated intensity of use from its location adjacent to an urban high-density mixed-use district. Andersen described the proposed park as "a new front yard for the city of Columbia."

Market Feasibility and Economic Impact. John Lumpkin properly questioned the market feasibility of the proposed Innovista plan in a project work session during the early phases of planning. In response, the planning and design team recommended that a real estate market assessment be carried out by Economic Research Associates. Concurrently, Dr. Donald L. Schunk, a professor of the Moore School of Business at the university, carried out a comprehensive economic impact assessment of construction activity, employment, and retail sales from the potential commercial space and the property tax revenues that the new commercial and residential construction would potentially generate.

Dr. Schunk's report suggested that new real estate development in the Innovista Master Plan would have an estimated value of $1.3 billion (as of 2006) at full build-out. The cumulative economic impact from this construction activity was estimated to be the creation of nearly $2.3 billion in local economic output, 27,651 jobs, and $942.7 million in household income. At full build-out, property tax revenues to local governments were estimated to be $25.6 million annually. At the 15-year mark the Innovista area was projected to generate $17.7 million in annual property tax revenues to local government, which includes schools, Richland County, and the City of Columbia.(14)

Critical Planning Issues. The newly formed partnership between the university and the Guignard interests launched the university into the public arena and the complexities of urban public planning, an activity outside the University of South Carolina's core mission. The proposed project immediately presented three critical issues.

First: how could the two parties, the university and Guignard Associates, assume responsibility for master planning an urban district containing multiple private property owners in addition to their own property holdings? The university had launched a planning process over a 500-acre area of the city without the engagement of the city's political leadership or the City of Columbia's professional staff. Mindful of the neighborhood conflicts it had created in the post–World War II period with its expansion into adjoining neighborhoods, the university recognized that it could not take the initiative without official public participation. Guignard heir Charles Thompson, representing a family that historically has tried to maintain a low profile within the Columbia community, said, "I can't be in the position of planning other property owner's lands."(15)

Second: real estate development projects of this magnitude are not part of a university's mission. The University of South Carolina recognized from the onset that it would need real estate expertise outside of its own resources to carry out the project. While the University Development Foundation has nominal responsibility for securing land for university purposes, it did not have the staff and resources to carry out the large scale, mixed-use real estate development envisioned in the Innovista Master Plan.

Third: who was to bear the burden of the cost of infrastructure and how was the cost of infrastructure and open spaces within the Innovista Master Plan to be financed? The cost of infrastructure, streets, and utilities is typically a public expense. The cost of infrastructure in the Innovista Plan, including streets and utilities, was estimated at $42.7 million, and the proposed parks and open spaces were estimated to cost an additional $75.5 million.[16]

The Waterfront Steering Team. John Lumpkin, one of Innovista's principal "boosters," recognized the central issue of the partnership planning the property of other multiple private owners. At a project meeting in Rick Kelly's office he asked, "How are we going to do this?"[17] John acknowledged his "aha moment" at the Sasaki response: "You have to find champions outside of the University and the Guignard interests to sponsor the plan for you and you have to invest the City of Columbia and property owners into the planning process." This recommendation led to the formation of the "Waterfront Steering Team" with Bill Boyd as chair.

John Lumpkin and Lee Bussell took the initiative in assembling a "Who's Who" of regional business, community, and environmental leaders, and other property owners within the planning district, for the team. The team was chaired by distinguished lawyer Bill Boyd and included Lynett Alston, community advocate; Gayle Averyt, retired chair of Colonial Life; Steven Benjamin, lawyer and former president of the USC student body; Lee Bussell, chairman of Chernoff Newman; Clente Flemming, president of South Carolina Community Bank; Dr. Madilyn Fletcher, director of the USC School of Environment; Kester Freeman, former CEO of Palmetto Health; Chuck Garnett, former chair of the Greater Columbia Chamber of Commerce; Dr. William L. Graf, USC professor of geography; Alan Kahn, CEO of Kahn Development Company; Rick Kelly, USC vice president of finance; John Lumpkin, USC interim director of Innovista; Frank Mood, general counsel of SCANA; Cathy Novinger, Palmetto Agribusiness Council; Dottie Owen, community volunteer; Mark Robertson, executive director of the Nature Conservancy; Jasper Salmond, a member of the Richland County School District #1 Board; Jim Smith, chair of the River Alliance; Charles C. Thompson, managing partner of Guignard Associates; Gilbert Walker, executive director of the Columbia Housing Authority; and Thad Westbrook, Nelson, Mullins, Riley and Scarborough, LLC.

The Waterfront Steering Team, with Boyd as its spokesman, became the public face of the Innovista project. The committee met on a regular basis for the first several years. Boyd estimated that he and members of the committee made multiple presentations to community groups in Columbia. With the exception of Boyd and Lumpkin, who have continued to foster the implementation of the Innovista Plan, the effectiveness of the Waterfront Steering Team has lapsed.

A Real Estate Development Partner. Prior to the development of the Innovista Master Plan, a contingent of university and public officials led by President Sorensen, vice President Harris Pastides, Rick Kelly, John Lumpkin, trustees, members of the General Assembly, and other administrators visited the Research Triangle Park and North Carolina State University's Centennial Research Park in Raleigh, North Carolina. The tour convinced the group of the viability of university research parks as well as the need for the University to secure an experienced real estate development partner. President Sorensen also came away convinced that for a university research park to be successful, it had to be located adjacent to the campus and thus immediately accessible to university researchers.

Recognizing the need for real estate expertise, the university embarked on the process of selecting an experienced real estate development partner. Six responses were received after the university's public solicitation. A university selection committee chaired by Provost Jerry Odom unanimously selected Craig Davis Partners of North Carolina. Craig

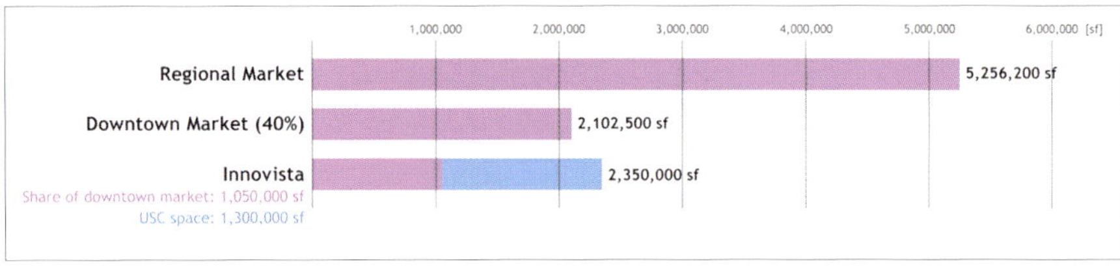

15-year office space development potential with a combination of market-driven growth and USC-led initiatives

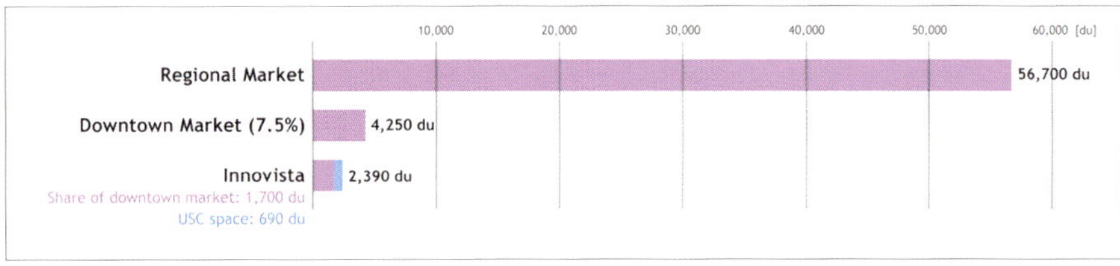

15-year residential development potential with a combination of market-driven growth and USC space (and average dwelling unit size of 2,000 gsf)

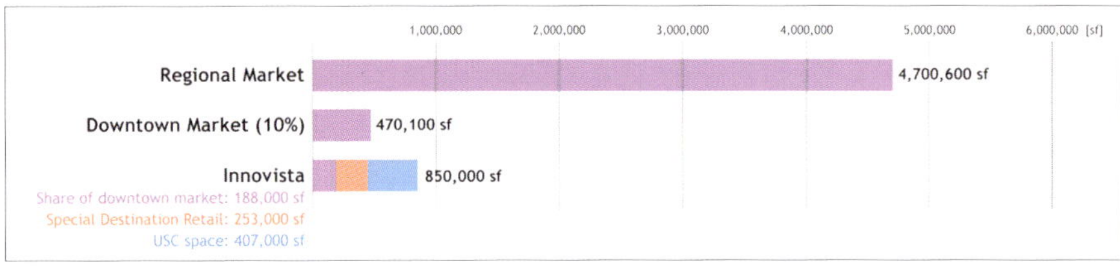

15-year retail space development potential with a combination of market-driven growth, special destination retail related to baseball, and USC space

Davis Partners had developed building facilities in the Research Triangle Park and North Carolina State University's Centennial Park.

Craig Davis Partners was contracted by the university on a fee basis to develop the university's research buildings, pair them with private office buildings, and secure private companies for the office buildings that would capitalize on the university's research activities. In order to coordinate its activities, the university appointed John Lumpkin as interim director of Innovista. John served until the university selected John Parks, an experienced research park executive, as its director of Innovista.

Financing Innovista. A comprehensive cost estimate had been prepared for the projected infrastructure improvements in the Innovista Master Plan. The total estimated infrastructure and open space development cost of the project in 2006 was estimated to be $120 million in 2006 dollars.(18) Because the university and its development foundation controlled most of the property east of the rail line and private property owners, including the Guignard interests, held most of the property west of the rail line toward the riverfront, the Innovista Plan was organized around an "Innovation District" to the east of the rail line and a "Waterfront District" to the west of the rail line. The total estimated cost of infrastructure improvements and open space included road and utility improvements, right-of-way and landscape improvements to existing streets, the creation of new streets, the proposed Congaree River Parkway framing the east edge of the park, and the creation of a pedestrian promenade along Greene Street.

The Master Plan recommended that a variety of funding streams be explored to construct the public infrastructure and parks within Innovista, including private funding, the federal Water Resources Development Act, tax increment financing (TIF), transportation funding, and local and state government funding sources. The plan also recommended exploring smaller funding streams such as the National Endowment for the Arts, historic preservation tax credits, and local philanthropic organizations.

View of Green Street in Innovista.

IMAGES COURTESY OF SASAKI ASSOCIATES, INC.

Public Unveiling. "A transformative vision" was the description applied to the proposed Innovista Master Plan by the *State,* Columbia's newspaper, following its public presentation at the State Museum on the afternoon of April 20, 2006. Prior to the public presentation the city and the City's professional staff were briefed on the development of the proposed Innovista plan. Bill Boyd, chair of the Waterfront Steering Team, John Lumpkin, Charles Thompson, Rick Kelly, and the project design team briefed property owners, and the business community. Lee Bussell played the key role in achieving the early public support for the project by arranging the briefing sessions with the property owners and a private briefing of the editorial board of the *State.* The briefing of the editorial board led to favorable front page coverage of the Innovista Plan in the paper and favorable support on the editorial page.

Before the public presentation at the State Museum, the Innovista Master Plan was presented to the full board of trustees of the university. The plan was warmly received by the board with trustee Darla Moore excitedly exclaiming that the board should write a check "right now" for the waterfront park.

At the State Museum, Boyd and other public officials led the presentation of the proposed plan and its projected economic impact. They were followed by the Sasaki team and the economists Patrick Phillips of Economic Research Associates and Dr. Donald Schunk, assistant professor at the Moore School of Business.

Dr. Sorensen Goes to Washington. In June of 2006, after the public presentation of the Innovista plan in Columbia, President Sorensen led a contingent to Washington. The objective was to keep the state's congressional delegation informed and to explore sources of federal funding. The group, which included Bill Boyd, John Lumpkin, Charles Thompson, and the planning and design team, waded through the crowds of lobbyists at each door in the Senate and House office buildings. Senator Edward Kennedy of Massachusetts was sighted in the crowd taking his pair of noisy Portuguese Water dogs for a walk down the corridor. In small standing-room-only conference rooms the Innovista Master Plan was presented to Senators Lindsey Graham and Jim DeMint and the majority whip of the House, Congressman Jim Clyburn. It was also presented to Congressmen Joe Wilson, Gresham Barrett, Bob Inglis, and John Spratt. ■

State Capitol
State Museum
Arena
Congaree River
Baseball Stadium

Chapter 10

Realizing the Vision

A New Beginning. Announced with great fanfare in 2006 as a "transformative vision" for the city of Columbia, development of Innovista initially floundered. The failure of the university's first real estate development partner, the "Great Recession," and the university's inexperience with real estate development were the primary causes. The initial failure led to the public labeling of Innovista as "the name that results in failures."[1] However, 2014 saw a complete reversal of fortune. The private real estate market had responded to the growth of the university and the promise of Innovista. The university has since fielded a new experienced team under the leadership of President Harris Pastides. A proactive marketing program has been launched and the university is partnering with new real estate development partners.

The Development Team. Within the administration, President Pastides's strategic planning team includes Ed Walton, senior vice president and chief operating officer; the late Russ Meekins, executive director of the University of South Carolina's Development Foundation; and Bill Kirkland, who heads the Office of Economic Development. Derrick Huggins, vice president of facilities and transportation, and Derek Gruner, university architect, are charged with carrying out the project design work attendant to the Master Plan.

Trustee Miles Loadholt served as chairman of the board of trustees through the challenging years from 2008 to 2012.

Pictured Left to Right
Harris Pastides
Miles Loadholt
Ed Walton

Harris Pastides. (2008 to –) With President Sorensen's resignation in 2008, the trustees selected the dean of the Arnold School of Public Health, Dr. Harris Pastides, a distinguished scientist, researcher, and prolific fund raiser, as its new president. President Pastides began his tenure shortly after the onset of the Great Recession in the spring of 2008. His tenure was greeted with enthusiasm by the trustees. "We are really, really, happy with Harris. We felt really comfortable with him."(2)

Miles Loadholt. A member of the board of trustees since 1996, Loadholt chaired the board from 2008 to 2012, during the period when Innovista was perceived as a failure. In speaking to the launching of the Innovista Master Plan, Loadholt said, "The timing could not have been worse with the onset of the Great Recession. There is no question that we need experienced private real estate development partners."(3) Despite the difficult period when he served as chair, Loadholt went on to say, "My best experience as a Board member was the hiring of Harris Pastides as President. My worst experience is when a tragedy occurs with a student. It has been a privilege to serve on the Board and membership has provided me an opportunity to give back to the University."(4)

Ed Walton, Russ Meekins, and Bill Kirkland. In 2015, Ed Walton, Bill Kirkland, and Russ Meekins have taken the "point" position in developing the university's strategic initiatives to implement the Innovista Master Plan.

Ed Walton is the University of South Carolina's senior vice president and chief operating officer. He joined the university in 1997 and has served in a variety of financial roles including that of chief financial officer for the Research Foundation. He teamed with Russ Meekins and Bill Kirkland of the Development Foundation in developing the real estate deal for a mixed-use housing, retail, and office complex in Innovista. The first phase, 650 Lincoln, was completed in September of 2015. In response to an inquiry about Innovista's initial lack of success, Walton responded, "We were inexperienced and assumed that somehow these companies would come to Columbia for its University and quality of life. We didn't know how to recruit them."(5)

The late Russ Meekins headed the University of South Carolina Development Foundation. A seasoned and experienced businessman, Meekins had served as the foundation's chief financial officer before assuming the role of executive director in 2013 upon the retirement of Jerry Odom. The foundation serves as the university's real estate arm and under Meekins's leadership has moved aggressively in the last few years. In addition to the mixed-use housing, retail, and office complex, the foundation front-ended the engineering design of the Greene Street reconstruction in order to provide a "shovel ready" project that secured high priority for construction under the county-administered penny sales tax program. Most recently the development foundation under Russ's leadership has purchased 300 acres of land on the banks of the Congaree River near Williams Brice Stadium for much-needed student recreation fields. Russ anticipates that the foundation will participate in the development of additional student housing, utilizing the public/private partnership model.

Pictured Left to Right
Russ Meekins
Bill Kirkland
Derrick Huggins

Pictured Below
Derek Gruner

PHOTO COURTESY OF BILL KIRKLAND

Bill Kirkland heads the university's new Office of Economic Development. A gregarious and enthusiastic salesman, he is an experienced entrepreneur who has held executive management positions with IBM and Pfizer. Kirkland also serves as executive director of the USC–Columbia Technology Incubator, a 501(c)(3) independent entity supported by the university and the City of Columbia. The research and development components of Innovista are his responsibility. Kirkland has developed an innovative, proactive marketing program for the university as way of marketing Innovista to private companies who are citing the university's patents in their product development.

Derrick Huggins. Derrick Huggins has had an immediate impact on two key elements of the Innovista Master Plan. First, at the request of the board of the Regional Transportation Authority in Richland County, the university "loaned" Huggins to the authority with the mandate to streamline the authority's operation and introduce fiscal accountability. Changes to the authority were well received by the public, which led to a "penny sales tax" referendum for Richland County in 2012 for transportation improvements. Upon passage of the referendum, $32 million from bond sales has been targeted for infrastructure improvements in Innovista.

Second, working with the federal Department of Transportation, Huggins helped secure an 80/20 grant of federal funds for the redevelopment of Assembly Street between Blossom and Pendleton Streets. Improvements have enhanced the safety of pedestrian movement and a landscaped median and street trees have greatly improved the aesthetics of one of Columbia's principal streets.

An avowed environmentalist with degrees in botany and biology from the University, Huggins's major goals for his stewardship of the campus are the "greening" of the campus by removing small surface parking lots in the academic core, restoring the campus's historic southern gardens, and improving the bus transit serving the community as well as the campus. "We have enough parking. I don't want to build any more parking garages." [6]

Huggins has had a "Horatio Alger" career at the University of South Carolina. Entering the freshman class at USC in 1984, Derrick graduated with a biology degree with an emphasis in botany in 1991. He worked part-time jobs, included driving the campus shuttle bus, the "Shuttlecock." Upon graduation, Huggins joined the University staff, assuming ever-increasing responsibility for transportation, including the role of transportation coordinator, program coordinator, and budget manager until he was named as director of transportation. In 2014 Huggins was named vice president for facilities and transportation.

Derek Gruner. A genial, soft-spoken professional, Derek Gruner came to the university as university architect in 2011. Gruner fulfils a goal of the university and the trustees to have a design architect on staff. Gruner is responsible for managing the contracts of the engineering and design professionals responsible for the project design work for infrastructure projects in Innovista including Greene

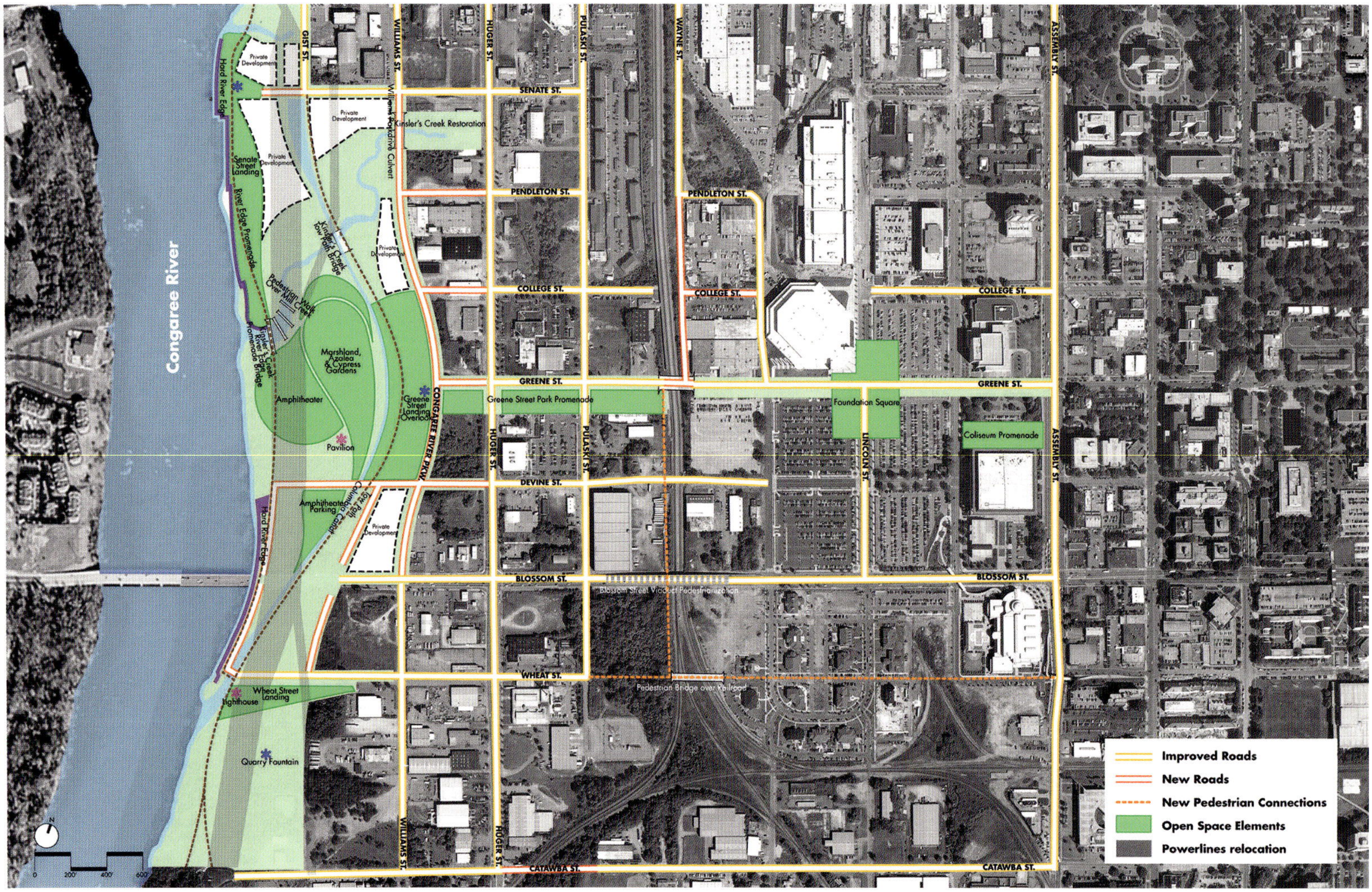

Innovista planning area showing street and open space improvements included in the conceptual cost estimate

IMAGE COURTESY OF SASAKI ASSOCIATES, INC.

Street and Foundation Square under. His professional architectural experience and understanding has brought order to the management of the university's project programming and design process. He manages the project design process under the purview of the university's design review committee. He echoed Charles Jeffcoat's sentiments about the facilities role, emphasizing the importance of managing the expectations of university stakeholders in the development of new facilities and the management of existing space.

The Community Partners. The Innovista concept moved the university outside the brick walls of its campus into the public arena and required them to enlist hundreds of partners to realize their plan. The State of South Carolina, the City of Columbia, Richland County, the Columbia Development Corporation, the River Alliance, the Army Corps of Engineers, the Guignard family, utility companies, and over 100 other private property owners and developers have either property ownership, a jurisdictional responsibility, or interest in the Innovista planning area. Each entity carries out its individual responsibilities and pursues its own goals and interests in the development of Innovista.

The vision of Innovista requires that the principal parties be proactive partners, acting in concert with each other. All the parties have to be "at the table" together in order to address issues such as financing infrastructure, funding the Congaree Regional Waterfront Park, and addressing the aspirations of a wide range of property owners and citizens.

The Waterfront Steering Team was initially formed to provide "champions" outside the university and the Guignard family and to carry the concept through its public unveiling and approval process. However, because the Waterfront Steering Team is an entirely volunteer group, it could not be expected to carry out the complete implementation of the plan, which is projected to take several decades to fully realize. The planners recommended that an organization along the lines of a not-for-profit permanent 501(c)(3) with a stable base of human and financial resources be formed to implement the plan.

Hunter Morrison, long-time director of planning for Cleveland, Ohio, was retained to advise the Waterfront Steering Team on organizational and implementation strategies. Morrison had successfully laid the foundation for the renaissance of downtown Cleveland with projects such as the downtown campus of Cleveland State University, the Cleveland Gateway Center sports complex, and the Rock and Roll Hall of Fame. Morrison confirmed the need for a non-profit organization that was professionally staffed, with a dedicated source of funding. He also recommended increasing the engagement of the City of Columbia and its staff, as well as the area's private property owners; identifying a dedicated revenue stream such as tax increment financing to fund infrastructure improvements; and building a public relations program to communicate the Innovista story again and again, expanding the story to clarify which development entities would implement the infrastructure elements and which would coordinate the private development.

At the time of publication a 501(c)(3) organization or its equivalent has not yet been developed to bring the principal partners together. At present the parties are acting independently of each other. The university's investment in Innovista has been limited to the development of university facilities on university-held properties; private property owners and private developers are currently bringing hundreds of new apartment units to the market.

Partnerships are served by mutual self-interest. Innovista could be described as the "perfect storm" of self-interest for the city, the university, Guignard Associates LLC, and the other property owners in the area. The university brings to the partnership the economic energy of a stable and growing institution—growth that is currently fueling a mini–real estate boom in downtown Columbia. The city brings the municipal authority, responsibility, and theoretical resources to implement the needed infrastructure improvements for utilities, streets, and public open spaces shown in the Innovista Master Plan. The property owners and their developers are the risk-takers and development catalysts and bring the private financing.

The university's self-interest includes the highest and best use of its largest reserve of undeveloped land for future growth of campus facilities, and the potential amenities of an adjacent mixed-use urban neighborhood offering job opportunities, walk-to-work housing, and access to the waterfront through a world-class park. By any measure this strongly benefits the recruitment and retention of university faculty, researchers, staff, and students, as well as graduates seeking to remain in the city of Columbia. Bill Kirkland, who heads the university's Office of Economic Development, describes the Innovista concept of a new downtown neighborhood within walking distance of the university as "incredibly important"[7] to the university's research and economic development program.

The city's self-interest lies in the need for a stronger tax base and the need to improve the quality of its downtown urban environment. At present an estimated half of Columbia real estate is held by non-profit institutions and public facilities and is untaxed. While university property is untaxed, the university is the city's prime employer and its $1.3 billion operating budget in 2014 underlies Columbia's current downtown real estate boom, which is adding to the city's taxable real estate base. Market analysis of the real estate development potential of Innovista estimated the cumulative economic impacts from construction activity to be $2.3 billion. Further, based on the real estate absorption estimates, Innovista has been estimated to generate $17.7 million in

Pictured Above Left Location of the proposed Congaree Regional Waterfront Park

IMAGE COURTESY OF SASAKI ASSOCIATES, INC.

Pictured Above Right View of an existing portion of the "Three Rivers Greenway"

IMAGE PROVIDED BY THE AUTHOR

annual property tax revenues for the Richland County School District, Richland County, and the City of Columbia by the fifteen-year mark.[8]

The City of Columbia and Richland County. Innovista requires the support of the city and county's political and business leadership. The City of Columbia has planning and zoning authority and the city, Richland County, and the Richland County School Board all share in the real estate taxes of the area. Any tax increment financing (TIF), for example, has to receive the approval of the city, Richland County, and the Richland County School Board. The city and Richland County have shown strong support for the Innovista concept.

In 2006 the Columbia City Council unanimously approved the Innovista Master Plan and a comprehensive new zoning ordinance for Innovista. The new zoning overcomes a major impediment to realizing the plan for Innovista. The existing zoning featured a patchwork of eight different zoning classifications, dominated by designations for industrial, commercial, and institutional uses. In order to develop new mixed projects under the existing zoning, each individual property owner had to go through a separate re-zoning process with the city. While the Guignard interests and the university were the largest property owners, controlling 40% of the developable area, over 100 other property owners held the other 60%. The planners recommended a new single comprehensive mixed land use zone for the area at the densities proposed in the Master Plan. The city's planning/zoning staff developed the new ordinance and the Columbia City Council approved it.

Prior to the approval of the new zoning, the area's property owners were briefed at a series of workshops organized by Bill Boyd and Lee Bussell. A distinctive feature of the Innovista Master Plan compared to other redevelopment plans was that it did not anticipate the taking of any private property by eminent domain—a lesson well learned after the neighborhood conflicts generated in Columbia's redevelopment programs in the post–World War II period. Most property owners saw the immediate benefits of the plan and the proposed new zoning ordinance, which allowed significantly more flexibility and more valuable land uses for their properties. Ben Arnold, an area property owner, said, "It's about time. If this is done right, it could really open this town to more development."[9]

The new mixed-use zoning ordinance classified existing light industrial uses as allowable, but did not permit new industrial use. No height restrictions were imposed. One developer who owned 10 acres in separate parcels commented that a blanket rezoning would save him the time and money involved in getting the city to rezone the land one parcel at a time.

Identifying a source of funding for the needed infrastructure improvements—new roads, the Greene Street Viaduct, open space improvements, and the Congaree Regional Waterfront Park—has proven to be very difficult. A proposed TIF district developed by the Waterfront Steering Team has not yet received the city's support. A TIF would hold the real estate taxes due to the city in the planning area at the existing levels and would allow the increment of new taxes derived from new development in the district to stay within the district to pay for infrastructure improvements. The city's Vista redevelopment project provides an outstanding example of successful redevelopment utilizing a TIF to finance needed public infrastructure improvements. However, the city, rather than focusing its limited resources to create synergy between the existing centers of downtown activity, has allocated most of its current bonding capacity to a new minor league ball park, parking garages, and other infrastructure improvements on the old South Carolina Hospital complex on Bull Street, more than a mile away from downtown. Critics have characterized the city's business arrangement with the developer of the hospital complex as "giving away the store."

Some progress has been made in securing infrastructure financing through a county-wide sales tax. In 2012, a city/county initiative placed a one cent sales tax on the ballot for transportation improvements in Richland County, which includes the city of Columbia. The voters approved the referendum. A portion of the tax proceeds have been assigned to street improvements in Innovista, including the Greene Street Promenade, the viaduct bridging the railroad, and the Williams Street connector, which will define the borders of and provide public access to the proposed Congaree Regional Waterfront Park.

The Columbia Development Corporation. In addition to its existing staff resources, including public works and planning, the city has a real estate development arm in the Columbia Development Corporation. The Columbia Development Corporation (CDC), a 501(c)(3) organization, was formed in 1982 to implement the city's very successful redevelopment of the Vista. Supported by a TIF district, the Vista redevelopment program carried out the adaptive reuse of the city's historic mercantile buildings along the Gervais Street corridor, effected a comprehensive redevelopment of the supporting infrastructure and streets, and created a streetscape program throughout much of the Vista redevelopment area.

Theoretically the CDC could assume responsibility for implementing the Innovista Master Plan. However, its TIF financing has lapsed. Fred Delk, the executive director, is now a salaried employee of the city, with the CDC lacking a supporting staff and a dedicated source of funding. Currently the CDC selectively acquires and sells properties at the behest of the city in furthering the Vista redevelopment plan. One recent transaction was the purchase of the Palmetto Compress, an historic cotton warehouse in the Innovista planning area. Using its line of credit, the CDC acquired the property in

2014 for preservation from demolition. The CDC resold the property to a developer to recoup its investment. The developer has adaptively reused the warehouse for housing and retail facilities.

The State of South Carolina. The State of South Carolina General Assembly passed two significant pieces of legislation in support of the university's research initiative in Innovista. In recognition of the success that the neighboring state of North Carolina has achieved with the Research Triangle Park and North Carolina State's Centennial Park, the South Carolina Legislature passed "The Research Universities Infrastructure Act," which provided $220 million as seed money to the state's three research universities—the University of South Carolina, Clemson University, and the College of Charleston—for the development of facilities supporting their research initiatives. USC's allocated share was $70 million. Each university was required to match the state funds from the university coffers or other local sources. The University of South Carolina used its share of the state allocation to build two research buildings, Horizon One and Discovery One. The City of Columbia and Richland County stepped forward with the "match" by building two large parking structures to support the research buildings. The State Assembly's second legislative act, "The Centers of Economic Excellence Act," provided funding to enable the state's research universities to attract an array of internationally recognized research scientists.

The River Alliance. The River Alliance is a non-profit public sector partnership incorporated in 1995. It represents five local governments: Columbia, West Columbia, Cayce, Lexington, and Richland County. The purpose of the alliance is to link the amenities of the Broad, Saluda, and Congaree Rivers with the citizens of the region through the development of a twelve-mile-long linear park, the "Three Rivers Greenway," along the shorelines of the three rivers. The Broad and Saluda Rivers join the Congaree in a unique tuning fork configuration with an outreach to the larger metropolitan area. In Columbia, the planning concept for the Greenway encompasses the historic Columbia Canal as well as a complex of historic mills that have been adaptively reused for the South Carolina State Museum and Education Venture, the children's museum. To date over nine miles of the planned greenway system have been completed.

To finance the initial development of the Three Rivers Greenway, the City of Columbia, Richland County, and the Richland County School District extended the Vista TIF in order to use the tax increment to secure property and develop the trail system in Columbia. Cayce and West Columbia enabled a TIF district on the west banks of the rivers to finance the trail system through their communities. These funding steams have now lapsed. Mike Dawson, the chief executive officer of the alliance, reports that without a dedicated source of funding the alliance is dependent on grants and special funding to complete additional segments of the Greenway.

The keystone to completing the Three Rivers Greenway on the east bank of the Congaree River in Columbia is the Guignards' riverfront properties in Innovista, which extend six city blocks from Blossom Street to Gervais Street. The proposed Congaree Regional Waterfront Park in the Innovista Master Plan will complete the Three Rivers Greenway.

The Army Corps of Engineers. An area of approximately seventy acres along the east bank of the Congaree River (from Catawba to Gervais Street) was identified in the Innovista Master Plan as the proposed location of the Congaree Regional Waterfront Park. Much of the designated area is within the 100-year flood plain; some of it is within the floodway of the river. Land in the floodway and the floodplain triggers the jurisdictional responsibility of the Army Corps of Engineers, as well as statutory restrictions from the State of South Carolina and the City of Columbia on the use of the land. While park use is permitted, other land uses are encumbered with various restrictions or prohibited outright. As part of the planning process for Innovista, meetings were held with the corps in Charleston as well as on the site of the

View of Horizon One, the university's first research building in Innovista

IMAGE ©JEFF AMBERG

park to brief representatives of the corps and to solicit their assistance in developing the proposed park.

Sasaki identified the federal Water Resources bills periodically authorized by Congress and administered by the Army Corps of Engineers as a potential source of funding for the proposed park. Federal money from water resources bills had been a major funding sources for waterfront parks in Charleston, Indianapolis, Cincinnati, and other riverfront cities.

The need for a full-time professionally staffed organization responsible for implementing the Innovista plan was clearly demonstrated in April 2014. An inquiry was made to the university's representative in Washington, DC, as to whether the water resources bill passed by Congress in the spring of 2014 included funds for the proposed waterfront park. The response: money was not allocated for the Congaree Regional Waterfront Park because "there had not been a lot of push for that lately."

The Guignard Family. In their work with Charles Thompson in developing a concept plan for the family's waterfront land in Innovista, the planners documented, from experience elsewhere, the real estate values stimulated by the development of public parks. Thompson understood the potential real estate value that the proposed Congaree Regional Waterfront Park would generate and was an advocate for the larger public benefit of a "world-class waterfront park." As part of the implementation program for Innovista, Thompson was urged to consider making the land available to the City of Columbia for the park. It was pointed out that the lands in the floodway and floodplain that fell under the jurisdiction of the Army Corps of Engineers would be limited in real estate development potential. In making the recommendation that the land for the waterfront park should be "made available to the City," the planners recommended that funding be first assured for the construction, long-term operations, and maintenance of the park consistent with Charles Thompson's vision for an urban waterfront park of the highest quality.

2014 signaled a new beginning for Innovista. The University and private real estate interests are responding to the vision of Innovista with new research, residential and commercial facilities

In an extraordinary meeting in the offices of Haynsworth Sinkler Boyd, P.A., Thompson presented the potential benefits of a waterfront park to the majority shareholders of the LLC, which included other Guignard heirs. He described other cities in which public waterfront parks had leveraged property values and stimulated new real estate development. Charles cited the stimulus value of Charleston's Waterfront Park, which has generated an estimated $337 million in associated real estate development, and the Central Indianapolis Waterfront, which has generated some $425 million in associated development.[10] In this meeting, Thompson was seeking first and foremost to gain the shareholders' approval for the plan of the waterfront property with its proposed mixed-use development and park. Second, he sought the shareholders' preliminary commitment to "making the land available" for the park, subject to adequate funding for its construction, long-term maintenance, and operation.

Nearly a century before, in 1919, the landscape architectural firm of Kelsey and Guild had made a similar proposal to the Civic League of Columbia in their presentation of an "inner and outer" parks plan for Columbia. Their report documented the experience of other cities' investments in public parks and open spaces at the turn of the twentieth century: "Even at great cost, park systems almost invariably prove to be extremely valuable investments. In 1856 the assessed value of the three wards adjoining Central Park was $20,429,565. In 1873 that had increased to $236,081,515. A gain in 17 years of $215,651,950."[11]

Thompson successfully secured approval of the Innovista Master Plan and a conditional commitment from the family and shareholders of the LLC to "make the land available" for the park. As of 2016, funding sources have not yet been identified. In the meantime, at his own expense, Charles Thompson has carried out a forest management program on the property and cooperated with the local power company to consolidate its overhead power lines through the property.

Craig Davis Partners. The University of South Carolina's development concept for Innovista was to partner with a real estate developer who would utilize its real estate expertise to develop two university research buildings paired with two private office buildings. The university's real estate development partner, Craig Davis Properties, was obligated in its contract with the university to oversee the development of the university research buildings, to finance and develop the private office buildings, and to market the office buildings to private companies. The university planned to utilize the state grant from the "Research Universities Infrastructure Act" to fund the research buildings. The City of Columbia and Richland County had agreed to provide the "match" to the state grant by financing the development of two large parking structures to support the research buildings.

In the initial planning process for Innovista, the university inexplicably excluded its development foundation. The University of South Carolina Development Foundation is a legally separate 501(C)(3) corporation responsible to its own board. The foundation carries out real estate activities on behalf of the university. The university's website describes the foundation's function as follows: "The University of South Carolina Development Foundation acquires real estate and other special assets, by purchase or gift on behalf of the University and holds, develops, manages and maintains these assets to serve the University to achieve its educational objectives and improve its facilities through ongoing physical expansion."[12] Founded in the mid-1960s as the Carolina Research and Development Foundation, a private corporation, its primary function was to buy property for the university's expansion. The Carolina Research and Development Foundation was replaced by the University of South Carolina Development Foundation.

According to Russ Meekins, the executive director of the development foundation, the university's Master Plan guides its real estate initiatives and the foundation coordinates with the university through monthly meetings with the university's executive council. The executive council includes the president, chief financial officer, and provost. Meekins reported that there are "plenty of checks and balances in place."[13] He noted that major real estate initiatives require a complex review and approval process by the university administration, the University trustees, and the state's budget and control board.

In addition to the acquisition of land, the development foundation has carried out two notable real estate development projects in the preceding decades: the University Inn on Pendleton Street and the Adesso condominiums on Main Street. When carrying out development projects, the foundation partners with private developers who bring both their market understanding and their financing and construction experience to the partnership.

The foundation, which had been attempting to purchase land in the Innovista planning area since publication of the Bicentennial Master Plan back in 1994, was "completely in the dark and felt blind-sided" when the *State* newspaper reported an impending university research park for the area.[14] Whether or not inclusion of the foundation with their real estate development experience early in the planning process might have staved off the university's initial failure will never be known.

The administration approached the foundation after the Innovista Plan was announced and asked it to be the contracting agent with Craig Davis Partners, whom they had already selected as their real estate development partner. Upon review, the foundation, skeptical of the proposal and in circumstances that were described as "deadly internal politics," offered to prepare the "memorandum of understanding" (MOU) with Craig Davis Partners but refused to take responsibility for a contract. In response the administration formed a new foundation, the USC Research Campus Foundation, to contract with Craig Davis Partners.

The onset of the Great Recession caused Craig Davis Partners to lose their financing. According to Rick Kelly, Craig Davis Partners had prearranged their financing for the project

View of the university's new mixed-use building in Innovista with student apartments and 15,000 sq. ft. of retail space at street level

IMAGE COURTESY OF KEITH MCGRAW

through G.E. Capital Finance. After several meetings, Davis received a call advising that G.E. Capital was withdrawing its funding commitment because "it wouldn't work." In response to their loss of financing, Craig Davis Partners renewed their commitment to the university in a 2005 letter stating that they would build two private partner buildings adjacent to the two university research buildings.

The university followed through with the design and construction of its two research buildings, Horizon One and Discovery One, drawing upon $58 million of its $70 million state grant, with the "matching funds" provided by the city and county's investment put toward the adjoining parking structures. However, with the deepening recession Craig Davis Partners were unable to follow through with their commitment to finance and build the private partner buildings. The university terminated their contract.

Termination of the contract caused a firestorm of negative publicity; the terms of the contract disclosed a requirement for a large termination fee. Innovista as a brand reached its low point with the public when the *State* reported the payoff of $890,000. "The deal ends a controversial chapter for Innovista, a project meant to generate high-tech business and jobs from research work. About $100 million in state and local tax money has gone into Innovista, paying for two incomplete buildings and a pair of parking garages."[(15)] Ironically it was the university's development foundation that "bailed out" the university by paying the developer's termination fee. In response to the storm of criticism, Jerry Odom, director of the foundation at the time, responded, "I think that we made a good investment to help the University."[(16)] President Harris Pastides dissolved the USC Research Foundation shortly after taking office in 2008.

Two additional factors impacted Innovista's early problems. First, at the onset, university leadership perceived the Innovista project in terms of new buildings: "Build it and they will come." However, the university lacked the critical mass of research expenditures that would attract private companies. "We were trying to build a research park on connections. We didn't have the volume of research to support it."[(17)] In

2012 the University of South Carolina was ranked 96th by the National Science Foundation in its survey of "Higher Education R&D Expenditures," with expenditures of more than $214 million. By comparison, Johns Hopkins ranked first with expenditures of over $2 billion. For regional comparison, the University of North Carolina at Chapel Hill, part of the consortium of the Research Triangle Park, had expenditures four times those of USC at more than $884 million. The University of South Carolina has established a goal of $300 million per year for research expenditures.

A second factor was the transition of Innovista from the original concept of a university research park on the campus to a master plan for an urban district, designed with a mix of university facilities and private development. This transition launched the university into the public arena, required public support, and created the need to satisfy the interests of more than 100 separate property owners. This is a complexity that the university and city have not yet fully embraced.

Proactive Marketing and Development. The university's new development team, headed by Ed Walton, Bill Kirkland, and Russ Meekins, initiated a proactive approach to the development of Innovista. The Office of Economic Engagement, a new office established by President Pastides and the trustees, has assumed the research and development functions for Innovista. The university's website describes the new Office of Economic Engagement as follows: "Dedicated to encouraging statewide economic growth through the increased commercialization of cutting edge research, connecting new and existing businesses with university resources; and fostering an environment where entrepreneurial Gamecocks can thrive." The website goes on to say, "In the last five years the University of South Carolina has filed more than 370 invention disclosures on behalf of faculty, applied for more than 300 new patent applications, with 66 patents issued and executed 86 licenses representing 120 technologies. The USC/Columbia Incubator has graduated 40 companies and has 45 tenants."[18]

"President Pastides has taken a deep dive into economic development," according to Bill Kirkland.[19] In response, the university's Office of Economic Engagement has taken a unique proactive marketing approach to companies citing the university's patents in their product development. "The challenge was how to get the University out into the market. We are going to these companies and asking them whether they would like to license our [USC] patent or own it themselves."[20] When President Pastides said he would like to work with IBM in Columbia, Bill Kirkland arranged a meeting with IBM senior executives. Utilizing this approach led to the development of the IBM Center for Applied Innovation at the university. The new center is located in the new office building adjacent to the university's research facilities in Horizon One and will service multiple other institutions throughout the country. The university is also developing curricula to support the IBM program. Employment at the center is projected to grow from its present 72 employees to over 500 employees within five years.

Kirkland pointed to the critical importance of the creative work of the university development foundation in developing a feasible scheme for financing the new office building adjacent to Horizon One. "We wouldn't have the IBM Center if we didn't have the office building."[21] The university also received support from the state when the budget and control board supported the initiative with IBM by granting an exception to state's procurement code, allowing the university to negotiate the business arrangement directly with IBM.

The Office of Economic Engagement was also instrumental in fostering a new partnership between the Boeing Company and the McNair Center for Aerospace Innovation and Research. The new partnership with Boeing includes $5 million in funding for research projects to help create the next generation of aerospace technology. It also helps the university to remain on the cutting edge of scientific advancement and industry engagement. In support of the Office of Economic Engagement, the University of South Carolina Development Foundation has contracted with Holder Properties of Atlanta for development of two office buildings and a mixed-use housing and retail project on Lincoln Street. The first of the two private office buildings, which encompassed 130,000 square feet adjacent to the existing Horizon One research building housing the IBM Applications Center, was completed in 2016. In order to ensure the feasibility of the office building, the university is leasing 40,000 square feet of the building for its own use.

The mixed-use housing development on Lincoln Street is complete. Phase 1 has apartments with 582 beds for students, and 15,000 square feet of retail space. The six-story building features institutional-grade construction with residential apartments over ground-floor retail space. The second phase of the project was completed in the fall of 2016 providing a total of 800 beds for students. The overall project incorporates a total of 30,000 square feet of retail space, including two full-service restaurants at street level. While the foundation will manage the facility, the university's residential rules will prevail and apartments have been provided for university resident advisors. Ed Walton, the university's chief financial officer, foresees the university initiating additional projects with private real estate development partners, as well as a closer working relationship with the City of Columbia to satisfy mutual needs, including a source of funding for infrastructure improvements in Innovista.

The business arrangement for the mixed-use building features a ground lease from the university at market rates. The development foundation maintains a majority ownership and is accepting a lower rate of return of 4% on its investment, instead of the typical real estate return of 12% or higher, in order to enable an institutional-grade construction for the building.[(22)] Russ Meekins, executive director of the foundation, reported that the residences are fully leased. The housing and retail project has a projected cash flow of $1 million to the foundation, which is utilized to help finance the office building adjacent to Horizon One. While the mixed-use residential project has received a real estate tax exemption, the new office building is expected to pay $500,000 annually in real estate taxes to the City of Columbia, addressing a major concern of the city, which is financially starved by virtue of having more than 50% of its property qualified as tax exempt.

In developing the real estate concept Bill Kirkland noted that, "the hardest part is building the plan on paper."[(23)] The need for additional student housing was identified by a study carried out for the university by the consulting firm of Brailsford and Dunlavey. However, the same study also demonstrated that the university did not have the bonding capacity to build the housing. In view of the housing demand, Russ Meekins and Ed Walton felt the housing component was a low-risk real estate opportunity given the growth of the university and demand for on-campus housing. With the strong housing market as a foundation, Meekins and Walton together developed the concept of using the cash flow from the housing to help finance the long-sought office building adjacent to Horizon One. Other private businesses partnering with university researchers are expected to lease space in the building.

The university has also continued to make progress in developing facilities for its research programs. The "fitting out" of its two research buildings, Horizon One and Discovery One, is now complete and each is approaching full occupancy. In 2011 the university was able to secure the $11 million remaining in the state grant, despite Governor Nikki Haley's and the legislature's unhappiness with the university over Innovista's un-kept promises. Rick Kelly said; "I went to the Budget and Control Board and Governor and pointed out that 80 researchers and their assistants focusing on cancer and fuel cell research came to the University because of the State's support in building the two research buildings. The university got its $11 million."[(24)] The funding enabled the university to complete the fit out of its two research buildings.

The private real estate market is responding in dramatic fashion to the idea of Innovista and the growth of the university. Fred Delk, director of the Columbia Development

Site of the proposed Congaree Regional Waterfront Park in Innovista

IMAGE PROVIDED BY THE AUTHOR

Corporation, reports that through the support of a ten-year tax incentive from the City of Columbia, new apartments containing over 3,000 beds have been announced or are under construction in Innovista, including the university's new mixed-use housing project. An estimated total of $185 million in new university facilities and private commercial facilities are under construction or have been announced for the area. The latter includes the university's new Moore School of Business ($95 million) and its new research facility, Horizon II ($25 million). He anticipates that the resident population in downtown Columbia will grow from 1,350 persons in 2014 to over 5,000 in 2017. [25] ■

THE DELIBERATE CHOICE OF AN URBAN LOCATION FOR THE CAMPUS, IN THE STATE'S NEW CAPITAL CITY, WAS A REMARKABLE GESTURE AT THE TIME. DESIGNED TO HELP ACHIEVE A SOCIETAL GOAL OF BRINGING TOGETHER TWO IMMIGRANT CULTURES—THE ENGLISH MERCHANTS AND PLANTATION OWNERS OF CHARLESTON AND THE COASTAL PLAIN AND THE HUGUENOTS WHO FARMED THE PIEDMONT.

PHOTO COURTESY OF USC CREATIVE SERVICES

Section V

A CAMPUS IN THE CITY

View of Koger Center for the Arts
IMAGE COURTESY OF KEITH MCGRAW

Chapter 11

A Twenty-First-Century Campus

In 2009 the University of South Carolina initiated an update to its master plan. The "University of South Carolina 2010 Master Plan, Vision for a Sustainable Future," provides a single unifying vision for the University of South Carolina campus within the urban framework of John Gabriel Guignard's historic plan for the city of Columbia. The embrace of the city in the 2010 Master Plan is both a response to the South Carolina College founders' goal "to bring South Carolinians together" on the campus and a recognition of the essential role that the city plays in the university's mission of education and research.

The university's 2010 plan is also distinguished by its focus on environmental sustainability. The plan's environmental goals are articulated in a "Framework for Sustainability," which emphasizes the economic development potential of Innovista, promotes the efficient use of existing building space, advocates the adaptive reuse of existing buildings such as the Coliseum, and illustrates potential wide-ranging improvements to the public realm, including the quality of the public streets on campus. It also includes a comprehensive redevelopment plan for the area of South Campus that lies outside of Columbia's historic town plan.

Historic Mandate. The decision in 1801 to place South Carolina College in the heart of the new capital city of Columbia was a deliberate act of the college's founders. "The choice of Columbia was no accident, for a prime goal of the patricians who guided the bill of incorporation of the College through the general Assembly in less than a month was to unite up country and low country. If the future leaders of the Palmetto State formed classroom friendships, they reasoned, then some of the animosities troubling South Carolina life might be ameliorated."[1]

The deliberate choice of an urban location for the campus, in the state's new capital city, was a remarkable gesture at the time. Designed to help achieve a societal goal of bringing together two immigrant cultures—the English merchants and plantation owners of Charleston and the coastal plain and the Huguenots who farmed the Piedmont—the decision remains relevant today; the university embraces students from rural and urban areas across the state of South Carolina and from around the world. The location decision also gave South Carolina College a statewide mandate. Today the university's embrace of its statewide mandate is helping the state to secure economic and racial equality for its citizens.

The "City" as Campus. The campus of the University of South Carolina has been physically integrated within the urban fabric of the city of Columbia since its founding in 1801. The public streets and sidewalks that find their way through the campus house university, civic, and private commercial and residential facilities. Their sidewalks provide a "common ground" for the university community and local citizens.

Illustration of the potential enhancement of the Swearingen Engineering Center through the redevelopment of Rocky Branch Creek in South Campus GRAPHIC COURTESY OF SASAKI ASSOCIATES, INC.

Future leaders of the Palmetto State on the campus of the University of South Carolina

COURTESY OF USC CREATIVE SERVICES

The diversity and resources of the city of Columbia also serve as a "classroom" for the university. Academic programs and internship opportunities for the Arnold School of Public Health; College of Hospitality, Retail and Sport Management; College of Social Work; College of Education; and Darla Moore School of Business are drawn from, and in some instances dependent upon, the resources of the city. The university's new law school is located within a two-block walking distance of the state capitol. Surveys of students at colleges and universities in urban environments cite the value of the city's resources. The urban universities in Washington, DC, for example, attract students interested in government and politics. Oliva Goolkasian, a recent graduate in chemistry from New York University (NYU) reports that her classmates interested in finance sought NYU because of the internship opportunities on Wall Street. Others interested in fashion saw opportunities in the Garment District. Oliva, who is also an artist, found it particularly helpful that she could go from the art studios at NYU to experience the masterpieces found in New York City's great museums.

Schools whose focus is the arts have prospered in urban environments. The Savannah College of Art and Design (SCAD) created a campus from an abandoned department store, movie theatre, and other vacant commercial buildings in downtown Savannah, Georgia. SCAD has been the principal factor in the economic revitalization of historic downtown Savannah, helping to restore the city as a major tourist destination.

Georgia State University, with the University of South Carolina's former provost Mark Becker serving as president, is creating a remarkable campus in downtown Atlanta, utilizing high-rise commercial office and retail buildings abandoned by their owners in Atlanta's flight to its northern suburbs. As part of the analysis phase during its work preparing the master plan for Georgia State University, Sasaki Associates queried the student body as to the reason behind their selection of Georgia State. The survey showed that the great majority of students came to Georgia State for the diversity of its students, the ability to work part-time, and the amenities of the city of Atlanta.

The location of the University of South Carolina campus in the heart of its state's capital city, within walking distance of its downtown and located at the very core of its political power, is an extraordinary asset to the university's mission of education and research in today's urbanizing world.

Place. The Chicago Exposition at the end of the nineteenth century launched the "City Beautiful" movement in the United States. Cities such as Chicago, under the great Burnham Plan, and medium-sized cities such as Indianapolis, St. Louis, and Buffalo overlaid their urban fabrics with beautiful new public places—parks, squares, and grand boulevards. The age of suburbanization, which followed in mid-century and the post–World War II period, saw the physical deterioration and erosion of the quality of the urban core of these cities and others across the nation, which lead to the redevelopment programs of the post–World War II period.

With her book *The Death and Life of Great American Cities,* published in 1961, Jane Jacobs launched the conversation about the American city and "place"—its meaning, societal value, composition, and relevance to contemporary life. American cities of the twenty-first century that have survived the age of suburbanization and have reinvested in the quality of their urban public services, institutions, and public places are experiencing a remarkable renaissance.

The perception of "place" varies, from descriptions of physical sites such as historic urban districts, special streets, squares, and parks, to beautiful natural environments. The word "place" derives from the Latin platea. Webster's Dictionary defines place as "a particular [place], condition or relationship," and cites examples of a "square or court in a city, short narrow street, a space or room, a particular area, a city, town or village." Dennis Pieprz, internationally noted urban designer at Sasaki, defines place in the following way: "Memorable places have a physical dimension by virtue of extraordinary physical position, by being rooted in the form of the land, or through a beautiful man-made composition of buildings and open spaces. You will personally experience the place. You will know when you are there." (2)

Existing Carolina Coliseum and a view of a concept for the adaptive reuse of the Carolina Coliseum

IMAGE COURTESY OF SASAKI ASSOCIATES, INC.

Green space and water are among the primary elements in the creation of place. Some of America's most memorable campuses are celebrated for their "places" on the water, including Princeton University on Lake Carnegie in Princeton, New Jersey, the University of Wisconsin on Lake Mendota in Madison, Wisconsin, and Harvard, MIT, and Boston University on the Charles River in Boston, Massachusetts.

The greensward of the Horseshoe and the reflecting pool at the Thomas Cooper Library are the two most memorable "places" on the University of South Carolina campus. The beauty, shade, and extraordinary light of the Horseshoe provides an oasis in the heart of downtown Columbia. At the library, the reflected beauty of the framing landscape in the water's surface and the sounds of its fountains are

View of the Reflecting Pool at Thomas Cooper Library

COURTESY OF USC CREATIVE SERVICES

a compelling attraction to students and visitors alike. The proposed waterfront park in the Innovista district plan provides the university another exceptional opportunity to enrich its campus experience by extending the campus to the Congaree River.

Quality of Place. Author Richard Florida has advanced the thesis that "quality of place" as a means to attract talented workers has replaced traditional measures of location, natural resources, and the efficiency of labor as a source of wealth creation and economic growth. Florida brings an additional edge to his thesis in citing a 2002 *Wall Street Journal* survey of 4,000 college graduates wherein "three-quarters of them identified location as more important than the availability of a job when selecting a place to live. In the graduates' thinking, it made more sense to pick several different locations in which to live first, and then to go back and find potential employers in those locations." [(3)]

A cursory overview of capital/university cities where urban universities play a prominent role supports the theory of the attraction that cities hold for today's youth. Raleigh, North Carolina, Atlanta, Georgia, and Austin, Texas, for example, have shown significant growth in population and in their economies between 1990 and 2010. Raleigh's population has increased 72% since 1990, Austin's 71%, and Atlanta's 25%. During the same period, the city of Columbia has had a relatively slow pace of growth, experiencing a modest 10.7% growth in population to 125,000 persons as of 2010.

The University of South Carolina has set forth a bold goal of growing student enrollment by an additional 5,000 students over the next decade. The growing student enrollment, coupled with societal trends, is accelerating the increase in the number of downtown Columbia residents.

Place and Urban Universities. The growing awareness of the importance of quality of place has led urban universities to engage with their host city's urban renewal and place-making programs. The aforementioned redevelopment efforts of MIT and the Universities of Pennsylvania, Chicago, and Notre Dame, while self-serving, are also a recognition by these institutions that their fates are interwoven with the quality of the fabric of their host cities. These institutions have been joined by a host of other public and private universities throughout the country. The University of Connecticut in Storrs, Connecticut, and the University of Rochester in Rochester, New York, are each developing their own "college towns." Ohio State, a large public university which also sits adjacent to its capitol complex, launched Campus Partners for Community Redevelopment with the help of real estate development partners in 1995 to revitalize and stabilize the commercial and residential neighborhoods adjacent to its campus in Columbus, Ohio. The University of Florida is engaged with its host city of Gainesville, Florida, to enhance its "college town" characteristics.

The University of Pennsylvania in Philadelphia, Pennsylvania, and Ohio State in Columbus, Ohio, have utilized the broadest array of traditional real estate strategies and public/private incentives to join with their host cities in bringing about needed change. Others have capitalized upon unique opportunities. Georgia Tech partnered with the City of Atlanta and the Atlanta Olympic Organizing Committee for the Summer Olympic Games of 1996 to effect dramatic changes within the city and on the Georgia Tech campus.

View of the restored "garden" quality of Gibbes Green

IMAGE COURTESY OF KEITH MCGRAW

President John Patrick Crecine of Georgia Tech (1987-1994) volunteered his university as the site of the Olympic Village for the games, despite the strenuous objections of many faculty members. Georgia Tech housed thousands of athletes from around the world in new apartments that reverted to Georgia Tech at the conclusion of the Summer Games. Georgia Tech, which had some of the poorest quality student housing in the Georgia system before the Olympics, had some of the highest quality housing after the games. The Atlanta Olympic Organizing committee contributed $30,000 per bed for the construction of the new housing on the Georgia Tech campus. Georgia Tech also benefited from the millions of dollars of free advertising it received in serving as the Olympic Village for the Games.

The host cities of urban universities have also recognized that the universities are economic powerhouses and potential partners in their physical revitalization programs. The hue and cry of the city council in Cambridge, Massachusetts, in the 1950s and 1960s about the cost of servicing tax-exempt Harvard University and MIT has disappeared with the economic and real estate boom generated by these two universities in the city of Cambridge. In 2014 MIT's mixed-use research park, University Park, contributed $11 million to the City of Cambridge in real estate taxes.[4]

Herein lies the promise of Innovista for the University of South Carolina and the City of Columbia: a plan for a distinctive urban district for innovation and contemporary living within walking distance of the university, State Capitol complex, and Main Street. Innovista is a plan projected to generate millions of dollars of new tax revenue for the city and the county, a plan that will bring the existing activity centers of downtown together, a plan that celebrates the city's founding on the Congaree River with a great public waterfront park—it is the city's new "front yard."

Place-Making. Historically, most American cities have periodically engaged in "place-making"—physically renewing themselves as they mature. In South Carolina, Charleston, Greenville, and Columbia have all utilized

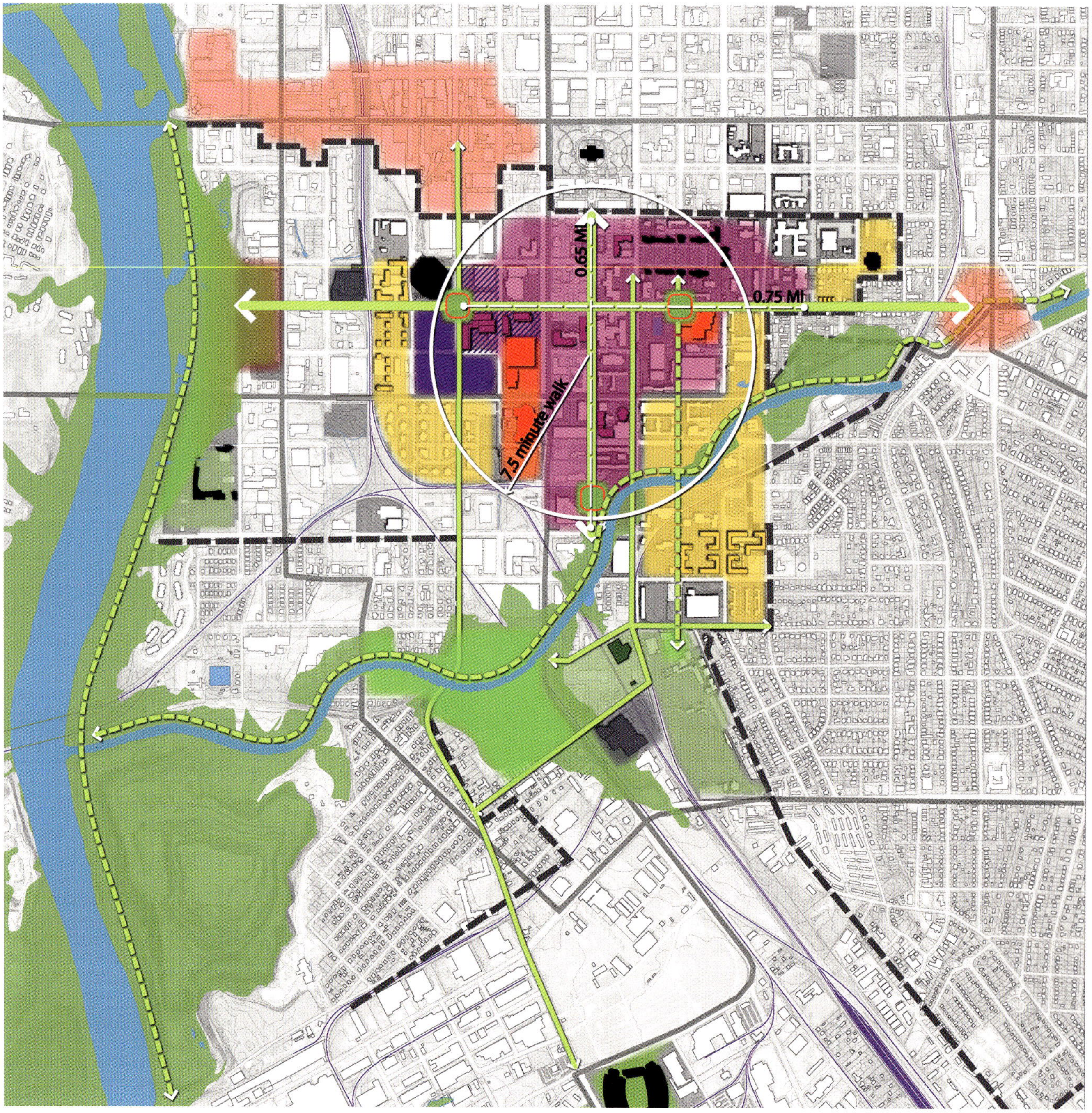

Illustration of land use for the 2010 Master Plan showing the academic core in purple, framed by housing in yellow, open space in green, and the principal connecting pedestrian ways

IMAGE COURTESY OF SASAKI ASSOCIATES, INC.

redevelopment programs in renewing parts of their cities. Charleston's redevelopment of the city's historic district with its investment in a beautiful new waterfront park and a mixed-use hotel and retail complex, Charleston Place, triggered private re-investment throughout the city's historic district. Charleston's "place-making" program has helped to make the city an international tourist destination. At a somewhat smaller scale, Greenville initiated a downtown revitalization program encompassing the Reedy River that has created a beautiful destination experience for the city's residents and visitors alike.

Columbia has a sporadic history of "place-making." The Kelsey and Guild report to the "Civic League of Columbia" in 1919 featured an "Inner and Outer Parks and Reservations Plan for Columbia and a Capitol Park and Mall for the State Capitol." The proposed parks plan envisioned a waterfront park on the Congaree River. The Capitol Park and Mall created a civic center for the expansion of the capitol facilities along south Main Street, with an extension of the university's historic Horseshoe westward through the mall to Assembly Street. The post–World War II period saw a series of redevelopment projects, including Arsenal Hill, Wheeler Hill, Ward One, and the successful redevelopment of the city's restaurant and entertainment district, the Vista.

Columbia's efforts, however, have been scattered and have failed to bring the existing downtown centers of activity together to create a vibrant urban place. Downtown Columbia is composed of four centers of activity: the State Capitol complex is at the center with the university on its southern flank, the banking and business center on Main Street on its north side, and the Vista, the city's entertainment district, on its western flank. The lack of vibrancy is reflected in the vacant lots on Assembly Street adjacent to the capitol building. Public gathering and green space amenities, except for the university grounds and the landscape area around the capitol building itself, are wanting in the immediate downtown area. A city that is still married to the automobile, Columbia has wide streets that physically separate the existing centers of activity and mitigate against pedestrian movement between the centers. The city's "great divide," Assembly Street, with its 150-foot right-of-way and six lanes of fast-moving traffic, has been a particularly divisive barrier separating the downtown centers of activity from the Vista and the Congaree River, and separating the university from its growing campus in Innovista.

The university's master planning, beginning with the Bicentennial Master Plan of 1994 and continuing with the Innovista Plan of 2006 and the comprehensive 2010 Master Plan, has promoted "quality of place" by introducing a series of place-making elements into the urban fabric of downtown Columbia. The Bicentennial Plan with its vision for the development of the campus west to a waterfront park on the Congaree River foretold the Innovista district plan. The Innovista Master Plan incorporates the conceptual design of a series of new public places: the Greene Street Promenade, Foundation Square, a sculpture park, and a large public waterfront park on the Congaree River. The university's 2010 Master Plan has proposed the redevelopment of Rocky Branch Creek as a linear greenway from the existing Maxcy Gregg Park to the Congaree River. The proposed new greenway along Rocky Branch Creek is designed to bring the structuring order and the amenities of a linear park to an area of the city that lies outside the orthogonal order of its historic town plan.

Downtown Columbia and the campus of the University of South Carolina will be judged not by the buildings alone but by the character of the city's streets: their aesthetics and the quality of their pedestrian environment. The Innovista

Illustration of the redevelopment potential of Rocky Branch Creek in South Campus for recreation and flood control

IMAGE COURTESY OF SASAKI ASSOCIATES, INC.

CAROLINA

district's plan extended the historic street grid where it had been obliterated and proposed a hierarchical system of streets, designating some streets primarily for pedestrian movement and others for traffic movement that would serve the Innovista neighborhood. The Innovista Master Plan also proposed bridging the "great divide" of Assembly Street by removing the center island parking and undertaking lane reduction, the creation of improved pedestrian crossings, and an extensive streetscape program. Five blocks of the street were redeveloped in 2014. Greene Street, designated as the principal "pedestrian primary" street in the Innovista Master Plan, is being reconstructed with broad tree-shaded sidewalks and dedicated bicycle lanes.

Robert Campbell, correspondent and architectural critic for the *Boston Globe,* in a critical commentary of new development in Boston said, "Cities are made of streets and parks. From the point of view of urban design, the buildings are there to shape those public spaces and feed them with energy." He goes on to say, "Architecture is the art of making places, not primarily an art of making things. It's the art of using building and landscape to shape space. A place can be your bedroom or your street or your neighborhood or a garden or a park or a city. It can be any space that human beings have created for habitation. The best city is the one with the most livable places." [5]

Pictured Above
The current conditions on Greene Street

IMAGE COURTESY OF JEFF AMBERG.

Facing Page
Proposed redevelopment of Greene Street showing lane reductions and the introduction of bike lanes and new landscape

IMAGE COURTESY OF SASAKI ASSOCIATES, INC.

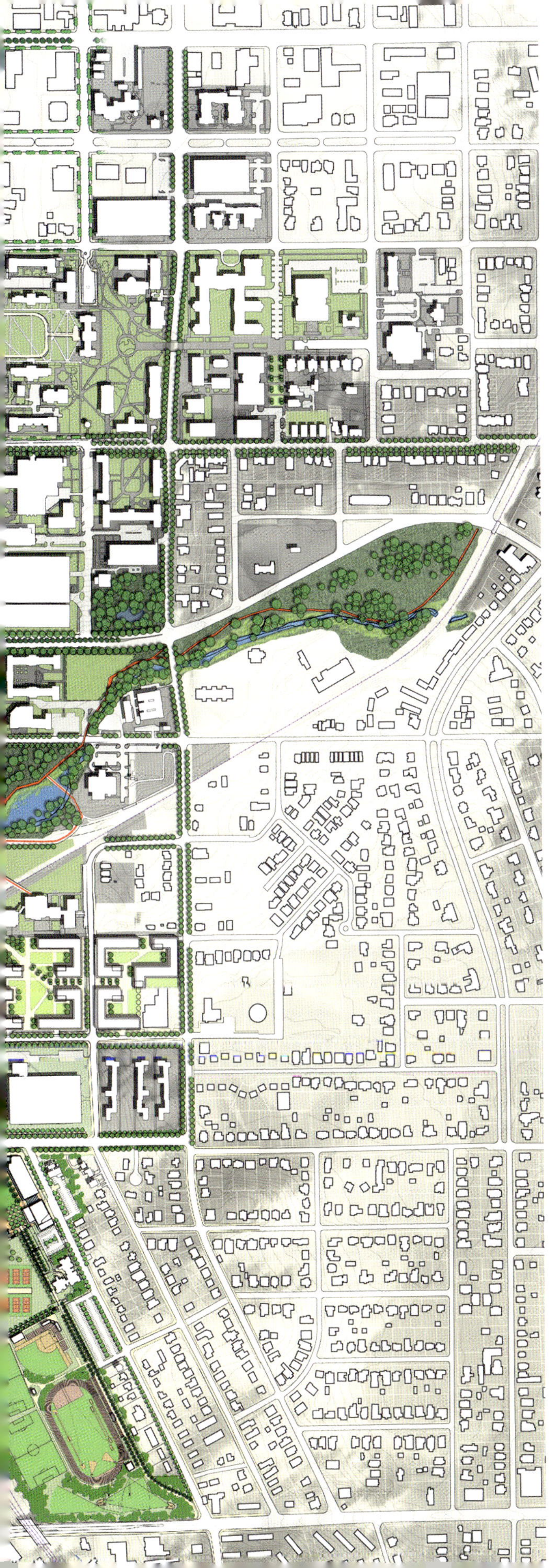

John Gabriel Guignard set forth a vision for the new capital city of Columbia in 1786—a plan composed of a classical orthogonal grid of streets. In 2006, 220 years later, the Innovista Master Plan builds upon that historic plan and sets forth a vision for the future of a "campus in the city" that springs from that grid of streets. The streets and open spaces are the framework that will give form to the University of South Carolina's twenty-first-century campus.

The University of South Carolina enters the twenty-first century with a strong tradition of campus master planning that sets forth a clear and bold vision for the university's future within the city of Columbia. Trustee William Hubbard articulated the importance of Innovista to the university's mission when he said, "USC has a unique role to foster economic, social, and artistic progress. To achieve that goal we must attract great faculty and the best students. This effort, Innovista, gives us a chance to make Columbia a place where people want to live." [6]

The "power of the plan" for the University of South Carolina lies in its ability to project a vision for the future and provide a receptacle for the passions and talents of its "builders" in creating a twenty-first-century campus within the city of Columbia. ■

The University of South Carolina Master Plan: "University of South Carolina 2010 Master Plan: Vision for a Sustainable Future." The plan illustrates the university's growth westward through Innovista to the Congaree River and the redevelopment of South Campus and Rock Branch Creek IMAGE COURTESY OF SASAKI ASSOCIATES, INC.

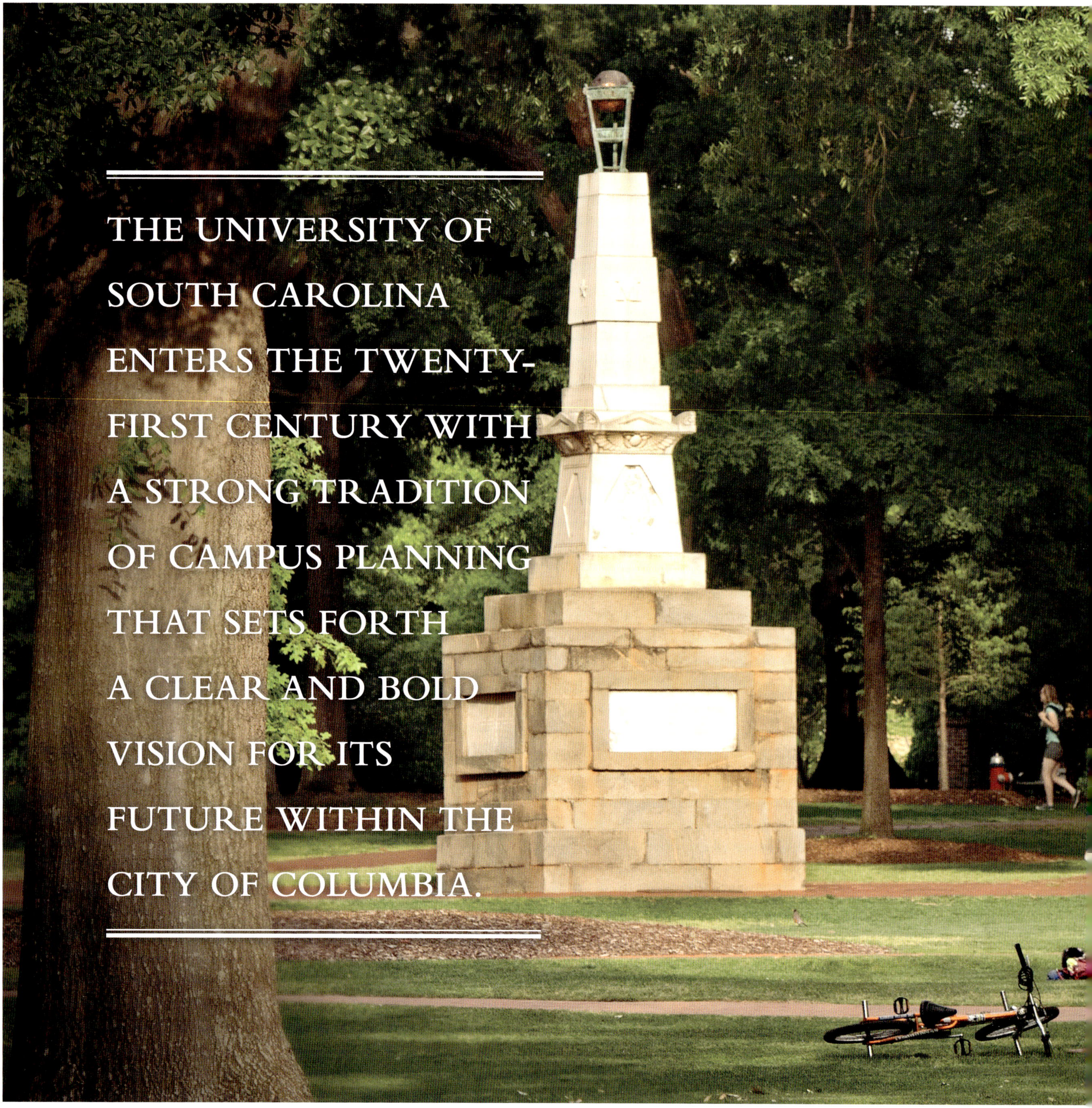

THE UNIVERSITY OF SOUTH CAROLINA ENTERS THE TWENTY-FIRST CENTURY WITH A STRONG TRADITION OF CAMPUS PLANNING THAT SETS FORTH A CLEAR AND BOLD VISION FOR ITS FUTURE WITHIN THE CITY OF COLUMBIA.

PHOTO COURTESY OF USC CREATIVE SERVICES

RESOURCES

NOTES

INTRODUCTION

1. Richard Florida, *Cities and the Creative Class,* Routledge 2005, 50
2. John Hammond Moore, *Columbia and Richland County: A South Carolina Community, 1740–1990,* University of South Carolina Press 1993, 101
3. Author interview with William Hubbard, 1/10/14

SECTION I. A NEW CAPITAL CITY FOR SOUTH CAROLINA

Chapter 1. The Planned City of Columbia 1786

1. Author interview with Charles Thompson, 1/8/14
2. Ibid.
3. Ibid.
4. John Hammond Moore, *Columbia and Richland County: A South Carolina Community, 1740–1990,* University of South Carolina Press 1993, 119
5. Kelsey & Guild, "The Improvement of Columbia South Carolina, report to the civic League of Columbia South Carolina," Mt. Pleasant Press, J. Horace McFarland Co. Harrisburg, PA, 7
6. Ibid., 8

Chapter 2. The Legacy of the Congaree River

1. Kelsey and Guild, The Improvement of Columbia South Carolina, *Report to the Civic League of Columbia South Carolina, Mt. Pleasant Press,* J. Horace McFarland, Harrisburg, PA, 25
2. John Hammond Moore, *Columbia and Richland County: A South Carolina Community 1740–1990,* University of South Carolina Press 1993, 91
3. Ibid., 303
4. Ibid., 304

Chapter 3. A New Public University—South Carolina College

1. Paul Venable Turner, *Campus: An American Planning Tradition,* The Architectural History Foundation New York, The MIT Press, Cambridge, MA, and London England 1984, 18
2. Ibid., 23
3. Blake Gumprecht, *The American College Town,* University of Massachusetts Press 2008. Printed and bound by Sheridan Books Inc., 20
4. John Hammond Moore, *Columbia and Richland County: A South Carolina Community 1740–1990,* University of South Carolina Press 1993, 100
5. *Rememberingt he Days: An Illustrated History of the University of South Carolina,* The Institute for Southern Studies, The R.L Bryan Company, Daniel W. Hollis, "A Brief History of the University" 1982, X
6. John Morrill Bryan, *An Architectural History of the South Carolina College 1801–1855,* University of South Carolina Press, 12
7. Ibid., 14
8. Ibid., 28
9. Arthur interview with Justin Fay, 5/6/15
10. Arthur interview with Derek Gruner, 1/8/14
11. Blake Gumprecht, *The American College Town,* University of Massachusetts Press 2008. Printed and bound by Sheridan Books Inc., 19
12. Ibid., 41
13. Ibid., 67

SECTION II. BEST LAID PLANS

Chapter 4. The University of South Carolina in the Twentieth Century

1. Henry H. Lesesne, *A History of the University of South Carolina 1940–2000,* 2001, University of South Carolina Press, 3
2. Ibid., 32
3. Ibid., 36
4. Hal Brunton, *Renovation and Restoration of the USC Horseshoe: A Memoir,* Caroline McKissick Dial Endowment,

University of South Carolina, South Caroliniana Library 2002, ix
5. Ibid., xii
6. Ibid., xii
7. Author interview with Thomas Stepp, 1/10/14

Chapter 5. Conflict

1. Author interview with John Stucker, 9/23/14
2. Ibid.
3. David C. Perry and Wim Wiewel, *The University as Urban Developer: Case Studies and Analysis,* The Lincoln Institute of Land Policy, Cambridge, Massachusetts, M.E. Sharpe Armonk, New York and London, England 2005, 68
4. Boyer, 1999, "Hyde Park Herald", 1954, quoted by Henry S. Webber in "The University of Chicago and Its Neighbors: A Case Study in Community Development" in Ibid., 69
5. David C. Perry and Wim Wiewel, *The University as Urban Developer: Case Studies and Analysis,* The Lincoln Institute of Land Policy, Cambridge, Massachusetts, M.E. Sharpe Armonk, New York and London, England 2005, 69
6. Ibid., 70
7. Ibid., 72
8. Judith Rodin, *The University and Urban Renewal: Out of the Ivory Tower and Into the Streets,* University of Pennsylvania Press 2007
9. Ibid., 41
10. Ibid., 48
11. Ibid., 48
12. Ibid., 54
13. Ibid., 78
14. Author interview with Timothy Sexton and Gregory Hakanen, 5/21/14
15. Henry H. Lesesne, *A History of the University of South Carolina 1940–2000,* University of South Carolina Press, 93
16. Author interview with Bobby Donaldson, 12/08/14
17. Henry H. Lesesne, *A History of the University of South Carolina 1940–2000,* University of South Carolina Press, 154
18. Ibid., 154
19. Ibid., 185
20. Ibid., 186
21. Author interview with John Stucker, 9/23/14
22. Ibid.
23. Ibid.
24. Ibid.
25. David C.Perry, and Wim Wiewel, *The University as Urban Developer: Case Studies and Analysis,* The Lincoln Institute of Land Policy, Cambridge, Massachusetts, M.E. Sharpe Armonk, New York & London, England 2005
26. Henry H. Lesesne, *A History of the University of South Carolina 1940–2000,* University of South Carolina Press, 260
27. Ibid.
28. Author interview with Lee Bussell, 10/1/14

SECTION III. A VISION FOR THE VISTA

Chapter 6. The Bicentennial Master Plan

1. Author interview with C. Edward Floyd, 10/20/14
2. Ibid.
3. Author interview with William Hubbard, 1/10/14
4. Author interview with Herbert Adams, 7/3/15
5. American Council of Trustees and Alumni (ACTA) www.goacta.org
6. Ibid.
7. Author interview Rick Kelly, 9/24/14
8. Author interview Chris Corr, 6/15/14
9. Ibid.
10. Ibid.
11. Author interview with William Hubbard, 1/20/14
12. Author interview with Miles Loadholt, 3/12/15
13. Ibid.
14. Author interview with C. Edward Floyd, 10/20/14
15. Author interview with Mack Whittle, 10/30/14
16. Henry H. Lesesne, *A History of the University of South Carolina 1940–2000,* University of South Carolina Press

17. Author interview with C. Edward Floyd, 10/20/14
18. Author interview with Mack Whittle, 10/13/14
19. Author interview with William Hubbard, 1/10/14
20. Author interview with Lee Bissell, 10/1/14
21. Author interview with C. Edward Floyd, 10/20/14
22. Author interview with Lyles Glenn, 9/22/14
23. Ibid.
24. Author interview with C. Edward Floyd, 10/20/14
25. Author interview with William Hubbard, 1/10/14
26. Author interview with Rick Kelly, 9/24/14
27. Author interview with Fred Delk, 3/18/15
28. "Bicentennial Plan for the Carolina Campus 1994," Sasaki Associates Inc.
29. Author interview with Dennis Pruitt, 1/6/15
 New York Times, 12/02/03 National/02, KERR.htm
 Clark
31. Ronald G. Ehrenberg, *Tuition Rising: Why College Costs So Much,* 209
32. Author interview with Derrick Huggins, 8/14/15
33. Author interview with James Doolin, 1/16/15
34. Dr. C. Edward Floyd, "Bicentennial Plan for the Carolina Campus 1994", Sasaki Associates Inc.
35. Author interview with William Hubbard, 1/10/14

Chapter 7. A Decade of Planning

1. Author interview with Mack Whittle, 10/30/14
2. Author interview with Herbert Adams, 7/3/15
3. Author interview with Dennis Pruitt, 1/6/15
4. Author interview with Jerome Odum, 10/26/15
5. Author interview with Shirley Mills, 12/21/15
6. Ibid.
7. Author interview with Thomas Quasney, 12/17/14
8. Author interview with Charles Thompson, 1/8/14
9. Author interview with Dennis Pruitt, 1/6/15
10. Adam Goodheart, *The New York Times Magazine,* 5/21/2006, 82
11. Werner Sensbach, *Planning for Higher Education,* Vol 20, Fall 1991, 15
12. Ibid., 11
13. Harris Pastides, "Grand Opening of Darla Moore School of Business," Sept. 12, 2014 www.sc.edu/about/our_leadership/president/speeches/index.php

Chapter 8. Setting the Stage for Innovista

1. enwikipedia.org/wiki/Morrill_land-Grants.Acts
2. en.wikipedia.org/wiki/Georgia_Tech_Research_Institute
3. Ibid.
4. Ibid.
5. William M. Rohe, *The Research Triangle: From Tobacco Road to Global Prominence,* University of Pennsylvania Press, Philadelphia, 64
6. Ibid.
7. Author interview with Robert J. Wolfe, 11/18/14
8. Ibid.
9. Ibid.
10. Ibid.
11. Ibid.
12. Ibid.
13. Ibid.
14. Author interview with Peter Calkins, 11/20/14
 Boston Sunday Globe, 10/5/14
16. Author interview with Peter Calkins, 11,20,14
17. Author interview with Robert J. Wolfe, 11/18/14

SECTION IV. INNOVISTA: A NEW PARTNERSHIP

Chapter 9. A Research Park for the University of South Carolina

1. *State,* 10/23/05
2. Ibid.
3. Free Times, 9/13–19/06
4. *State,* 10/23/05

5. Author interview with William Boyd, 9/23/14
6. Ibid.
7. *State,* 10/23/05
8. Ibid.
9. Ibid.
10. "Innovista Master Plan," Columbia, South Carolina, Preliminary Report, July 2007, Sasaki Associates Inc.
11. Ibid.
12. Ibid.
13. *State,* Jeff Wilkerson, 7/29/07
14. "Innovista Master Plan," Columbia, South Carolina, Preliminary Report, July 2007, Sasaki Associates Inc.
15. Author interview with Charles Thompson, 1/8/14
16. "Innovista Master Plan," Columbia, South Carolina, Preliminary Report, July 2007 Sasaki Associates Inc.
17. Author interview with John Lumpkin, 1/9/14
18. "Innovista Master Plan," Columbia, South Carolina, Preliminary Report, July 2007 Sasaki Associates Inc.

Chapter 10. Realizing the Vision

1. Author interview with Rick Kelly, 9/24/14
2. Author interview with C. Edward Floyd, 10/20/14
3. Author interview with Miles Loadholt, 3/12/14
4. Ibid.
5. Author interview with Ed Walton
6. Author interview with Derrick Huggins, 8/14/15
7. Author interview with Bill Kirkland, 3/25/15
8. "Innovista Master Plan," Columbia, South Carolina, Preliminary Report, July 2007, Sasaki Associates Inc.
9. *State,* 7/29/07
10. "Innovista Master Plan," Columbia, South Carolina, Preliminary Report, July 2007, Sasaki Associates Inc.
11. Kelsey and Guild, "The Improvement of Columbia South Carolina, Report to the Civic League of Columbia South Carolina," Mt. Pleasant Press, J. Horace McFarland Co., Harrisburg, PA
12. www.sc.edu/foundations/development/index.shtml
13. Author interview with Russ Meekins, 4/1/15
14. Ibid.
15. *State,* Andrew Shain, 5/14/10
16. Ibid.
17. Author interview with Rick Kelly, 9/24/14
18. University of South Carolina Office of Economic Engagement
19. Author interview with William (Bill) Kirkland, 3/25/15
20. Ibid.
21. Ibid.
22. Ibid.
23. Ibid.
24. Author interview with Rick Kelly, 9/24/14
25. Author interview with Fred Delk, 3/18/1

SECTION V. A CAMPUS IN THE CITY

Chapter 11. A Twenty-First-Century Campus

1. John Hammond Moore, *Columbia and Richland County: A South Carolina Community, 1740–1990,* University of South Carolina Press 1993, 100
2. Author interview with Dennis Pieprz
3. Richard Florida, *Cities and the Creative Class,* Routledge 2005
4. Author interview with Peter Calkins, 11/20/14
5. Robert Campbell, *Boston Sunday Globe,* 3/1/15
6. Author interview with William Hubbard, 1/10/14

BIBLIOGRAPHY

Primary Sources: Oral History by Author, 2014 and 2015

1. Mr. Herbert Adams
2. Mr. Igor Andersen
3. Mr. William C. (Bill) Boyd
4. Mr. Lee Bussell
5. Mr. Peter Calkins
6. Mr. Chris Corr
7. Mr. Mike Dawson
8. Mr. Stuart (Stu) Dawson
9. Mr. Fred Delk
10. Mr. Bobby Donaldson
11. Mr. James Doolin
12. Mr. Justin Fay
13. Ms. Gayle Farris
14. Mr. Alan Fisher
15. Mr. C. Edward Floyd
16. Mr. J. Lyles Glenn
17. Mr. Derek Gruner
18. Mr. Gregory Hakanen
19. Ms. Krista Hampton
20. Mr. William C. Hubbard
21. Mr. Derrick Huggins
22. Mr. Charles (Chuck) Hulstrand
23. Mr. Charles G. (Charlie) Jeffcoat
24. Mr. Richard (Rick) Kelly
25. Mr. William (Bill) Kirkland
26. Mr. Miles Loadholt
27. Mr. John Lumpkin
28. Mr. Russ Meekins
29. Ms. Shirley Mills
30. Mr. Jerome (Jerry) D. Odom
31. Mr. Harris Pastides
32. Mr. Dennis Pruitt
33. Mr. Joe Rogers
34. Mr. Thomas Stepp
35. Mr. John Stucker
36. Mr. Charles Thompson
37. Mr. Alan Travis
38. Mr. Mack I. Whittle Jr.
39. Mr. Robert J. Wolfe

SASAKI ASSOCIATES, INC. DOCUMENTS

1. Bicentennial Master Plan for the Carolina Campus 1994
2. University of South Carolina Columbia Campus Wide Space Needs Analysis December 1993 with Paulien Associates
3. University of South Carolina, Columbia Campus Master Plan Update 2001 with The Boudreaux Group
4. University of South Carolina Westward Expansion Master Plan; University Research Park January 2005
5. Coliseum Reuse Study June 2006
6. University of South Carolina Athletics Master Plan August 2006
7. Proposed Congaree Regional Waterfront Park September 2006
8. National Advocacy Center Program Accommodation Study March 2007
9. Innovista Master Plan, Columbia South Carolina July 2007
10. Proposed Congaree regional Waterfront Park February 2007 Update
11. Foundation Square Design Concept Innovista, City of Columbia, SC, January 2008
12. University of South Carolina Design Guidelines February 2008
13. University of South Carolina Vision for a Sustainable Future 2010 Master Plan

PUBLISHED SOURCES

1. Brunton, Hal, *Renovation and Restoration of the USC Horseshoe: A Memoir,* Caroline McKissick Dial Foundation at the South Caroliniana Library, University Libraries, University of South Carolina
2. Guignard, John Gabriel, *Guignard Memories* Vol. 1, *1832–1913 Recollections by His Son the Reverend Sanders Richardson Guignard,* Transcribed by Jane Guignard Curry Sanders R. Guignard Jr. Columbia, South Carolina 1996
3. Moore, john Hammond, *Columbia and Richland County: A South Carolina Community 1740–1990,* University of South Carolina Press 1993
4. Bryan, John Morrill, *An Architecutral History of the South Carolina College 1801–1855,* University of South Carolina Press
5. Lesesne, Henry H., *A History of the University of South Carolina 1940–2000,* University of South Carolina Press
6. Florida, Richard, *Cities and the Creative Class,* Routledge 2005
7. Perry, David C. and Wiewel, Wim, *The University as Urban Developer: Case Studies and Analysis,* Lincoln Institute of Land Policy, Cambridge, Massachusetts; M. E. Sharpe
8. Bradley, Jennifer and Katz, Bruce, *The Metropolitan Revolution: How Cities and Metros are Fixing Our Broken Politics and Fragile Economy,* Brookings Institute Press, Washington, DC
9. Rohe, William M. *The Research Triangle: From Tobacco Road to Global Prominence,* University of Pennsylvania Press, Philadelphia
10. The Institute for Southern Studies, *Remembering the Days: An Illustrated History of the University of South Carolina,* the R. L. Bryan Company Columbia, South Carolina
11. Sennema, Martha D and David C. *Columbia South Carolina: A Postcard History,* Arcadia Publishing Charleston SC, Chicago Il, Portsmouth NH, San Francisco CA
12. Allen, Katharine Thompson, *The University of South Carolina Horseshoe: Heart of the Campus,* University of South Carolina Archives, University Libraries, University of South Carolina
13. Chapman, Perry M. *American Places: In Search of the Twenty-First Century Campus,* American Council on Education, Praeger Publishers, Westport, CT 06881
14. Dumont, Ricardo, Kenney, Daniel R., and Ginger, *Mission and Place: Strengthening Learning and Community through Campus Design,* American Council on Education, Praeger Publishers, Westport, CT
15. Gumprecht, Blake, *The American College Town,* University of Massachusetts Press, Copyright 2008 by Blake Gumprecht, Printed and bound by Sheridan Books Inc.
16. Ehrenberg, Ronald G. *Tuition Rising: Why College Costs So Much,* Harvard University Press Cambridge Massachusetts and London England, Copyright 2000 by the President and Fellows of Harvard College.
17. Turner, Paul Venable, *Campus: An American Planning Tradition,* The Architectural History Foundation New York, The MIT Press Cambridge, MA, and London England 1984
18. Jacobs, Jane, *The Death and Life of Great American Cities,* Vintage Books, A Division of Random House, Inc., New York December 1992
19. Sensbach, Werner, *Planning for Higher Education* 20, Fall 1991
20. Goodheart, Adam, *Expanding on Jefferson,* Copyright 2006 Moore Ruble Yudell Architects & Planners
21. Afofsin, Anthony, *The Struggle for Modernism, Architecture, Landscape: Architecture, and City Planning at Harvard,* W. W. Norton and Company New York London
22. *Chronicle of Higher Education,* "Campus Architecture," March 25, 2005
23. Rodin, Judith, *Out of the Ivory Tower and Into the Streets,* U Penn Press.
24. *State*
25. *Boston Globe*
26. *New York Times*

ACKNOWLEDGMENTS

To my wife, **Mary Anne Galehouse,** who provided three years of encouragement and unconditional support.

I wish to acknowledge and express the deepest appreciation and thanks to the many women and men whose talent and support were essential to the development of this book. At Sasaki Associates: **Mr. Mark Dawson**, **Gina Ford**, and **James Miner**, Sasaki Partners for their support of this endeavor; **Sasaki Associates** for their generous support and sharing of their talents; **James McCown**, who served as coach and critic, provided editorial advice and line editing; **Terri Dube** and **Ryan Collier**, Sasaki Graphic Designers, who brought beauty to the book, and **Neda Movaghar**, who helped conceive the graphic design concept; **Aliza Leventhal,** Sasaki Archivist, for securing historic documents and drawings; and **Ali Eaton** for her administrative support and Cambridge Editors for their editorial support.

At the University of South Carolina: **Thomas Stepp** for his generous contribution of his time and advice; **Linda Fogle**, Assistant Director of Operations for the USC Press, for her patience and advice; **Keith McGraw Jr.** for his beautiful photography; **Elizabeth Cassidy West**, University Archivist for the South Caroliniana Library, for her editing and enabling the use of the library's archival material; and **Bob Lowder** of the University Creative Services for helping to secure essential photography for the book.

I am especially indebted to **Stacie Davenport** for her unfailing support in providing information and liaison for facilitating interviews with trustees, senior administrators and other university officials.

Sasaki Associates, from whom this work is drawn, is a multidisciplinary planning and design firm located in the Boston, Massachusetts, area. The firm was founded in 1956 by the landscape architect Hideo Sasaki, who was Dean of the Department of Landscape Architecture at the Harvard Graduate School of Design. The planning and design work presented in this book is the work of an extraordinary group of Sasaki professionals: planners, urban designers, landscape architects, architects, engineers, and graphic designers with whom I have been privileged to partner over the last 25 years. They have provided the analytic foundation and master plan vision for development of the campus, beginning with the Bicentennial Master, published in 1994 though the development of the Innovista Master Plan and the 2010 Master Plan Vision for a Sustainable Future. The passage of time has permitted many Sasaki professionals an opportunity to contribute their talents to the development of the campus.

From 1992 to 2000

Donald H. Olson, "Don," Sasaki Principal, was the designer of the Bicentennial Master Plan published in 1994. A Harvard-educated landscape architect and urban designer, Don has retired and is living in Woodstock, Vermont. **James B. Doolin, "Jim,"** was the project manager for the Bicentennial Master Plan. Mr. Doolin is now the Chief Development Officer for the Massachusetts Port Authority. He is responsible for the development of Massachusetts Port Authority properties in the Innovation District of South Boston. **Greg Haven**, architect/planner, was the project planner for the Bicentennial Master Plan. Greg currently heads Sasaki's institutional planning practice. **Nancy Freedman**, architect, authored the university's first computerized building information program for space management and setting capital improvement priorities. **Carol Moyles** provided project landscape architectural design services and **Jonathan Austin** served as architectural designer for the East Quad residential complex, the university's first student apartment–style housing. The Bicentennial Master Plan was an interdisciplinary team effort and included **Charles Hultstrand**, architect, who was a principal of the Columbia firm of Boudreau, Carter and Hulstrand at the time. Mr. Hultstrand served as project architect and project coordinator in Columbia for the Bicentennial Master Plan. Mr. Hultstrand was also an architect of record with Sasaki as Design Architect for the East Quad student housing. Mr. Hultstrand is now a Principal with LS3P Architects in Greenville, SC.

Dan Paulien, CEO of Paulien Associates of Denver, Colorado, carried out the first comprehensive space use analysis of academic facilities at the university, providing an analytical foundation for managing requests for new space and allocating capital funds for new projects. **Swygert Crowder Consulting Engineers** of Cayce, South Carolina, provided cost estimating services for the infrastructure and new buildings identified in the Bicentennial Master Plan.

From 2000 to 2015

Igor Andersen, architect and urban designer, was Sasaki's project designer for the decade of intensive planning and design which began in 2000. Igor was the lead designer for the Innovista Master Plan, site designer for the baseball park and the Athletics Village Master Plan, and the author of the "University of South Carolina Design Guidelines." Igor could boast of having one of Boston's first "green roofs" on the roof of his fifth floor Beacon Hill walk-up condominium. Igor has followed his Swiss wife and family back to Geneva, Switzerland, where she is Dean of Architecture and Planning at the Swiss Institute of Technology. Igor heads the urban design studio of Urbaplan in Geneva. **Jack Robinson** was project manager/planner for Sasaki's assignments at the beginning of the decade, working with Igor Andersen and other team members. Jack's exceptional project management skills kept the planning and design team focused. Jack left Sasaki to pursue and receive a doctoral degree in planning at the University of Pennsylvania. **Justin Fay**, a Yale- and MIT-trained architect/planner has succeeded Jack Robinson as project planner for Sasaki's work with the university. Justin's outstanding team-building skills, and his ability to develop consensus on planning and design concepts, have been essential to Sasaki's continuing planning and design work at the University of South Carolina.

Other Sasaki professionals who have made significant long-term contributions to planning and design for the university since 2000 include **Andy McClurg**, Cornell-trained transportation planner, who provided the transportation and parking analysis for the Innovista Master Plan and the university's 2010 Master Plan. **Stuart Dawson**, Fellow of the American Institute of Landscape Architects and Principal Emeritus of Sasaki, was the principal landscape designer for the proposed Congaree Regional Waterfront Park in the Innovista Master Plan. Stuart is the designer of Charleston's famous Waterfront Park. **Stephen Kun**, GIS planner and steward of the university's mapping. **Varoujan Hagopian**, civil engineer and expert in marine science, advised the design team on the concept plan for the proposed Congaree Regional Waterfront Park and cost of infrastructure for the Innovisata Master Plan. Varoujan also advised the Waterfront Steering Team on the legal issues associated with the Army Corps of Engineers' jurisdiction over the Congaree River and wetlands in the Innovista plan. **Patrick Phillips**, now CEO of the Urban Land Institute in Washington, DC, and former CEO of Economic Research Associates, a national real estate consulting practice, provided the market analysis of the real estate development potential for Innovista. **Don Schunk**, university professor in the School of Business, prepared the beneficial fiscal impact analysis of the Innovista Master Plan. **Bill Winkler**, architect, and **Trey Sasser**, engineer, developed the facilities program for the Athletics Facilities Master Plan leading to the design of the Athletics Village. **Elke Berger**, landscape designer, was responsible for development of the design concept for Foundation Square. **Pablo Savid**, principal architect who developed the design concept for the adaptive reuse of the university's Coliseum. **Neda Movaghar** served as graphic designer for the Innovista Master Plan and the University of South Carolina Design Guidelines.

The 2010 Master Plan, with its focus on sustainability, also engaged additional professionals: **Greg Janks**, principal at the time who was responsible for the space use planning; **Nathalie Beauvais** and **Phillip Bruso**, planners; **Stephen Gray**, Project Urban Designer; **Robyn Reed**, Project Landscape Architect; **Elizabeth Hixson**, Designer; **Amy Houghton**, Project Landscape Architect; **Matt Kanaraus,** Graphic Designer, and **Richard York**, Designer.

ABOUT THE AUTHOR

Richard "Dick" Galehouse currently resides in Lexington, Massachusetts, with his wife Mary Anne. They are parents of five grown children and have nine grandchildren. Dick received his architectural degree from the University of Notre Dame in 1956. Upon graduation he served in the United States Navy as an instructor at Saufley Field, Pensacola, Florida, teaching meteorology and aircraft engineering in the ground school to naval officers in flight training. Upon completion of his military service he entered Harvard University where he received a master's degree in city and regional planning from the Harvard Graduate School of Design. Upon graduation he joined Sasaki Associates in 1961, a professional services planning and design firm founded by the landscape architect Hideo Sasaki.

His professional practice as a principal at Sasaki Associates has ranged across a broad array of institutional, corporate, and public planning and design assignments. His institutional planning and design work has included master plans for universities and colleges throughout the United States. His public planning practice included planning for the modern Olympics in the United States including Lake Placid in 1980, Los Angeles in 1984, and Atlanta in 1996, where he led Sasaki's work in planning the Olympic Village at Georgia Tech. His urban planning and design assignments include the new community of "Southwood" in Tallahassee, Florida, the master plan for the "Riverwalk" in Ft. Lauderdale, Florida, and Princeton University's mixed-use research park, "The Princeton Forrestal Center."

Project work for which he has been responsible at Sasaki Associates has received awards including a Global Award for Excellence from the Urban Land Institute, for the Presidio Trust Management Plan in San Francisco, and from the Congress for New Urbanism for the Innovista Master Plan at the University of South Carolina.

Dick has held teaching assignments and lectured at colleges, universities, and professional organizations and has written extensively for publication in professional journals including *Urban Land and Landscape Architecture.* He has provided community service to over 15 communities in the United States and abroad through the Urban Land Institute's Advisory Services Program.

At the University of South Carolina Dick has served as Sasaki Associates' principal-in-charge for the firm's planning and design work since 1992. Notable assignments for the university include the "Bicentennial Master Plan," published in 1994, the "Innovista Master Plan," published in 2006, and the "2010 Master Plan, Vision for a Sustainable Future."

Dick retired from full-time professional practice at Sasaki in 2014 but continues to consult on selected professional assignments with Sasaki. He currently serves on the Board of the Girl Scouts of Eastern Massachusetts and is a member of the American Planning Association and an active member of the Urban Land Institute.

INDEX